*A Diplomat Looks Back*

# *A Diplomat Looks Back* by Lewis Einstein

Edited by Lawrence E. Gelfand, with a Foreword by George F. Kennan

New Haven and London, Yale University Press, 1968

Designed by Sheila L. de Bretteville,
set in Baskerville type,
and printed in the United States of America by
Connecticut Printers, Inc., Hartford, Connecticut.
Distributed in Great Britain, Europe, Asia, and
Africa by Yale University Press Ltd., London; in
Canada by McGill University Press, Montreal;
and in Latin America by Centro Interamericano de
Libros Académicos, Mexico City.


Library of Congress catalog card number: 67–24497

# *Contents*

*Foreword* by George F. Kennan vii
*Lewis Einstein: American Diplomatist* by Lawrence E. Gelfand xv
*Editor's Note* xxxi
*Preface* by Lewis Einstein xxxiii

*1. The Algesiras Conference* 3
*2. Constantinople under Abdul Hamid* 25
*3. Diplomatic Life and the Turkish Revolution* 55
*4. Peking Days* 83
*5. Costa Rican Interlude* 108
*6. Constantinople in Wartime* 118
*7. Sofia during the War* 144
*8. Prague Memories* 173
*9. A Diplomat Bows Out* 207
*10. A Spectator Gazes at the War* 221

*Biographical Directory* 233
*A Bibliography of Lewis Einstein's Published Writings* 251
*Index* 257

*Illustrations*

Lewis Einstein circa 1907. *Harris & Ewing, Washington, D.C.* frontispiece

Lewis Einstein in his apartment in Paris, 1960. opposite p. 207

# *Foreword* by George F. Kennan

In a foreword written a half-century ago to another book by the author of these present memoirs, ex-President Theodore Roosevelt described him as "one of the men whose work has kept alive the fine tradition of the union between American diplomacy and American letters which is illustrated by such names as those of Lowell and Motley, of John Hay and Maurice Egan." The description was not overdrawn. Even at that early date, in addition to a diplomatic career which had taken him to Paris, to Algeciras, to Constantinople, to Peking, and to San José, Lewis Einstein already had behind him a respectable measure of literary achievement. It included a book on the Italian Renaissance in England, written at the age of twenty-five, before he had entered the diplomatic service; another on Napoleon III and American diplomacy at the outbreak of our Civil War; the editing of a volume of selections from the thoughts of Leonardo; and a book of memoirs about life in wartime Constantinople.

In the years to follow, this list would continue to grow and to reflect a refinement and diversity of interests worthy of that very Italian Renaissance to which Einstein was himself so devoted. There would be a volume on Tudor ideals; a chapter on Lewis Cass for the series *American Secretaries of State and Their Diplomacy;* an intellectual biography of Theodore Roosevelt himself; two volumes of poetry; a theoretical monograph on the subject of historical change, for inclusion in a series published by the Cambridge University Press; a study of the experiences of Americans in London during the American War of Independence; and a study of Italian gardens in Prague. Finally, the 1960s would see the appearance of a volume of items from the intimate personal correspondence which Einstein conducted for nearly thirty years with Justice Oliver Wendell Holmes, a body of letters in which those from the pen of Einstein (relatively few, unfortunately) in no wise lag behind those of his distinguished friend in wit, grace of language, and pithiness of content.[1] And all this would be in addition to further years—not as many as there might and should have been, but no small number—of distinguished service in a diplomatic capacity.

The little volume to which Theodore Roosevelt contributed his foreword deserves special note. Entitled *A Prophecy of the War,* and published in 1918 by the Columbia University Press, it included only two small articles from Einstein's pen. Both had previously seen magazine publication: one in January 1913 and the other in November 1914. They had appeared in an English review, after it had proven impossible to find an American publisher interested in printing them. Roosevelt cited them in his foreword as "proof of a prescience in world politics very rare among American statesmen." This, too, was no overstatement. One could search long in the American political literature of the period for anything equal to these documents in maturity of judgment, mastery of material, analytical power, and brilliance of insight.

The first of the two articles was written, one must suppose, at some time in the summer or early autumn of 1912—scarcely later. The outbreak of the World War was still two years off. Einstein was then serving as American Minister to Costa Rica—a position which could scarcely have been replete with outside stimulus and in which, one may imagine, the pondering of the problems of Europe may well have been a lonely occupation.

In this article, Einstein pointed to the curious contrast between the active interest American statesmanship displayed in Latin America and the Far East and the relative indifference it showed toward the affairs of Europe. This seemed to reflect, he noted, an assumption that the United States had no vital or important national interest in European developments—an assumption which he then proceeded to demolish with thoroughness and cogency. America, he pointed out, owed its security very largely to the existence of an adequate balance of power on the European continent—a balance that had been maintained throughout the nineteenth century mainly by British effort. Yet this balance of power was now in jeopardy. A sense of unrest was spreading across Europe. Armaments were piling up with frightening

1. *The Holmes-Einstein Letters: Correspondence of Mr. Justice Holmes and Lewis Einstein, 1903–1935,* ed. James Bishop Peabody (New York, St. Martin's Press, 1964).

rapidity. The growing power of democratic opinion and of the press was tending to inflame rather than to moderate the passions out of which war would be likely to flow. Special danger lay in the mounting rivalry and ill feeling between Great Britain and Germany. This situation was dangerous precisely for the reason that it rested on no specific differences, such as might be susceptible to adjustment by negotiation and compromise—on nothing more than general mistrust and uneasiness about the position of the other party. Neither of the two governments would deliberately precipitate a war, but there was serious danger "lest, in an atmosphere as surcharged as is the present, with the deep-rooted feeling of hostility existing on both sides, some petty cause of friction . . . inflaming public opinion, should induce either Government to prefer a foreign war which it might regard as inevitable to domestic humiliation." In this case, France would also be involved, and the fields of Belgium could "again witness a struggle where the descendants of Napoleon's and Wellington's men will this time stand side by side against Blücher's."

War, then, had to be regarded as likely, and the United States had to take cognizance of the possibility of its breaking out at an early date. Contrary to prevailing opinion, there was no reason to suppose that such a war would necessarily be a short one. It was more likely to be long and exhausting. This would place a great strain on our neutrality. Our economic interests would unavoidably be heavily engaged. It was not absolutely inevitable that we would become militarily involved. But we would probably be obliged at some point either to intervene or to mediate. Whichever we did, we would need military strength, if we were to be effective. It was not too early to begin to strengthen our military power.

And it was also not too early to begin to mobilize our thoughts—to think seriously, in particular, about our stake in the outcome of any European war. Our interest in the preservation of a European balance of power was a vital one. That balance was "a political necessity" which alone could make possible for the United States "the continuance of an economic development unhandicapped by the burden of extensive armaments." The undisputed paramountcy of any nation would inevitably make that power "a menace and a peril to every other country." The balance of power would probably not be greatly affected by a British victory, for Britain's insular position debarred her from continental ambitions. Even a defeat of England could conceivably be endured, provided the general balance was preserved. But if the results of the war were such as to upset "what has for centuries been the recognized political fabric of Europe, we can remain indifferent thereto only at our own eventual cost . . . The disappearance or diminution of any one state in Europe would be a calamity to us, varying with its degree . . . If we then neglect to observe that the interests of the nations crushed are likewise our own, we shall be guilty of political blindness which we will later rue."[2]

I shall not pursue this summary. What has been cited is enough to show that one had to do here with political insight of a very rare and superior order—insight which, if heeded and respected, could well have altered our relationship to the coming European war in a manner greatly beneficial to ourselves and to the future peace of Europe. And this insight, it should be noted, was forthcoming from a man already in government service, whose experience and intellectual distinction were wholly at Washington's disposal, had Washington wished to avail itself of them.

Washington, only too obviously, had no such wish. The appearance of the first of these articles was followed almost immediately by the appointment as Secretary of State of William Jennings Bryan, than whom (as Einstein points out in these memoirs) it would have been difficult to find anyone in American public life more ignorant of world affairs. Einstein himself, after a period in which his services were not used at all, was packed off, during the war he had so brilliantly forecast, to handle the dreary details of prisoner-of-war protection in Turkey and Bulgaria. After the war, he served for nine years as American Minister at Prague. In 1930, President Hoover put an abrupt end to his governmental service by accepting, without explanation, a resignation he had never tendered, thus relegating him to that honorable and numerically impressive company of men who have faithfully served successive American presidents and secretaries of state in a diplomatic capacity, often at considerable personal sacrifice, only to find themselves one day suddenly and mysteriously discarded

2. This passage should be noted in connection with the eventual fate suffered, as a consequence of the war, by the Austro-Hungarian and Russian empires, and the resulting instability in Eastern and Central Europe, which offered Hitler his great possibilities.

and often to receive the first intimation of their dismissal from the public prints. In most instances, it must be said, the men thus affected have contrived to accept this treatment philosophically; and Einstein was no exception, although he does mildly observe in these memoirs that "there could have been more courteous ways of dismissing an old public servant." It would have been unseemly for him to say more. But the historian, not being under the same restraints, is at liberty to recognize this termination of a distinguished diplomatic career as a singularly shocking example of what Einstein himself refers to, albeit in a different connection, as "that light-heartedness which so often characterizes the waste of human resources in America."

It would be pleasant to be able to record that ensuing decades had done something to diminish this cheerful prodigality of official Washington toward the nation's resources of diplomatic talent. Mr. Einstein's experience would not suggest that it did. He wrote from time to time, during the 1930s, to Secretary of State Cordell Hull, giving him impressions of developments on the international scene. On one occasion he attempted, with indifferent success, to communicate some of these impressions orally to F.D.R. In neither case was there any detectable effect on official American outlooks or policies. During the Second World War, being then resident in England, he offered his personal services to Ambassador Winant in London and vouchsafed to him some very cogent suggestions about the need for giving attention to the political problems of Eastern and Central Europe before the Russian advance made it idle to discuss them at all. But all of this—the offer of service and the policy suggestions—was received with cryptic unresponsiveness, and Einstein devoted himself philosophically, for the remainder of the war, to the feeding of pigs in Scotland. He leaves untreated in these memoirs the question of what he might have done in government service had anyone been interested. He observes only that he found the feeding of pigs a useful occupation. Pigs, after all, were "reasonably intelligent, easy to handle, and providing they are properly fed make no further demands."

The diplomatist or ex-diplomatist whose memories go back a respectable number of years cannot read these memoirs without a sense of nostalgia for certain of their features which he associates, involuntarily, with an earlier period of diplomacy. The bland urbanity of word and conduct; the graciousness of manner; the wit; the good humor; the refinement of taste; the breadth of cultural interest; the largesse of perspective; the shrewd and skeptical view of men and governments; the appreciation for the values, in diplomacy, of elaborate indirection; the keen sensitivity to irony (without which no understanding of international life can achieve profundity): these are not qualities that were universally present among an earlier generation of diplomatists, nor are they universally lacking among those of the present age. But they were more highly valued and more generally cultivated in the days (the end of Charles E. Hughes' incumbency as Secretary of State might mark the turning point) before the great democratizers began to address to the Foreign Service those attentions with which they have never since ceased to encumber it.

More than just these qualities is admittedly required for the tasks of diplomacy in the 1960s. The contemporary diplomatist has need of a sterner schooling in economic and social fields, of training in the analysis of whole societies, not just courts and governments, and often of specialized expertise in individual geographic and functional disciplines. Nor would it be possible today to try to restrict the recruitment of diplomatic initiates to such as have had the good fortune to be schooled to the social and intellectual graces by superior breeding in superior homes. But many of us will part with reluctance from the view that the qualities Lewis Einstein's memoirs betray have lost none of their usefulness in the diplomacy of the present age; and we will continue to sigh for a Foreign Service in which the cultivation of these qualities would meet with the understanding and support, rather than the incomprehension, of those various Washington figures, legislative and executive, on whose interest and level of understanding the administration of the service depends.

Outside of this, there is little to be said by way of introduction to these memoirs. They speak for themselves. Like the interests and the career of their author, they deal with a wide variety of subjects. The shrewd judgments and observations woven through them are distributed impartially over a wide spectrum of historical situations. Some of the most valuable appreciations relate to the final years of the old Turkish and Chinese empires and to the Algeciras Conference of 1906. These are phases of international life from which we are separated now by an appalling profusion of spectacular, and often tragic, historical changes. They have become, in this way, largely eclipsed from even the educated consciousness of our time. It is startling to hear them discussed by a contemporary who was also an eye-witness to them all, for Lewis Einstein is today unique in this respect. But it is precisely in this quality that their greatest value lies. We have other books of impressions of all those phases and episodes of history, emanating for the most part from the period itself, and bearing the stamp of its outlooks and its myopia. We have none other from the pen of one who has also witnessed the entire drama of intervening events, who can recall the happenings of this turn-of-the-century period in the light of these intervening events, and who can recount his memories, in 1968, with a freshness and youthfulness of spirit that makes them, in the fullest sense, a part of the literature of the modern age.

There are three qualities of these memoirs to which, in conclusion, particular attention might suitably be drawn: their skepticism, their realism, and their modesty. It is not by chance that these qualities find themselves mentioned together. Sigmund Freud noted somewhere that it takes a modest man to distinguish what is real from what is unreal on this planet. And Lewis Einstein has quoted Holmes as observing that "the skeptic is more humble than all the other devotees of the sects." Holmes' skeptical attitude became in this way, Einstein observes, "the groundwork of his own modesty"; and he goes on to point out that modesty "perhaps is more frequently met with among the cultivated who have learned of other men's attainments in other ages, and measured their own talent accordingly, than it is among self-made men who are only aware of the present time." It is a measure of his own modesty, as well as of his generosity of spirit, that in making this observation, he was plainly oblivious of its relevance to himself.

# *Lewis Einstein: American Diplomatist*
# by Lawrence E. Gelfand

Lewis Einstein was already twenty-six years of age when he entered the United States Diplomatic Service in 1903. At least by the standards of the time, his preparations and general qualifications could hardly have failed to impress his examiners as well-nigh impeccable. He had graduated with honors from Columbia College and had gone on to earn a Master's Degree in history. He was fluent in French, German, and Italian and had already published two book-length studies of the Renaissance. But intellectual capacity was not the most important prerequisite for a career in diplomacy in 1903. His large family, including his uncles as well as his parents, had amassed considerable wealth from several textile manufacturing enterprises and newspapers which it controlled in New York and New Jersey. The family's social position afforded an opportunity for acquaintance with politicians and business leaders in New York City.

A merit system of sorts, including a qualifying examination, had recently been instituted by the Department of State for lower-grade diplomatic appointments, but there remained a broad area in which Executive discretion could be exercised in appointments, assignments, and promotions. The Einstein family's long personal friendship with leading New York Republican Party officials certainly did not prove any handicap, particularly as two close friends happened to be Theodore Roosevelt and Elihu Root. During the years immediately following Einstein's appointment to the Diplomatic Service, occasional letters from members of the family reached friends in Washington just to make sure that Lewis would not be overlooked for choice assignments. Representative R. N. Arthauer of New York, for example, wrote to Lewis Einstein in 1905, at the time he was transferred from Paris to London:

> In talking over the matter of your transfer to London with the President [Theodore Roosevelt] which he was very ready to grant

> for he has taken a great interest in you and your work, he wanted me particularly to advise you not to seek to become too permanently connected with our diplomatic service. He felt, that after you will have had a few years experience in London, that you should get back to this country amid American surroundings and not permit the influences surrounding you abroad to gain so strong a foothold as they have done with some men in like position, men who started out to prosecute literary work, but ended up by becoming permanently attached to our diplomatic service. You surely have enlisted the President's and Secretary Hay's interest, for they would not give any consideration whatever to the demands of a dozen Senators for the London billet.[1]

Lewis Einstein's diplomatic career reads almost like that of the proverbial foreign correspondent who just happened to be on the scene at the precise moment when the big news was breaking. His first real opportunity came in 1906 when he was appointed Secretary to the American Delegation to the First Moroccan Conference at Algeciras, a position for which he had applied. At the time Britain and France, traditional foes in the European power struggle, were pulling together not so much because of common interests as because of their common opposition to the rising might of Germany. The Anglo-French Entente of 1904 had provided a tangible indication of this changed course of international affairs. But the next year the Kaiser's government put the Entente to a severe test when it challenged French paramountcy in Morocco. The issue was clear: would the British government, by supporting France's interests in Morocco, risk a possible war with Germany? As was customary prior to 1914, whenever tensions threatened to reach the breaking point the governments concerned arranged an international conference at which diplomats thrashed out the issues in dispute and resolved the crisis without resorting to force.

True to form, an international conference was called in late 1905, at the height of the Moroccan Crisis, to meet in Algeciras in southern Spain. The question might be raised: Why did the United States send delegates to a conference concerned with Morocco? The United States

1. Letter from R. N. Arthauer to Einstein, Jan. 26, 1905, Einstein Mss, University of Wyoming Library. See also Letter from Einstein to Elihu Root, May 3, 1911; Letter from Root to Einstein, Nov. 14, 1905; Letter from Caroline Einstein to Root, Feb. 2, 1906; all in the Elihu Root Mss, Library of Congress.

government was supposedly adhering to a doctrine of noninvolvement in purely European affairs. In 1880, however, President Hayes had accepted an invitation to a conference concerned with Morocco and had appointed an American delegate to the Conference of Madrid in the same year.[2] Since the Conference of 1906 was designed to bring together the same parties that had met in Madrid in 1880, the United States was included.

President Theodore Roosevelt, anxious to prevent any shift in the European balance of power, was not reluctant to take part in the conference in any case. His instructions to the American plenipotentiaries indicate that he was sympathetic to the German desire to maintain the Open Door of commercial opportunity and the independence of Morocco, while at the same time he definitely favored placing the weight of American influence on the side of France and England.

Besides Einstein, who served as Secretary, the American delegates at Algeciras were veteran diplomat Henry White and the United States Minister at Tangier, Samuel Gummere. There, young and inexperienced, Lewis Einstein carefully observed the work of Europe's most skilled diplomats. In the excellent collection of his papers at the University of Wyoming Library is a memorandum that Einstein composed under the date of March 31, 1906, the day the conference reached its settlement. In this memorandum he made the following observations:

> The cause of peace has thus in reality been strengthened by the Conference not so much by any of its direct results as by its indirect action. France stands today in a far stronger military position than six months ago and no longer invites attack by her weakness. Furthermore, she has been able to parade openly to the world on the one hand the English Alliance, on the other the Italian defection from Germany. But lastly it would appear as if the German Emperor had realized the mistakes of demanding a conference in which he has been unable to gain such advantages as he could have obtained by direct negotiations, nor is he likely soon again to risk a war so unpopular with his subjects as the one over Morocco would have proved. . . . Morocco except for the ports will doubtless remain

2. Selected documents concerning American participation in the Conference at Madrid are published in *Papers Relating to the Foreign Relations of the United States, 1880* (Washington, Government Printing Office, 1880), pp. 897–930.

> in its present anarchy profiting no one, until a few years time when the sharpness of the present crisis has been forgotten, Germany, surrendering a situation from which she can derive no benefit, will possibly follow the example of England, Italy and Spain, in making an arrangement with France which while amply confirming the previous guarantees for her commerce, will give France free rein in her Moroccan ambitions, in return for advantages exchanged elsewhere.[3]

Events were not to bear out Einstein's optimistic prognosis, but the delicate balance of power in Europe was maintained for the time being.

Einstein's next assignment took him to Constantinople just when the young Turkish nationalists were stirring the winds of revolt in the Ottoman Empire. For the highly impressionable diplomat there was no better location from which to observe the developing European power struggle. Einstein's duties were those of First Secretary of the Legation, or, after its status was upgraded in 1908, the Embassy. From that vantage point, he had the opportunity to meet and discuss the Near Eastern Question with the large number of foreign diplomats accredited to the Sultan's Court.

United States interests in the Ottoman Empire at the outset of the twentieth century were relatively minor. The flow of American trade and investment was hardly what could be called substantial. In some respects, the American stake in Turkey and the Middle East was limited to the activities of the Christian missionary organizations which had successfully established educational institutions in the area. Robert College in Constantinople was the most noteworthy example of this kind of philanthropic enterprise.

Einstein perceived how important it was, however, to maintain a delicate balance of power in the Near East if America's economic and cultural interests were to be preserved without military involvement. He even proposed to his superiors in Washington that an international banking consortium be established with American participation for the purpose of preventing or at least retarding the breakup of the Ottoman Empire. In the process, American business would be assured

3. Einstein's handwritten Memorandum, Mar. 31, 1906, Einstein Mss, University of Wyoming Library.

of equal access to the markets of the Empire, and American interests in the Empire generally would be secured.[4]

This notion, which approximated what would later be called Dollar Diplomacy in the Taft Administration, came logically and easily to Einstein, given his assumptions. The United States was not likely to defend or assert its interests in Turkey by the use or threat of military force. How then could diplomacy devise a substitute for military power? By neutralizing the area through an international consortium of bankers supervised and even guaranteed by the great powers. If all the powers had approximately an equal stake, no one nation would be disposed to take advantage of the others. A device providing for parity among the powers gave promise of preserving the status quo.

His work at Constantinople allowed Einstein ample opportunity to take a good, hard look at the explosive tinderbox of Balkan politics. He was not optimistic about Turkey's chances of remaining landlord in southeastern Europe for long. But just as he was beginning to become acquainted with the intricacies of Turkish affairs, he learned that he was to be transferred to China as Secretary of the Legation in Peking.

Einstein's arrival in China late in 1909 coincided with the beginnings of Dollar Diplomacy in that country. I believe it can be clearly established that Dollar Diplomacy was the handiwork of the young career men in the Department of State during these years—Huntington Wilson, William Phillips, Henry Fletcher, Willard Straight, and Lewis Einstein. Its goals were the containment of Japanese commercial penetration in China, the provision of economic assistance to the tottering Manchu Empire, and the development of a healthy balance of power among the nations possessing substantial interests in China. Dollar Diplomacy, in the words of President Taft, aimed at substituting dollars for bullets by means of an international banking consortium whose function would be to channel the flow of foreign investments into a vast network of railroads, currency stabilization, and other enterprises designed to strengthen the economy of China. An important aim was to revitalize the concept of equality of commercial opportu-

4. [Lewis Einstein], *American Foreign Policy by a Diplomatist* (Boston, Houghton Mifflin, 1909), pp. 149 ff. See also Marcia Zimmerman, "Lewis Einstein: Twentieth Century Diplomat and Critic of Foreign Policy" (M.A. thesis, University of Wyoming, 1962), pp. 25 ff.

nity in China for all nations, thus discouraging Japan and Russia from continuing their race for special concessions. Einstein met in Peking the man who was without doubt the moving force in Dollar Diplomacy—the American Willard Straight. Correspondence between Straight and Einstein indicates that the two men were never close friends, but did recognize a common ground in their approach to American policy.[5]

In several letters addressed to Secretary of State Philander Knox, Einstein pointed to Japanese efforts toward domination of southern Manchuria:

> To you least of all [Einstein wrote Knox on July 2, 1910] is it necessary to say how the flood of Japanese settlers, the growth of Japanese industrial enterprise and the Japanese state-aided railroads, public works, post offices and savings banks are continually sapping the remaining bases of Chinese sovereignty. It is certainly unfortunate that at a critical time like the present so little is being done by the Chinese to assert their rights. . . . The Japanese have certainly the upper hand at the present time and are not likely to allow any opposition to their interests to assert itself if they can possibly avoid it.[6]

To Einstein, even Turkey at its worst could not equal the ignorance, the corruption, and the inefficiency of the central government in Peking. Under the circumstances, he proposed that the United States join with England in a common venture aimed at creating a sphere of influence in the valley of the Yangtse where the Open Door could be effectively guaranteed.

In the fall of 1910, Einstein learned that he was again to be transferred, this time as United States Minister to Costa Rica. Though this was a promotion for him, he took up his assignment with misgivings. Only two years before he had declared that there was little hope of improvement in the American Diplomatic Service in Latin America until the government provided decent residences and adequate salaries for diplomats serving there in isolated capitals under difficult living

5. In particular see Letter from Willard Straight to Einstein, Jan. 11, 1911, Einstein Mss, University of Wyoming Library.

6. Letter from Einstein to Philander C. Knox, July 2, 1910, and Letter from Einstein to Knox, Oct. 17, 1910, both in the Einstein Mss, University of Wyoming Library.

conditions.[7] The $10,000 per annum salary of the Minister to Costa Rica had been unchanged since 1854.

Costa Rica probably had the most progressive and politically stable government in all of Central America, and provided a sharp contrast to other Caribbean countries whose unstable situations had frequently invited American military interventions. Costa Rica enjoyed a profitable foreign trade, exporting coffee, bananas, and cacao. President Jiménez's regime had won a popular mandate, and Costa Rica's friendliness toward the United States was unquestioned. In fact, no serious or difficult problems arose in the relations between the two countries during Einstein's tour of duty in San José. Perhaps the most important event was Andrew Carnegie's offer to donate $100,000 to rebuild the permanent center for the Central American Court of Justice at San José, following the destruction of the earlier structure by earthquake.

Einstein did not remain long at San José. Because the high altitude (almost 4,000 feet) seemed to affect Mrs. Einstein's health adversely, he was granted an indefinite leave of absence in January 1912, and left Costa Rica for England, where he proceeded to indulge an ever-present urge to write, producing several articles on American foreign policy.

Like almost every ranking career officer in the American Diplomatic Service during the prewar decade, when Anglo-American marriages and strong transatlantic family ties were prevalent, Lewis Einstein was an Anglophile. He himself married in 1904 a British woman of Greek background, the former Helen Ralli, who helped the fledgling diplomat find his way in English society. But it is safe to say that other factors also influenced his attitude.

In a brilliant article, "The United States and Anglo-German Rivalry," published in 1913, Einstein argued that American security had not been the product simply of geographical isolation from the European continent.[8] Rather, he declared, the United States had been able to preserve its peaceful existence, which in turn had permitted its impressive internal development, only because of the continued maintenance of Europe's balance of power. "It has been far less the distance

7. *American Foreign Policy by a Diplomatist,* pp. 96–97.

8. Einstein, "The United States and Anglo-German Rivalry," *National Review* (January 1913), pp. 746–50; reprinted in slightly altered form in Einstein, *A Prophecy of the War* (New York, Columbia University Press, 1918).

which allowed our previous weakness than it has been the division of Europe into two warring camps." The balance of power, he wrote, "has been such a permanent factor since the birth of the Republic that Americans have never realized how its absence would have affected their political status." As arch-sponsors of the balance of power, the British had performed an invaluable service to American interests. England's naval superiority had safeguarded America's security.

> Towards England, the clearest dictates of reason impel us to turn —not because of the intimate ties of language, blood and civilization, nor because the two nations have shared a common past. Bonds of sympathy and kinship have never prevented fratricidal strife; where conflicting interests oppose they offer a poor foundation upon which to base an understanding. Identical interests undivided by divergent ambitions afford a far safer basis for friendship between nations.[9]

Common interests did not exist, Einstein firmly insisted, in German-American relations. From America's standpoint German domination of the Continent would augur a dangerous future. Europe's balance of power would almost certainly be destroyed. "A disastrous defeat inflicted by any opponent [upon England] unwilling to use moderation in his victory should invite on our part a friendly mediation which in the last extremity might have to be converted into more effective measures."

Lewis Einstein's published writings at the outset of the First World War reflect an almost unique appreciation of America's historic stake in the European community. He urged that United States foreign policy be based on a thorough understanding of its long-range interests. In previous generations the existence of a European balance of power had allowed the United States the luxury of not maintaining an expensive military and naval establishment, which would have required it to conscript its citizenry for years of national service and tax their wealth. This happy fortune was not geographically determined by the mere presence of two great oceans separating the Western from the Eastern hemisphere; it was due to an historic relationship of nation-states that had prevented a single nation from exercising such disproportionately immense power as to pose a menace to the United States

9. Ibid., pp. 49–50.

and the Western Hemisphere. But, Einstein predicted, when the war ended and a single power had gained preponderance on the continent of Europe, this situation "will require steps of an entirely different order" if American security was to be assured.

During these years while Einstein endeavored to awaken public opinion to the critical implications of international events, his own experience drew his attention to the ills that affected the American Diplomatic Service. Between 1903 and 1913, he had moved from assignment to assignment with a frequency that barely permitted him to develop effective familiarity with government leaders or the institutional life of the countries to which he was accredited. At no time was he brought back to Washington for a tour of duty in the Department of State. Even on vacation, he was as likely to be abroad as in the United States. It was easy for a diplomat to lose touch with trends of thought in his own country. As early as 1909, Einstein urged that appropriate administrative reforms be adopted for the merging of the diplomatic with the departmental services of the State Department in much the same manner that the Army had integrated its line and general staffs.[10] This reform was ultimately incorporated in the reorganization of the Department during the early 1950s.

The coming of war in 1914 found Einstein still living in London. He had not been reassigned following his departure from Costa Rica, having fallen victim to a partisan purge that took a heavy toll in the ranks of the nation's professional diplomats.[11] A staunch Republican and admirer of Theodore Roosevelt, he was out of favor with the Democratic administration elected in 1912. Confronted with numerous Democratic aspirants for diplomatic appointments, President Woodrow Wilson and his Secretary of State, William Jennings Bryan, simply replaced many Republicans with Democrats. During the crisis with Mexico in 1914, Einstein wrote to President Wilson volunteering his services,[12] but he did not receive an encouraging response.

10. *American Foreign Policy by a Diplomatist,* pp. 167 ff.

11. Warren F. Ilchman, *Professional Diplomacy in the United States, 1779–1939* (Chicago, University of Chicago Press, 1961), pp. 119–31; William Barnes and J. H. Morgan, *The Foreign Service of the United States: Origins, Development and Functions* (Washington; Department of State, 1961), pp. 184–85.

12. Letter from Einstein to President Wilson, Apr. 27, 1914, Einstein Mss, University of Wyoming Library.

Within the year, however, he was asked to serve at the Embassy in Constantinople.[13] Accepting this call of duty at a time when war was spreading into Eastern Europe, he found new and complicated problems awaiting him. By 1915 Turkey had joined the Central Powers. As representative of a neutral government, Einstein observed the abortive attempt by the British fleet to capture the Straits. And he was present, too, to witness continuous persecution and atrocities perpetrated by the Turks against the Armenians. The systematic destruction of an entire people could not be taken casually. Einstein gave expression to his deep revulsion:

> Enough has been said to indicate the gruesome nature of the vast tragedy. Details have been published elsewhere and will for long continue to filter through. But the fiendish spirit in which the death of some six hundred thousand human beings was perpetrated can never adequately be realized. In all this war of horrors nothing has equalled the silently planned destruction of a race, nor can German officialdom easily escape its terrible share of responsibility for association by acquiescence in this crime. The Armenian race in Asia Minor has been virtually destroyed.[14]

Einstein remained in Turkey only until the fall of 1915, when the newly appointed Secretary of State, Robert Lansing, chose him to serve as Special Agent to Sofia, to assist the United States Minister in Roumania, Charles Vopicka, in caring for British interests in Bulgaria, a responsibility that had fallen earlier to the Dutch Minister.[15] It will

13. Letter from Secretary of State William J. Bryan to Einstein, Feb. 1, 1915, Einstein Mss, University of Wyoming Library.

14. Einstein, "The Armenian Massacres," *Contemporary Review* (April 1917), p. 494. See also *Inside Constantinople: A Diplomatist's Diary During the Dardanelles Expedition, April–September, 1915* (London, John Murray, 1917), pp. v, 159.

15. Concerning Einstein's experiences in Sofia, see his unpublished Sofia Diary, which will be deposited with his papers at the University of Wyoming Library. See also Telegram from the British Secretary of State for Foreign Affairs to the U.S. Ambassador to England (Walter Hines Page), Feb. 5, 1916, Department of State File 18416/16/P, Copy in Einstein Mss, University of Wyoming Library. Sir Cecil Spring Rice, British Ambassador to Washington, wrote to Einstein on June 22, 1916:

> I have today sent to the Secretary of State an official note expressing Sir Edward Grey's regret at hearing that you have left Sofia and that your return is not anticipated. The note points out the valuable services which you rendered to

be remembered that, though Britain declared war on Bulgaria, the United States remained neutral. Einstein's task was to visit British prisoners of war in camps and check on their treatment. He also maintained a close watch on British commercial institutions. But his mission came to an abrupt end when a jurisdictional dispute arose between Einstein and Vopicka over the issue of whether Einstein had to report to the Department of State through Vopicka's office, as the latter insisted, or could report directly. In the end, Secretary of State Lansing sided with Vopicka, and Einstein resigned.[16]

From late 1916 through the end of the war, the Einsteins lived in a villa located in the hills outside Florence, where the American journalist Ray Stannard Baker, then serving on a special mission for President Wilson, visited him. We are indebted to Baker for the following description of the visit:

> At 12 Mr. Acton came to me in his car & we drove out to the matchless Florentine hills toward Vallombrosa where I was to dine with Lewis Einstein. He has a charming villa, one mentioned by Boccaccio in his stories, with a fine garden & orchard. He makes his own wine & oil. We walked about the place & were much interested in hearing about & seeing Italian farming methods. . . . Mr. Einstein has had a long & interesting diplomatic career & is a handsome man with a somewhat Hebraic cast of countenance, a fine big head and very bright dark eyes. His wife is . . . very beautiful—still beautiful at

---

the British interests committed to your charge, and expresses Sir Edward Grey's gratitude.

A copy of this note will no doubt be sent to you in due course, but I also wish to write to you personally to tell you how very deeply I appreciate the splendid and successful work that you did on behalf of the British prisoners in Bulgaria who have cause to remember you with gratitude as long as they live. One of the few bright pages in the story of this unhappy war has been written by yourself and the United States Ambassadors in Berlin and Vienna whose action on behalf of our prisoners and whose effective sympathy will, I trust, never be forgotten by my fellow countrymen. It has been a source of untold comfort to many an anxious home and of unqualified satisfaction to the whole country to know that British interests were confided to such hands.

16. Concerning the dispute, see Letter from Einstein to Secretary Lansing, Nov. 22, 1915; Letter from Charles Vopicka to Einstein, Nov. 19, 1915; Telegram Number 189 from Lansing to the U.S. Legation at Bucharest, Nov. 19, 1915; Telegram Number 191 from Lansing to the U.S. Legation in Bucharest, Nov. 12, 1915; Telegram Number 4 from Einstein to Secretary Lansing, Nov. 21, 1915. Copies of all are located in the Einstein Mss, University of Wyoming Library.

> 55 years. . . . A woman of power & fascination; all black, all white—no smudgy grays, a woman who can hate desperately & love passionately, believing in the beauty of excess, the utter being of life. Her husband's career, everything, went for her! And probably without regret. They have a beautiful, though small villa & the dinner I had was matchless. No better dinner *could* be served, or, I think ever was served. The fame of their table resounds throughout the valley of the Arno. Much good talk.[17]

The enjoyment of leisure at his villa was not an altogether satisfying life for a diplomat when his own country was at war. During the months following American intervention, Einstein wrote to Colonel House volunteering his services for the new organization that House was forming which would prepare the American case for the eventual peace conference, the organization known as the Inquiry.[18] His overture was, however, not encouraged.

Undaunted by what he could have taken as a rebuff from his government, he addressed another letter to Colonel House a year later, in 1918, from Scotland. This time he expressed grave concern over the possible ramifications that could flow from American policies in the Far East. Although he appreciated that the military intervention by the United States in eastern Siberia could exercise a moderating influence upon Japanese military activities there, at least while the war continued, Einstein feared that the United States could easily become so overcommitted in northeast Asia that no honorable withdrawal would be possible. To a later generation troubled by dangers of far greater magnitude in South Vietnam, Einstein's letter of 1918 holds a timely significance.

> The hope doubtless exists that our intervention will exercise a moderating influence to [restrain the Japanese]. May it not, however, produce the opposite effect? Once the German threat has been parried in Siberia, will not the result of our joint action, with its inevitable ramifications be to leave us face to face with Japan engaged together in a venture where our interests may clash and from which

17. Ray Stannard Baker Mss Diary, Box 124, Library of Congress. Entry for Dec. 1, 1918.

18. Letter from Einstein to E. M. House, Oct. 12, 1917, and Letter from House to Einstein, Nov. 12, 1917, House Mss, Yale University Library.

we can no longer honorably withdraw? With our initial policy as allies already tinged with suspicion, what result is to be expected? . . . The elements of an eventual conflict have step by step been created in a land where geographical conditions place us from the start at a disadvantage.[19]

With the end of the war and the beginning of the peace negotiations at Paris in 1919, Einstein's participation in the national political debates gathered momentum. It seems clear that even though he was a professional diplomat he had no intention of remaining silent during the heated political controversies that raged over international affairs in the United States during 1919–20. Until Theodore Roosevelt's death, Einstein maintained a regular correspondence with the ex-President.[20] He served as a consultant to several Republican senators, including Henry Cabot Lodge and Philander Knox.[21] That he did not oppose America's participation in a League of Nations is clear. But he was an early advocate of some broad definition of national rights within the framework of the League's organization. At the end of 1918, he declared that differences between Democratic and Republican views of the League were matters more of detail than of principle. To satisfy those critics who believed that American participation in the world organization would bring about a substantial loss of national sovereignty, Einstein went so far as to propose a reservation that would safeguard American interests. His all-inclusive reservation read as follows:

That the United States (1) understands and construes the Covenant of the League of Nations as in no way affecting the right of the United States to any military or other action involving expenditures or interference in respect to the affairs of other nations without in each case obtaining the Consent of the Congress of the United States; and (2) further reserves full liberty of action in respect to all provisions of this treaty, which may contain or later be found to con-

19. Letter from Einstein to House, July 30, 1918, House Mss, Yale University Library.

20. There are several letters between Roosevelt and Einstein in the Einstein Mss, University of Wyoming Library.

21. Letters from Einstein to Lodge, Oct. 16, 1919; Einstein to Knox, Dec. 11, 1919; and Elihu Root to Einstein, Dec. 24, 1919; all in the Einstein Mss, University of Wyoming Library.

tain any infringement on the rights hitherto enjoyed by American citizens.[22]

During the presidential campaign of 1920, Einstein was back in the United States serving in the capacity of foreign policy consultant to the Republican nominee, Warren G. Harding. Among his contributions to the Harding victory can be included the section of the Republican Campaign Text Book which blasted the Wilson administration for destroying the effectiveness of career diplomats, for damaging the overall administration of the Department of State, and for resorting to the use of numerous Executive agents rather than diplomatic personnel for diplomatic assignments.[23] He also took exception here to the proposal that the United States should accept a mandate over Armenia. On this question his reasoning was simply that the responsibilities of the mandatory in Armenia would so extend America's political commitments in the Middle East that this country would become hopelessly involved beyond any justification by national interests. Concerning Armenia he wrote: "The most certain way to keep a daily casualty list in our newspapers would be to accept an American Mandate for Armenia."

Under the pressure of the campaign, various charges were leveled at Wilson's foreign policy. Along with other Republicans, Einstein criticized the Democrats for accepting the Japanese occupation of Shantung, for the loss of American prestige in Mexico, for negative policies that contributed to the success of Bolshevism, for failure to register effective protests during the height of the Armenian massacres, for "misplaced interference in the Adriatic willfully prolonged unrest throughout Italy and southern Europe." And at the Paris Peace Conference, Wilson had, in Einstein's view, "wasted the greatest constructive opportunity in history and by an insistent meddlesomeness alienated from America the gratitude of Europe."[24]

Following the return of the Republican Party to power in 1921, President Harding appointed Einstein United States Minister to Czechoslovakia, where he remained until his retirement to private life in 1930 at the age of fifty-three. He took ample advantage of his oppor-

22. Einstein, "One Reservation Only: A General Statement to Cover Debatable Treaty Points," Letter to the Editor, *New York Times,* Dec. 27, 1918.

23. *Republican Campaign Text Book for 1920,* pp. 231–32, 115–17.

24. Ibid., p. 231.

tunity there to become familiar with the complicated status of various minorities. Later, during the fateful years of the 1930s, his was one of the earliest voices to speak out clearly and unequivocally concerning Hitler's blueprint for the mastery of Europe. Article after article, letter after letter to leading journals and newspapers in Europe and the United States contained Einstein's diagnosis of the ills that were rapidly spreading throughout Europe.[25] He urged that the democratic nations adopt a firm policy of containment of the Axis powers. As writer and publicist, he continued into the postwar years to use his long experience and vast knowledge of international affairs toward the end of making his fellow Americans aware of their vital interests in a world continuously beset by tensions and crises.

25. Among Einstein's many letters and articles of these years, see his letters to Secretary of State Cordell Hull, July 19 and 22, 1933, in Einstein Mss, University of Wyoming Library (the originals of these letters are in the Hull Mss, Library of Congress); Einstein, "The Cult of Force," *North American Review* (December 1933), pp. 501–07; "Herr Hitler's Middle Europe Plans," *The Spectator* (January 1934), pp. 39–40; "The German Question to Czechoslovakia," ibid. (July 24, 1936), pp. 135–36.

# *Editor's Note*

Lewis Einstein wrote these memoirs during the 1940s and early 1950s. They were among his papers when he presented the collection to the University of Wyoming Library in 1962. With only slight alterations, the manuscript is here published just as Mr. Einstein wrote it. One chapter in the original version, having to do with his relations with Mr. Justice Oliver Wendell Holmes was deleted because it seemed not entirely relevant to a work otherwise concerned with diplomatic affairs. Moreover, the omitted chapter covers much of the same subject matter that has already appeared in the published volume of the Holmes-Einstein correspondence (New York: St. Martin's Press, 1964). It may be of more than passing interest to observe that where alternative American and English spellings exist, Mr. Einstein invariably chose the English forms, and these have been preserved here.

I have added an introductory essay which it is hoped will contribute some additional clarification and perspective. Brief notes have also been prepared for the purpose of identifying many persons and places mentioned in the text. It was not always possible to find the desired biographical or explanatory information. Unfortunately, there are few adequate biographical reference works apart from the *Dictionnaire Diplomatique* (Paris and Geneva, Académie Diplomatique Internationale, n.d. but ca. 1954), Volume V, and the limited number of directories which provide data concerning diplomats of the early twentieth century. I can only ask for the reader's indulgence and trust that the admittedly incomplete notes may prove useful.

In preparing these memoirs for publication, I have received valuable assistance and advice from many persons. I appreciate the willingness of George F. Kennan to take time from a busy schedule to write the Foreword for the volume. Henry Andrews of England, long-time friend of the Einsteins, has been an unfailing source of encouragement from the outset. I also want to acknowledge the enthusiastic cooperation of Gene M. Gressley, director of the Manuscripts Division of the

University of Wyoming Library, who generously allowed me the freest use of the Einstein papers in his custody. Mrs. Jasper Streater of Oxford, England, very graciously shared her vast knowledge of Turkish politics during the early twentieth century by providing many of the notes for those chapters concerned with Mr. Einstein's work in Constantinople. I want also to express my deep sense of appreciation to numerous reference librarians who helped me at the Library of Congress, the Yale University Library, the Cleveland Public Library, the Hoover Institution at Stanford, California, and the University of Iowa Library. I have relied on the wise counsel of Marian Neal Ash, managing editor of the Yale University Press, who has devoted much time to seeing these memoirs through to publication.

I want to express special acknowledgment to Lewis Einstein himself. I think it must be rare indeed to find an author of memoirs who allows such complete latitude to an editor. Mr. Einstein's many letters to me over the past several years have provided a real inspiration and much assistance. His willingness to entrust his extensive manuscript collection and these memoirs to me when I was at the University of Wyoming has been a source of great personal satisfaction. Hopefully, the papers will continue to benefit historians, who will find much that is significant.

*Lawrence E. Gelfand*

Iowa City, Iowa
August 29, 1967

Lewis Einstein died on December 4, 1967, in Paris, at the age of ninety. His friend Henry Andrews had shown the page proofs of these memoirs to him shortly before his death.

# *Preface* by Lewis Einstein

Diplomacy is a profession which lies on the borderland between history and gossip, for every diplomat desires to make history and few can avoid gossip. These memories contain a little of both, for the two are without any natural dividing line and nearer to each other than is commonly suspected.

When Minister at Prague, I recall a conversation with a retired Austrian cavalry general who frequently came to the Legation and liked to chat about the old army. We talked that day about a mutual friend who, after having been an officer in the general's regiment, resigned to become a diplomat. I asked why. The old soldier explained that our friend understood there was no future open to him in the cavalry; he really was far too stupid for a military career, so he became a diplomat. I smiled; the general apologized.

After spending the best years of one's life in diplomacy, it is hard to keep many illusions regarding the present state of the profession or its still more doubtful future. The old career looked at life through the window of a chancery with something of the detached aloofness with which the aged look at people in the street. Its secret wickedness was a romantic myth, its plotting intrigues fantastic tales, and its principal sins were those of Sybarites. Its morals were not always Puritan, but it kept a high standard of honesty. It believed in its ability to give disinterested advice, to act as a convenient shock absorber, and to serve as a mollifying intermediary. The world today, when diplomacy is carried out often by threat and insult, has less and less use for intermediaries who understand each other's language and are personal friends. Politicians have become as indifferent to the smiling and sceptical honesty of the courteous old diplomacy as the latter had once been to the crowd's applause.

For anyone to put down his recollections on paper contains an unfortunate assumption of self-importance; the writer implies that he has something to say, and the reader wonders if this is true and hopes that he will at least be indiscreet. Yet the author is the last person whose opinion has any value on either point. If in these pages there is an attempt made to record certain experiences, it is because of the wish to preserve memories of public men and of events witnessed and of incidents I have been concerned with. Recollections that cover many unconnected topics, trivial and otherwise, pertain to the career, and there are few diplomats in recent years who have not had occasion to touch some of the fringes of great questions. Everyone who is past middle age sees his map of life today divided like Caesar's Gaul into three parts—that which came before the First World War, the War, and all that has happened since, for the Second World War has really been a delayed continuation of the First. There are things that pertain to all three parts in this book.

It is in the order of life that those familiar with that reputedly Elysian period which reached its end in 1914 should daily grow fewer. No one is now alive of the leading diplomats who discussed futilities at Algesiras,* while an expectant Europe trembled. Turkish sultans have gone their way. Abdul Hamid has become almost a legendary figure; the eunuchs and the scallywags who formed his incredible court have been forgotten. But whoever tries to dig up the roots of the Great War will find not a few of these lying deep in the soggy soil on which Yildiz† was built. That is why I have roughly tried to sketch a little of the life that went on around the Red Sultan, for I passed several years at Constantinople in the time of that potentate's splendour, and later I was to witness his fall. Afterwards at Peking, during the last days of the Manchus, one could see the handwriting of the Revolution already written on the Wall. A brief interlude in Central America and then Turkey again, during the epic of the Dardanelles and the massacre of the Armenians. I was then sent to Bulgaria, in charge of British interests, and soon found myself the most unpopular neutral at Sofia. Today, only to recall these memories is also to recall something of the old diplomacy, for until those who once formed its ranks have left the scene they can still trim the wicks of their flickering lamps.

* Einstein here employs the French spelling; the common English spelling is Algeciras. A resort community, it is located in the extreme south of Spain, in the vicinity of Gibraltar, and was the scene of the conference on Morocco held in 1906.

† Imperial residence situated northeast of Constantinople. During the reign of Sultan Abdul Hamid, Yildiz attained its greatest size, with about 12,000 inhabitants.

*A Diplomat Looks Back*

# 1. *The Algesiras Conference*

The first thunderclap of the Great War exploded over Algesiras. After the Kaiser had landed at Tangier,* on the last day of March 1905, Prince Radolin, the German Ambassador in Paris, baldly announced to the French government that his Imperial master stood with all his strength behind Morocco. Europe unexpectedly discovered a first-class crisis, and France found that she was threatened with war at a moment which could hardly have been worse, for her army had just passed through the painful aftermath of the Dreyfus affair, while Russia, exhausted by her struggle against Japan and seething with revolution, could offer no help. The diplomacy of the Wilhelmstrasse had counted on this precise predicament. The gamble for Berlin was only to know if British battleships were ready to replace Cossacks and if the freshly cemented *Entente*† could stand a real strain.

The German grievances over Morocco were largely symptoms of a smouldering resentment felt by a great power which was overconscious of its strength and bitterly jealous of the fact that less populous nations had found better opportunities for enjoying the world's resources. Deliberately, Germany made trouble not because she cared about the Shereefian Empire‡ but because she felt ill-tempered at her place in the world. She did not want war, but in the menacing way of handling this question she acquired the dangerous habit of a willingness to pro-

* The Kaiser announced upon his arrival that Germany wanted Morocco to have an independent status so that all the powers would enjoy equality of commercial opportunity. The German sovereign's statement was interpreted as a deliberate counter to recent French attempts to gain hegemony over Morocco.

† The diplomatic understanding, known as the *Entente Cordiale,* reached between England and France and embodied in several conventions signed on April 8, 1904. Included were arrangements for the future of Madagascar, the New Hebrides, and Siam, but by far the most important had to do with Morocco and Egypt: the British were given a free hand in the latter and the French in the former. In settling most of their outstanding disputes, Britain and France, traditional diplomatic rivals, effected a diplomatic revolution of the first magnitude.

‡ Derived from Sherif, or ruler, of Morocco, hence the Empire of Morocco.

voke a crisis, which owing to her military superiority she did not fear, and then left on other nations the burden of reducing the consequences of her truculence.

The first introduction to my colleagues at the conference took place in the train on the way to Algesiras. Early in the morning I was not the only one to be puzzled by a trickle of water that ran down the corridor of the sleeping car. Everyone was at a loss to account for this until the conductor discovered that it came from the compartment of Count Sforza, who was indulging in his morning tub. This was my first introduction to perhaps the most brilliant member of the conference, who was afterwards to become a valued friend.

Largely owing to President Roosevelt's secret diplomacy, the French had been persuaded to accept a Moroccan Conference, which met at Algesiras in January 1906. The small Andalusian city which gave its name to a famous conference is prettily situated on the northern shore of the Bay of Gibraltar. Behind the town are cork woods, but before these are reached there lie fields which already in January were bright with daffodils dancing in the sunshine that made one forget we were still in winter. In contrast to the countryside, the windswept town that was to be our residence during the next three months was as drab and somnolent as is the usual small Spanish city. The streets were always deserted, and the few inhabitants who were visible showed no sign of occupation, although rumour had it that the principal local industry was smuggling. One associates Spanish smugglers with the music of *Carmen,* but there was too much indolent detachment about these people to suggest anything operatic or picturesque. Without actually being rude, the Algesirans appeared to be as indifferent to our presence in their town as all the rest of the world, trembling in fear of a conflict, was just then interested. The inhabitants, who might have stepped out of Zurbaran's* canvases, were not in the least curious about foreign ambassadors nor were they concerned by such trifles as an international conference which was then about to meet in their town in order to avert a war. Their own mysterious affairs seemed to be of far greater importance than a mere European crisis, but what these affairs were I was never able to discover.

* A Spanish painter (1598–1668) noted for his canvases of still life and portraiture. Some of his best-known existing work decorates the chapel and sacristy of the monastery at Guadalupe.

The courteous Spanish officials sent from Madrid made profuse apologies for the scanty resources offered by a small town like Algesiras and tried hard to accord us at least the more conventional signs of welcome. The Governor greeted the delegates on their arrival at the station with Castilian grandiloquence. Spain possesses some of the finest tapestries in the world, but only a shabby red baize was found to adorn the Town Hall in which the sessions of the conference were held, and even that embellishment worthy of a village fair looked as if it had been grudgingly applied. Later a few wretched bulls were massacred in our honor at a *Corrida,* and a cinema performance was given for our entertainment of a nature that scandalized the Moorish delegates and left the Africans more than ever perplexed regarding the merits of European civilization.

At the Hotel Reina Cristina, where the members of the conference were to reside for three months, the diminutive flags of many nations were placed, as in Swiss hotels, over the dining-room tables of the different delegations. The *table d'hôte* form taken by an international conference, although not particularly impressive, was yet a symbol of the proximity in which the delegations were obliged to live and which put human intercourse on its most practical basis. Frenchmen and Germans might be on the eve of war, but meanwhile they slept under the same roof and grumbled together over their fare in the same public rooms. Long ago it was said that cooks can accomplish more than ambassadors, and at the Reina Cristina an aggrieved attitude toward the monotony of the hotel dishes certainly united potential foes in a common complaint. There was something slightly ludicrous in despatching to a remote corner of Spain a number of diplomats who were obliged to inhabit the identical hotel while at the same time they tried to settle a dispute of grave international dimensions. Along with diplomatic discussions, something which might almost be described as a hotel *esprit de corps* developed. This was mainly of a negative kind, for it was grounded on certain common complaints and the nearness in which we lived made these real. Everyone in fact jostled everyone else continually. A careless ambassador would drop his confidential papers in the most awkward localities, and once I earned the momentary gratitude of the Spanish Delegation by returning a secret memorandum that I had picked up in a corridor and which would have proved embarrassing if it had fallen into some journalist's hands.

The press provided the link between our cloistral isolation and the outside world. While Europe was waiting in anxious suspense to know whether war or peace was coming from the conference, a number of prying newspapermen swarmed like hornets around us ready to distort any half-baked bit of information. From this mass of international journalists Walter Harris, the Tangier correspondent of the London *Times,* stood out as one of the most amusing talkers in the world. The disordered state of Morocco had made it too dangerous for Harris to live in the fine house which he had lately built for himself on the beach near Tangier, and he professed to discover his principal interest in the Moroccan question in being able to return to his home. Actually he was greatly enjoying the humour of finding his own domestic difficulties enmeshed in a European crisis, nor was he averse to establishing a connection between the kidnapping Moorish brigands and a tortuous German diplomacy. Beyond such quips Harris possessed a remarkable insight into the native mind and took an impish delight in every tribal squabble. These were his particular hobby, for he spoke Arabic like a Moor, and although he possessed much shrewd knowledge of diplomatic questions, these interested him less, I suspect, than the sheep-stealing politics of the native clans. He followed these in all their intricacies, for he was an orientalist and a traveller who some years before, disguised as a native, had visited at great risk such mysterious localities as the Talfilelt,* where before him no white man had ever ventured, but which he described as being singularly uninteresting and unpicturesque. Harris was also one of the few men I have ever known with enough humour to tell a story even against himself. Once the Sultan had expressed his satisfaction to him that so remarkable a liar should not be counted among his subjects. At least Harris told me this merely for the pleasure of relating his rejoinder, which was typical of the man: "Had I been a Moor with such a talent for lying I certainly would have become Your Majesty's Grand Vizier!"

Before the conference met, a sensible agreement had been reached between Paris and Berlin that the delegations should so far as possible be composed of career diplomats. The real advantage which this arrangement offered was probably the one least considered at the time. Public opinion, which was everywhere excited by the press and fright-

* An oasis and district in the southern part of Morocco on the northern edge of the Sahara and the southeastern edge of the Atlas Mountains.

ened by the gloomiest forebodings, needed to be allayed, and diplomats could do this more satisfactorily than politicians, for it is one of the merits of the career that its members, like players for the Davis Cup, learn to fight without any personal animosity.

American diplomats are frequently recruited by methods mysterious to Europeans, but at the Moroccan Conference the United States Delegation was constituted along highly orthodox lines. Henry White, at that time Ambassador at Rome, was Chief, Samuel R. Gummere, Minister at Tangier, was the second delegate, and I was Secretary. After Mr. Choate, the late Ambassador in London, had declined the post, President Roosevelt offered the appointment of first delegate to Mr. White. A common American belief looks to lawyers for diplomats, in contrast to England where the advocate is not thought to make the best negotiator. Among White's other merits was the fact that he was not a lawyer. Moreover he had always lived in a world which hardly extended beyond a somewhat narrow circle in London and New York. Although his sympathies were not wide, he possessed a natural amenity of manner, a conscientious sense of duty, and a vast amount of common sense. As a chief I always found him considerate, well balanced, and painstaking. At the conference White was from the start in a strong position, for the United States had made no previous commitments and desired no selfish advantage. Also the fact of representing Theodore Roosevelt helped him to carry out to general satisfaction the task of a disinterested peacemaker.

Roosevelt was then at the height of his fame, with a prestige immensely enhanced by his recent success in having brought the Russo-Japanese war to an end. This may explain why the Kaiser tried to enlist the President's help, without stopping to realize that Roosevelt's private views about the Moroccan question had already been formed. The latter liked the French and sympathized with their ambition to take up another "White Man's Burden"; he distrusted German policy which he had recently discomfited in Venezuelan waters.* The President shortly before had in fact described the Kaiser's sudden interest

* Einstein refers here to the Venezuelan Debt Dispute of 1902. When the Castro regime in Venezuela would not meet its obligations to European creditors, several governments, the German in particular, acting as "collection agencies" for their bondholders, threatened to use naval force. President Theodore Roosevelt intervened for the United States on the side of Venezuela, forcing Germany to abandon its "gunboat diplomacy," and the crisis subsided.

in Morocco as his "latest pipe dream." For Roosevelt understood European politics in a way which few American presidents have done, and he dreaded lest Germany might blunder into war all the more lightheartedly because of blustering confidence in her own strength. He knew that a real danger lay in the Imperial Government being so convinced about its military superiority that it might refuse to back down from a position once this had been assumed. He also foresaw that the Kaiser would have to be humoured. The opinion was at that time widely held in Berlin that the mere threat of war would be sufficient, although at Algesiras the second German delegate, Count Tattenbach, delicately hinted that his country might be obliged to crush the French "like cockroaches." Eight years later the world was to discover the consequences of this kind of arrogance. If proof of this did not come during the Moroccan crisis, much of the merit of saving Europe from a vast disaster was due to the diplomacy of Theodore Roosevelt.

The United States was a signatory of the first Moroccan Conference which had been held in the early eighties and had dealt with such controversial topics as the control of the lighthouse on Cape Spartel.* That Washington would be asked to attend the second conference was certain, but it was less so that the invitation would be accepted. American opinion in principle strongly favours international congresses but was until lately inclined to become less enthusiastic, always suspicious, and usually refractory as soon as anything which had political implications was discussed. The belief was then more widely entertained in the United States and not least in the Senate that American diplomacy falls an easy victim to foreign blandishments and that an unsuspicious innocence may cause an administration to stray into the most perilous entanglements. That is why the eminently successful steps to keep the peace of the world taken by an American President at a European conference regarding an African empire, instead of being announced as a triumph by the Administration, had to be kept secret most of all from the American people. What Roosevelt then did was kept secret even from his own delegates at Algesiras.

* An extensive summary of the sixteen sessions of the Conference, prepared by Lucius Fairchild, U.S. representative at the Conference, was published in *Papers Relating to the Foreign Relations of the United States, 1880* (Washington, Government Printing Office, 1880), pp. 893–929.

In August 1905, nearly six months before the conference opened, the President had written privately to Henry White, who had not yet been appointed a delegate, to say that although he proposed to keep an even keel in the Moroccan crisis his personal sympathies were entirely for France. At the conference itself, all the telegrams and despatches addressed to the American delegation at Algesiras passed through my hands as Secretary and I have since looked through the Henry White papers at the Library of Congress. Except for the abovementioned letter, I have never been able to discover that the President took any further steps, either before or during the course of the conference, to enlighten his representative, who was also an old personal friend, about his talks on the Moroccan crisis with the German and French ambassadors, Baron Speck von Sternburg and M. Jusserand, or that he ever informed White about the highly important communications which he then addressed to the Kaiser and the French government. The only Americans in fact acquainted at this time with the details of Roosevelt's secret diplomacy were Senator Lodge and Secretaries Taft and Root.

After White's appointment to Algesiras, Secretary Root wrote to him privately to "keep friendly with all. Help France get what she ought to have but don't take the fight on your shoulders. Help limit France when she ought to be limited, but don't take that fight on your shoulders."* This sybilline piece of advice from the pen of a great lawyer was almost too wisely unilluminating. In spite of an old personal friendship and the official confidence reposed in him by the President and his Secretary of State, White was kept very much in the dark regarding the important triangular secret negotiations which had led up to the conference and which were continued during its progress; nor did he learn any of the details about these until some time afterwards. Whatever the reason may have been for this neglect, the first American delegate at an international congress was left singularly uninformed concerning many important matters and remained unaware until much later of the extraordinary correspondence which had been exchanged between the White House and the Kaiser. Only after the conference was over, when such knowledge possessed merely an his-

* The text of the letter is published in Allen Nevins, *Henry White: Thirty Years of American Diplomacy* (New York and London, Harper, 1930), p. 268. *L.E.*

toric interest, did Roosevelt, who felt justifiably proud of the influence for peace which he had exerted in Europe, describe the steps he had taken in a confidential letter which he addressed to Whitelaw Reid and of which he sent White a copy.*

On one subject only did the American Delegation receive from the President specific and pressing instructions. Mr. Jacob Schiff, the New York banker, had addressed a lengthy memorandum, obviously prepared from German sources, perhaps with the idea of stirring up some further trouble, although this possibility was unsuspected by Mr. Schiff, in order to solicit Roosevelt's aid in ameliorating the condition of the native Jews in Morocco. The idea appealed warmly to the President as a reformer and a politician, and White, enlightened by a private letter from Root, mentioned that the President was more interested in this than in anything else at Algesiras. Shortly before the conference opened, I had gone to Tangier to enquire into this question and discovered, to my astonishment, that the last thing which the Moroccan Jews would have welcomed was a complaint about grievances which were then principally nonexistent. The injustices that Mr. Schiff's memorandum movingly described were either no longer in force or else were open to interpretations which were far from making these the hardships represented. Furthermore, in recent years a series of liberal reforms had been carried out much to the advantage of the native Jews. The latter were grateful for these ameliorations and only desired the conference to offer its congratulations to the Sultan on the enlightened policy which His Shereefian Majesty had pursued toward his Jewish subjects. This agreeable duty was easily arranged, as the delegates, after having given so many hard kicks to the Moroccans, felt pleased to stroke them with a friendly pat. The little pink-cheeked, blue-eyed Moroccan envoy, Mohammed El Torres, who was always as dignified as he was dumb and who remained seemingly unaware that the fate of his country was being decided, obtained in this way his only success. Even the Czar's envoy, Count Cassini, himself of Italian origin, who it was said barely knew a word of Russian and

* Published in J. B. Bishop, *Theodore Roosevelt and His Time, Shown in His Own Letters* (London and New York, Hodder and Stoughton, 1920), *1*, 467–505. See also *Selections from the Correspondence of Theodore Roosevelt and Henry Cabot Lodge,* ed. H. C. Lodge (New York and London, Scribners, 1925), passim. *L.E.*

whose brother was an Austrian admiral, expressed a wish to have Roosevelt, who particularly distrusted him, informed of the personal pleasure with which he adhered to so humane a resolution. Everyone became unexpectedly complimentary, and the mischief which Mr. Schiff's excellent intention might have led to was safely buried with flowers.

Closest to Henry White in sympathy was the British delegate, Sir Arthur Nicolson, later to become Lord Carnock. I had known him already in Tangier, where for years he had fought a skilful rearguard action to obstruct the advance of the French. Nicolson had been left so long in Morocco that he felt the usual fear of diplomats who serve at distant posts, lest he should be forgotten by his Foreign Office. Paradoxically his reward came when his government reversed everything that he had done in Morocco in order to give France a free hand in exchange for no longer opposing England in Egypt. After the *Entente Cordiale* was signed, it became impossible for Nicolson to remain at Tangier. Promotion took him first to the Embassy at Madrid. From there Nicolson went to Algesiras, no longer to block the French but to help them to stay in Morocco, which he did with a loyalty to his government's now reversed policy that infuriated quite as much as it impressed the Germans. No one worked harder for the success of the conference, and in addition to the duties common to all he had to write everything twice over to his Foreign Office, the first time in the gelatinous style suitable for future parliamentary Blue Books, with a second uncensored version for the Foreign Secretary's private enlightenment.

This little bright-eyed, stoop-shouldered man, already bent by a painful arthritis which later was to cripple him, displayed at the conference not merely ability but the rarer quality of character. He talked with an old-world courtesy which brought to my mind a statesman of the same breed as Walsingham,* and I could picture Nicolson wearing a doublet and a ruff around his neck and advising the Virgin Queen. He was old-fashioned in his courtly manner, but he was at heart surprisingly liberal, and after the general election in England which took place during the conference I heard him express pleasure at the number of seats which Labour for the first time had won. Above everything

* Sir Francis Walsingham (1530–90), an English diplomat during the reign of Elizabeth.

else Nicolson was an honest man who cared nothing for popular applause. This old-fashioned diplomat, brought up in a supposedly cynical school, afterwards refused to have anything to do with Sir Edward Grey's curious plan to buy off Germany by offering her support for the reversionary rights to the Portuguese colonies which Great Britain had guaranteed.*

By a striking though accidental coincidence, which at the time must have escaped the attention of Berlin, the location of the conference at Algesiras could not have been better selected to bring out in a most impressive way the full value of England's support. Across the Bay and in full sight of the hotel in which we lived rose the Rock of Gibraltar as a mighty symbol of British sea power. The French have never been willing to admit the immense debt which they owed at this time to the English fleet. Also the Kaiser in his various messages to Roosevelt seemingly allowed himself to be persuaded by the President's cajoling diplomacy. But the thick flattery which the White House then doled out to Potsdam might have been less persuasive without the British battleships which loomed against the horizon. At Algesiras a German remarked to me that the French who looked for a Napoleon had found him in the English Navy. I never knew if it was by accident or by design that Prince Louis of Battenberg, the German-born Admiral of the Mediterranean fleet, sailed into the Bay of Gibraltar at the head of the great squadrons under his command. Prince Louis, with Lord Charles Beresford and several other high British admirals, came over next day to dine at our table as guests of Henry White. I am convinced that my chief's invitation contained no ulterior purpose. But only a few feet away sat the German delegates, and it was not hard to guess at the thoughts which then entered their heads.

To be a grand old man implies certain vague qualifications both of age and of eminence. The title is rarely given, but from time to time every country discovers that it possesses some venerable hero who answers these requirements, and many were then prepared to recognise as

* Einstein refers here to the Anglo-German Convention of August 1913 concerning the Portuguese colonies. As his biographer-son has written, Nicolson believed profoundly in the "German menace." He was convinced that Germany wanted to dominate other countries, including England. His strategy for avoiding military conflict was to strengthen the Entente. See Harold George Nicolson, *Sir Arthur Nicolson, First Lord Carnock* (London, Constable, 1930), pp. 329 ff.

the Grand Old Man of Europe the first Italian delegate at the conference, the Marquis Visconti Venosta. This aged statesman was himself almost an epitome of nineteenth-century history, for he had begun his career in Vienna as an attaché under Metternich, left the diplomacy of the Habsburgs to join the *Carbonari** in his native Lombardy when it was still an Austrian province, and then abandoned their republican conspiracies in order to take service under Cavour. At the time of our Civil War he had already been Minister for Foreign Affairs, and in 1906 he was the last survivor of the great generation which had created a united Italy.

His long white beard, which extended like a reversed aureole, gave the Italian delegate the look of a more distinguished though less benevolent Father Christmas. Even his warmest admirers would hardly have dared to call him a dear old man. Age may have withered his sensibilities, for I still recall him gazing fixedly at dying horses in a bull fight while younger men slunk away in disgust from that revolting spectacle. In spite of his courteous surface, I suspect that the Marquis felt hardly more kindly toward his fellow delegates than he did to the horses in the arena. Certainly not many at Algesiras met with his favour, and he took few pains to conceal the poor opinion in which he held most of his colleagues at the conference. After all the delegates had been presented to him and the customary compliments had been exchanged, his comment made in private was, "They told me there were to be ambassadors here. I see only lawyers."

The Marquis was treated with a deference which is rarely given to men until they are past their prime. But when the aged statesman tried to assume the rôle of mediator he met with no success. Everyone knew that he had been sent to evince a mild sympathy for the French in exchange for future support that France had pledged Italy in Tripoli, and that he proposed to carry out what Prince Bülow wittily described as a *"tour de valse."* The result was a bit disappointing, and an irreverent Italian journalist remarked that the Marquis was certainly an eagle, although a stuffed one. This was not quite fair, for the old gen-

* Members of secret revolutionary societies in Italy during the early nineteenth century, who first appeared at the time of Napoleonic rule. Members were drawn mainly from the nobility and governing classes. Their most spectacular achievement was the Neapolitan Revolution of 1820.

tleman retained all the graces of his exceptionally rich cultivation. Public affairs, I suspect, finished by interesting him less in his old age, and his principal pleasures then came from a taste for roses and a love for ancient pictures. Renaissance art was his favourite topic of conversation, and he made me searching questions to know if I had come across any trace in Spain of Francesco da Salerno, who was one of Leonardo da Vinci's more obscure followers.

The Secretary of the Italian Delegation was Count Sforza, who after both world wars became Minister for Foreign Affairs. A brilliant and an agreeable talker, who also knew how to listen, Sforza possessed a flashing and incisive wit, which he could not always restrain even in his own interest, and an Irish streak of boyish humour which at times came out unexpectedly and was both spontaneous and deliberate. In the off hours of the conference his pranks enlivened many a dull day. I remember one afternoon when a few of us walked over to a neighbouring beach where we lay on the sand. The waves rippled gently at our feet and behind us rose an amphitheatre of cliffs to frame a scene of wild beauty in which no human habitation blotted the horizon. There always is something pagan about the blue Mediterranean landscape that suggests the nearness of the ancient gods, and this we felt when Sforza unexpectedly appeared on horseback. He disturbed the classical reverie which we imagined ourselves to be in; one of the ladies then observed that instead of modern man she would far prefer to see an ancient centaur dashing through the waves. Sforza disappeared at once after this remark, but a few minutes later the rider showed himself as a fleeting silhouette against the setting sun, galloping madly along the water's edge but without a stitch of clothing on his back. This was the lighter side of a brilliant man who since has shown that he possesses gifts of character and of courage as well as of statesmanship.

The French Delegate, M. Révoil, possessed a carefully curled moustache of the kind formerly seen in English comic papers whenever they attempted to depict an excited Frenchman. M. Révoil never betrayed excitement, though it would have been pardonable for he must have passed through anxious moments. He was an able lawyer who possessed a thorough technical grasp of every question and did a good job yet obtained strangely little credit for it. Although the conference turned out to be a much greater success for France than at first seemed likely, the French delegate never received his deserts. His personality failed to inspire much confidence among his slower-witted Anglo-Saxon colleagues who were otherwise extremely friendly to the French cause. He was overglib and amiable when a solid massiveness and restraint would have been more impressive to men of English speech. The dialectic subtlety of his legal mind, although imposed by the vacillations going on in Paris, had the effect of disquieting his allies and made them distrustful of his arguments. The French wished to justify the intended "Tunisification" of Morocco on legal grounds, which was not too easy, so that Révoil grew all the more voluble. The second French representative, M. Regnault, who was abundantly endowed with the calm composure of the northern French *bourgeois* and who was able to conceal without trying to explain his anxieties, enjoyed far greater personal sympathy among the English-speaking delegations. The able French Secretaries were Aynard, who was to meet a soldier's death at Verdun, and two future ambassadors in Berlin and Tokyo, de Margerie and de Billy, who would address each other familiarly as "Marjory" and "Billy."

Berlin had started with an excellent case to make trouble over Morocco. The Shereefian Empire was visibly falling into anarchy and in one way or another order had to be restored. Why, the Germans asked, should France claim this exclusive right except for the small northern coastal strip which she had agreed to reserve to Spain? Why should not Morocco remain a fair field for all instead of being grabbed only by one country? The Kaiser professed his own disinterestedness in this question, expounded "Open Door" to Roosevelt, and expected American sympathy for a doctrine which the United States only shortly before had preached in China. The Emperor William furthermore posed as the protector of the Moslem world, and had publicly announced his friendship for the Sultan of Morocco. Behind these two avowed motives a third one was kept in the background. Berlin has always been obsessed by the fear of encirclement, and above everything the Wilhelmstrasse wished to deal a shattering blow to the new and painfully born *Entente Cordiale*. The Kaiser wanted Paris to know that in a real pinch England would be of no use to her, and he counted on finding some support in France for this idea. Many Frenchmen in 1905 still smarted at the thought of Fashoda,* remained highly distrustful of Albion, and would have preferred a continental security guaranteed by Germany to a colonial security guaranteed by England. Not a few of his countrymen had severely blamed the energetic and daring M. Delcassé for having been bold enough to map out a forward Moroccan policy without consulting Berlin.

Germany's rise as a great power came so suddenly that her foreign policy has often been characterized by a startling abruptness which emanates from her military background. She has been the only great nation never to feel quite certain of her position and therefore alternating with an uneasy violence between extremes of effacement and of dangerous arrogance. Among some of the Germans who were at Algesiras I noted this misgiving, which went with a disposition to criticise the Kaiser for embarking too late on the Moroccan adventure. The flashy versatility of William the Second stood him in bad stead whenever things went wrong, and because of this he has met with some unfair blame. The real truth about his attitude toward Morocco came out with the publication of Bülow's memoirs,† which related that the Emperor made his memorable landing at Tangier most reluctantly and against his own better judgement. Prince Bülow was far too cautious to wish for war, but clever as he was and European as he liked to pose with much cynical humour, the Junker in his background left him not disinclined to resort to that peculiar Teutonic stridency which always alarms Europe. At first he had scored heavily by asserting Germany's right to be consulted. Then with Roosevelt's help he had forced an unwilling but unprepared France to accept his plan for a conference. But after this he had needlessly humiliated a proud country by demanding the dismissal of Delcassé. Then, holding most of the trumps in his hand, the German Chancellor felt less certain which one to play.

Any one of four possibilities were at that time open to Bülow. Germany might have made war on France, whose army was unprepared,

* In July 1898, during the campaign of Kitchener against the Mahdists in the Sudan, a French expedition from the Congo had occupied Fashoda (renamed Kodok in 1904), a site on the Nile claimed by both Britain and France. The incident precipitated an Anglo-French struggle from which the French ultimately withdrew.

† *Denkwürdigkeiten* (Berlin, Ullstein, 1930).

with every prospect of victory on land. Or, until the last moment, the Wilhelmstrasse could have negotiated a most profitable arrangement with the Quai d'Orsay, for the Rouvier Cabinet was prepared to pay a very high price in order to obtain a free hand in Morocco. A third alternative was for the Kaiser, after so many professions of disinterestedness, genuinely to become the advocate of the "Open Door" and to lead the world against what he had pilloried, not without some reason, as a French imperialistic grab. Lastly, having successfully displayed the strength of her position, Germany could have shown herself conciliatory and prepared the way for an eventual alliance with France which might then have killed the tender plant of the *Entente* and have ended by making the Kaiser master of Europe. A friendly gesture at this time, a little less blatancy and arrogance, and a little more care to avoid senseless humiliation of a neighbour, would have been far more serviceable to Berlin than the blustering threats she made or the petty colonial advantages she could hope to squeeze.

With an excellent case, Bülow overplayed his hand and was never able to decide on the precise line he wanted to take. The wish to grab and yet to defend the "Open Door," the desire to humiliate France and yet to separate her from England, were contradictory aims that were interwoven in a confused jumble at the Wilhelmstrasse and which left German policy before, during, and after the conference loud but vacillating, apparently strong and actually ambiguous and obscure. In the most critical moments the tortuous German movements seemed to flounder without possessing any clear sense of direction. All this time, the Quai d'Orsay was skilfully extricating itself by judicious concessions from its early difficulties. After Rouvier's original offer to negotiate privately with Berlin had been unceremoniously rejected, Paris, pressed with friendly insistence by Roosevelt, reluctantly but wisely accepted the plan of a conference. Then, just before Algesiras, Germany tried to be bought off in a secret negotiation. It was now the turn of the French to talk virtuously about an internationalized Morocco and declare that their earnest wish to preserve the "Open Door" would be incompatible with any such private arrangement.

Herr von Radowitz, the German Ambassador at Madrid, was the Kaiser's tired and disillusioned representative at Algesiras. In public he was always courteous in that bristling and mandatory Prussian way which looks either up or down but rarely sees others on a level. It was somehow not easy to reconcile this old man's starched military politeness with the blustering intrigues of his government. During the progress of the conference the Wilhelmstrasse was persistently attempting to instil suspicion of England in the minds of the French, and the whisper went round that in private Sir Arthur Nicolson had blamed the latter. The memory of the British envoy's record at Tangier was too fresh in Paris for the dart not to strike home, and the French, for a time, were seriously perturbed by a suspicion which they could hardly admit about their ally's supposed duplicity. Nicolson, the most honourable of men, when he heard about this outrageous aspersion on his loyalty, was furious, and in a letter to his wife he gave vent to indignation at what he called the German Ambassador's "unblushing lying and double dealing."* At a critical moment during the conference, Radowitz gave the British delegate his word of honor that he had made his very last concession—a statement which turned out to be quite untrue. The German Ambassador was, however, something of a figurehead, and may have been less a culprit than a victim of the Wilhelmstrasse, whose shifting tactics he must have found difficult to follow. He appeared to lack the assurance of an envoy who enjoys the full confidence of his Ministry and it was a little hard to understand why so seemingly effaced an old man should have been appointed to represent one of the principal powers at a great conference.

In the background lay the explanation. A minor official of the German delegation, an unpleasant little Prussian bureaucrat named Klehmet, whom Bülow later tried to use as a scapegoat for the Kaiser's famous interview, had been sent to control Radowitz by Holstein, the mystery man of the Wilhelmstrasse, who had plotted the entire Moroccan crisis which soon afterwards was to cause his own undoing.

The second German delegate was Count Tattenbach, who enjoyed a European celebrity for his violent temper and a reputation for diplomatic trouble making, which, it is only fair to say, he did not live up to. The gentler disposition of the amiable Countess Tattenbach stood out in sharp contrast to her husband's irascibility. The Countess had discovered in the conference an opportunity to add still more autographs to fill the pages of an album which, in the fashion of an

* Nicolson, *Sir Arthur Nicolson*, pp. 186, 192 ff. *L.E.*

older generation, had become the companion of her long diplomatic career and which invariably she carried with her. Everyone in turn was invited to inscribe his name in an album that possessed a hierarchy of its own, for only ambassadors were requested to add to their signature the expression of an appropriate thought. Thus when the Countess asked the Marquis Visconti Venosta to inscribe some suitable reflection, the caustic Italian wrote in Latin: "Peace be to all men who come with good intent."

After the conference had ended, the Emperor William addressed a telegram to the Emperor Francis Joseph, which in the annals of diplomacy is still remembered as a model of what not to say. The venerable Habsburg sovereign, who was imbued with the pride of his ancient House and somewhat inclined to regard the Hohenzollerns as recent *parvenus,* received from his ally at Potsdam a message of thanks for the services that he had rendered at Algesiras as a "brilliant second." It would have been difficult to discover anything brilliant about the sad-faced Austrian delegate, Count Welserheim, beyond his enjoying a more direct descent from Charles the Fifth than even the reigning dynasty could claim. The Count would have been described in French as a *brave homme,* which implies some vague virtues wisely left undefined and usually taken on trust; certainly the diplomacy which the Austrian envoy practised at the conference added more to his reputation for innocence than for brilliancy. During the only real controversy ever permitted to rise to the surface the Count, who was Ambassador at Madrid, ingenuously proposed the one plan that was distinctly offensive to the irate Spaniards, for it assigned Tetuan to the French.

The second Austrian delegate, Count Koziebrodski, did not suffer from the self-effacement of his guileless chief. Some men pass into history with a phrase, and in his own service the Count was famous for his description of a cousin who bore the same name as being "also a diplomat and also very good looking." In order to mark still more the importance of his activities, the Count never seemed able to enter the hotel dining-room without holding under his arm a vast portfolio conspicuously chalked "Confidential." A cultivated French correspondent at Algesiras, Joseph Galtier, having in mind the famous sonnet by Felix Arvers which begins: "Mon âme a son secret, ma vie a son mystère," gave me a witty parody that he had composed about the Austrian Count of which the first line ran "Kozie a son secret et Brodski son mystère."

According to the customary practise on similar occasions, His Catholic Majesty's Minister for Foreign Affairs, the Duke of Almodóvar, was elected president of a conference held on Spanish soil, after he had politely proposed that this honour should be offered to the Marquis Visconti Venosta. The Duke filled the office of chairman with a gracious, tactful, and somewhat indolent dignity, which might be expected from a grandee of Spain although his swarthy complexion and impeccable clothes gave him more the appearance of an Arab sheikh who dressed in Savile Row. His raven hair, always beautifully parted to the back of his collar, glistened with a peculiar brilliancy which caused an irreverent Parisian journalist to affirm that the Duke put his head outside the door every night to be polished with his boots. At meals numerous Spanish Secretaries would follow their chief into the dining-room, each one with hair brilliantly lustred in the same fashion. The Duke smiled with a gracious and languorous condescension and had an amiable word for everyone, but his activities were never oppressive. He was too much of a grandee to concern himself with the mere drudgery of daily business and left all such details to a remarkably able young Secretary named Hontoria, who was the real driving force behind the Spanish Delegation and later became Minister for Foreign Affairs. Almodóvar's Olympian services at the conference were rewarded when King Alfonso made him Duke of Algesiras.

At a moment when Europe was holding its breath, not knowing whether peace or war would issue from the conference, the opening session was marked by a skilful move on the part of the French. M. Révoil solemnly announced his government's aim to be the integrity of Morocco, the maintenance of the Sultan's authority, and the "Open Door." Benevolent professions habitually characterise the early stages of modern imperialistic acquisitiveness, and in the use of felicitous phrases the French easily scored over their heavier opponents. The well-founded objections advanced by Berlin seemed to lose much of their force and the conference much of its purpose as soon as the Quai d'Orsay proclaimed the very things which the Wilhelmstrasse had hitherto demanded. Everyone except the Germans breathed more freely, and the delegates then settled down to discuss a series of most humdrum details. It was difficult to discern a European conflict arising over such questions as the quantity of dried peas which could be imported into Morocco, or the export of its lean cattle, but no subject of a more controversial nature was allowed to occupy the attention of these early sessions. Even the problem of Belgian sporting guns shipped to Tangier did not seem likely to precipitate a crisis. Instead of discussing high politics the delegates were acting more like minor customs officials devising means to prevent the importation of smuggled cigarettes.

This was excellent diplomacy. In place of exciting drugs we were being deliberately treated to a dose of calming medicine. And all this time the French were keeping on the strictest defensive waiting until the Germans should unmask their batteries. No one knew when, how, or from what side the expected attack would be made, but it could hardly be supposed that the Wilhelmstrasse, which under the threat of war had forced the conference on a most unwilling France, did not have some positive programme of its own ready to launch at the opportune moment. But this programme, if it ever existed, was never presented. Occasionally the Germans raised objections to certain features of the French plan, yet for some mysterious reason they always refrained from taking any real lead and confined themselves to a negative obstruction. One day a Berlin journalist criticised his government's policy to me by making use of a delicate imagery in which Teutons excel. "We have spat in their soup," he declared, "but is this diplomacy?"

These minor and less explosive matters continued for several weeks to occupy the foreground at Algesiras, and only one dispute was at last allowed to come into the open. The unique question that caused an altercation at the conference table was the organization of the police, and the crisis came to a head over the issue regarding who should command the new forces of order which were to be created. In the controversy that followed, Germany found herself isolated and left with only Austrian support. The Wilhelmstrasse proposed to employ a neutral in order thereby to insert a wedge which would then block French control. It was left for Secretary Root's subtle brain, with superb casuistry, to render France an important service. On this point he advanced a highly specious objection to the plan of placing the police under some Dutch or Swiss inspector who was to exercise an independent command at Casablanca. White was instructed to object to this on the ground that it would suggest a division of Morocco into spheres of influence, which was the very thing the United States wished to avoid, and that it was far preferable for the French to bear the full responsibility for maintaining the Open Door. The Kaiser's previous attempt to win Roosevelt over to his side now became a boomerang, for at this critical moment the President let the Emperor know that if his own views were not accepted he would publish the private correspondence which showed that William the Second had offered, in case of future dispute, to abide by Roosevelt's decision.

Fortunately Berlin by this time was in a more conciliatory mood. After nearly three months of discussion, the Germans, like everyone else, were heartily sick of a conference which had brought them no benefit, and must have regretted ever having advanced those professions of disinterestedness which left their original pretence of virtue so distressingly unrewarded. Radowitz made no secret that his government was willing to yield on the police if given compensation elsewhere, and he wanted only to point to some concrete advantage in order to justify the noisy diplomacy of Berlin. At Washington, Baron Speck von Sternburg informed Roosevelt that "the immediate removal of all misunderstanding is far more important to Germany than the whole Moroccan affair." The discussion which had gone on in the great capitals simultaneously with Algesiras was therefore shelved until a decent interval had elapsed, when after some subsequent negotiations in Berlin between Kiderlen-Wächter and Jules Cambon, a corner of the French Congo, officially but not inappropriately known as the "duck's beak," gave the Kaiser the compensation for which he had cackled so loudly.*

The violent crisis which the Moroccan question provoked and the grave danger so nearly skirted had focussed world attention on the conference. It was fortunate that this could not be sustained indefinitely; excitement finishes by becoming ridiculous when it reaches an anticlimax. Day after day a series of vacuous deliberations over the most trifling questions were solemnly argued behind closed doors, whether in hotel drawing-rooms, in committee, or at public sessions. These masked the secret talks which went on in Paris and Berlin. The

* These negotiations took place in Berlin in 1911 in the aftermath of the Agadir Crisis.

trivial discussions that took place at Algesiras helped better than any eloquence to dispel the tension in Europe. Nothing could have been devised more useful to peace than the prolonged discussion of these futilities. The press could not continue to take an excited interest in something which produced nothing, and gradually it became apparent to the journalists of the world that nothing sensational would ever emanate from Algesiras. The real point at issue concerned the degree and extent of future French control, but this was hardly touched for the discussions had carefully avoided to mention anything so controversial. A result of primary importance had almost unconsciously been obtained, and the conference proved more serviceable to peace by the insignificance of its achievement than it could have been in any other way.

This negative outcome was no one's fault. If the delegates at Algesiras had been endowed with a far superior wisdom they could hardly have done more, and they were not to blame for accomplishing so little of any real value. It is a common fallacy to suppose that great results can only come from great men, for the reading of history suggests that the reverse can as justifiably be maintained. Years later, while Sforza and I walked one day amid the ruins of the Roman forum, we discussed our memories of the Moroccan Conference and he remarked to me how in the course of our careers both of us had seen some amazing mediocrities attain to the highest positions in the state. Like him, I was inclined to regard this circumstance as being fortunate for the world. But in 1906 I felt distinctly disappointed with the result of Algesiras. I was influenced by all I had read of the Congress of Berlin, when the towering figures of Bismarck and Disraeli had spoken with commanding authority. Undoubtedly I had expected too much from a few envoys greatly tied by their instructions and acting merely as agents for their governments. No one as yet recognised in this negative result that the stage was already being prepared for the excitable mass pressure that since the Moroccan Conference has been increasingly and detrimentally exercised on international affairs. In 1906 this pressure could still be kept in some restraint. That was why Algesiras turned out to be little more than an elaborate bit of stagecraft partly used to register certain results that were obtained elsewhere, and still more as a useful expedient which had extricated France and Germany from a highly dangerous muddle. There was no intentional design in this subterfuge, which was largely accidental, nor was the benevolent plot which turned a number of highly respectable ambassadors into innocent accomplices apparent at this time, least of all to themselves. Probably until long afterwards no such suspicion entered the delegates' heads, and if anyone had been offensive enough to make this insolent suggestion he would have been sternly and indignantly rebuked.

To a young diplomat, as I was in 1906, the conference brought some further acute disillusion. Hitherto, as a junior Secretary in Paris and in London, my contact with ambassadors had taken place at sufficient distance to preserve certain desirable illusions regarding the peculiar eminence of the heads of my profession. These were more difficult to retain after three months' experience of a conference which to an observer at close quarters seemed usually to act like a mountain in labour. It was a novel observation for me to remark that European diplomatists were far less Machiavellian and far more like ordinary mortals than I had ever suspected. In vain I searched for some hidden craft on their part, or for some secret illumination on my own, and failing to discover either I would ask myself if the fault was not due to my obtuseness and if there was nothing deeper in their art than the shallow rhetorician's trick of splitting hairs whenever they argued over formulas. With youthful arrogance I was not yet prepared to defer to the importance of solemnity in the discussion of what were obviously trifles. For I was still too inexperienced to understand the immense value of pompous and well-staged negativeness when this serves to allay political passion.*

* For other recent interpretations of the Algeciras Conference, see A. J. P. Taylor's "The Conference at Algeciras" in *From Napoleon to Lenin* (New York, Harper and Row, 1966) and Howard K. Beale, *Theodore Roosevelt and the Rise of America to World Power* (Baltimore, The Johns Hopkins Press, 1955), Chap. 6.

## 2. *Constantinople under Abdul Hamid*

Half-way through the Algesiras Conference came the news of my appointment as Second Secretary at Constantinople. I had once been there for a couple of days, on a tourist cruise during which one sees everything and understands nothing. The feeling of the East comes only by slow absorption, and I was to pass nearly four years on the Bosporus from the time of my arrival in 1906 to 1909, alternately loving and hating the place but never indifferent to it. More than a thousand times I crossed the clanking planks of the old Galata Bridge, which exists no more, and always with the feeling of entering another world. The sights of the city soon became familiar and many of them were commonplace. The wares in the bazaars were mostly gimcrack, the people were filthy, and the narrow alleys reeked with smells which had little in common with any perfumes of Araby. From every café creaky gramophones shrieked Turkish *manés* in minor key; on the bridge lepers held out their sickly hands, and in Stamboul vendors sang the delights of *halva,* and *hamals* performed their ablutions in the courtyard of the Valideh Mosque. Yet all of them brought a vision of the Orient with its squalor, some of its picturesqueness, its fatalism, and not a little of its poetry. Whenever I crossed to Stamboul, it was with the feeling of having stepped out of some tunnel into an Asiatic world. In the maze of its tortuous byways I made friends with Persian pedlars, roamed through the interior of every *han,* and in the course of these wanderings, as countless others have done before and since, I wove my own romance of the East.

At the Embassy the Chargé d'Affaires was Peter Jay, whom three years before I had succeeded as Third Secretary in Paris. Peter, like myself, was one of a group of young men, barely out of the university, whom Theodore Roosevelt had appointed to be diplomatic Secretaries when he laid the first foundation for an American career service. The President's innovation was gradual and passed unnoticed at a time when a small-town bureaucracy quite unsuspicious that there existed any world problems filled the intermediate ranks of the State Department. The Diplomatic Bureau which issued our routine instructions was composed at this time of four bearded clerks whose duties had never called them outside Washington. When I received my appointment, the Chief of this Bureau introduced me to his aged staff, and between two chews of tobacco described them as dividing the world between them. I still hear one of these greybeards, whose salary was $1,800 a year, commenting at his superior's pleasantry, "Yes, we divide the world but not its possessions!"

Jay and I were then imbued with our mission to reform American diplomacy. We discovered a common sympathy in an excessive love for the *carrière,* and with the assurance of much youthful inexperience we would discuss its problems like two old-world ambassadors, outline impossible Eastern policies for the United States, and argue about the intricacies of protocol as if our salvation depended on this. Modest about himself, Jay felt a kind of inherited pride as the fourth generation of his family to be a diplomat, although he admitted having slightly to bend the facts in order to establish an unbroken continuity. His taste for diplomacy, with an inordinate wish to slim, which had not yet become fashionable and which he alternated with occasional orgies of raw beefsteak, were the only excesses of a great gentleman who possessed a most lovable nature.

These were glorious days for young diplomats at Constantinople. We experienced there the pleasing sensation of having a new and unsuspected importance and the feeling that, being above the law in Turkey, we could do no wrong. In perfect innocence we acted in the most high-handed way; once when a band of singing Greeks disturbed Jay's slumbers at Therapia,* he put an end to their musical enthusiasm by firing a revolver over their heads and then having them all arrested.

Shortly after my arrival, William Jennings Bryan, who was then at the height of his fame, spent a week at Constantinople on a tour around the world, which he had undertaken as a suitable preparation before running again for the Presidency. Jay and I acted as his guides, which was easy, for the Great Commoner never embarrassed us by asking any

* On the west bank of the Bosporus almost half-way between the Sea of Marmora and the Black Sea.

question that a ten-year-old boy could not have answered. Bryan had no real wish to see mosques, though he was quite resigned to allow himself to be conducted to all the customary sights. In some mysterious way he connected his visit to the Turkish capital with an opportunity to talk about American politics, which was his unique interest; his customary conversation, whatever the hour of the day, was that of a public meeting, irrespective of the size or nature of the audience or the appropriateness of the locality. One night, as he stood by a lamp-post in the street outside the Pera Palace Hotel, he affirmed to me his political faith and declared with a magnificent outburst of eloquence that I was a Hamiltonian and he was a Jeffersonian but that he would sooner be wrong with Jefferson than right with anyone else. His admirers undoubtedly would have roared themselves hoarse could they have heard him; what I admired most was his seeming unconsciousness of the surroundings and his indifference to the quality of an audience which consisted solely of three barking dogs and myself.

Bryan possessed the politician's trick of professing to have a cure for everything and not bothering much about the merits of the remedy. He was a product of the American small town, as sincere as he was half-baked, and he made on me the impression of a likeable and kindly man who had a magnificent voice, spoke with deep moral fervour and fluency, and although he had singularly little general information, he possessed a shrewd and specialized knowledge of American political psychology. I doubt if he had more than the barest acquaintance with anything else, and he seemed as much at home in Abdul Hamid's Constantinople as a Yankee at King Arthur's Court. A week later, when I saw him off at the station, I mentioned that he would have an interesting journey through the Balkans. The future Secretary of State looked puzzled at me for a moment and then asked, "What are the Balkans?"

The Sultan took an Oriental potentate's delight in conferring decorations like the Order of Chastity of the Second or Third Class on passing matrons and would gladly have presented a celebrity like Bryan with the Grand Cordon of the Medjidieh, perhaps mounted on brilliants. But he restrained his munificence, for even an Eastern despot knew enough of American politics to understand that this honour might not be appreciated in the cornfields of Nebraska. In fact, the only remembrance of Constantinople which Bryan wished to take away was a rug. He asked me to accompany him to a carpet dealer in the bazaar, where the following conversation took place:

*Dealer: (his Levantine vanity showing off)* "I want to tell you, Mr. Bryan, that only last month Mr. Morgan came to see my collection with a number of ladies who were aboard his yacht. For me it was a problem of psychology, for I knew that I had to please one of his friends. But which one? I picked right and sold Mr. Morgan a million francs' worth of rugs."

*Bryan: (ignoring the difficulty of this psychological problem, dourly)* "That was money stolen from the people."

*Dealer: (taken aback, understands he must try another tack)* "Now, Mr. Bryan, I want to sell you a rug. Here is a very rare Gheordiz."

*Bryan:* "What does it cost?"

*Dealer:* "For you Mr. Bryan it will only be fifty pounds."

*Bryan: (stressing every word)* "Now we are plain people who live in a plain house and a rug of this fine character would certainly be out of keeping with the rest of what we have. I would like to see some plainer rug."

*Dealer: (determined to make a sale to a likely future President, even if he has to cut prices, brings out an almost identical rug)* "This rug, Mr. Bryan, is a little different, and because it is less rare I can let you have it for eight pounds."

*Bryan:* "I suppose that doesn't include the duty and delivery at my home in Lincoln?"

*Dealer:* "It will for you, Mr. Bryan. All I aspire to is the honour of your signature in my book."

*Bryan pretends not to hear: (audibly aside)* "Someone else will pay the duty."

For young Secretaries like ourselves, Bryan was something of a speculation, though it was plain that any career accomplishments in which we might take pride were wasted on the Great Commoner. Peter Jay felt worried as to his future and tried to discover what Bryan proposed to do with diplomatic Secretaries after he became President. One day as we stood in the middle of St. Sophia, he bluntly plumped a question regarding that momentous matter, but Bryan remained evasive and declared that he had not yet had time to consider. Fortunately Jay continued a career which twenty years later he rounded off as Ambassador to the Argentine. Before starting for Buenos Aires, Jay called on President Coolidge, whom he hardly knew at this time.

> *Jay:* "You know Mr. President that my salary as Ambassador is $17,500, and I will have to spend $15,000 on my rent."
> *Coolidge:* (*Yankee drawl*) "What are you going to do with the other $2,500?"

Soon after Bryan's departure, my new chief, John G. A. Leishman, returned from Washington. He had been Minister to Turkey for some years and had just obtained from Congress an appropriation to buy the building which we occupied at Constantinople and to raise the Legation to the rank of an Embassy. After this double success, for the purchase of any diplomatic residence was at that time an innovation, Leishman returned immensely pleased to be the first American Ambassador to Turkey. The Sultan, who was sufficiently plagued by the representatives of other powers, showed no early inclination to recognise an American envoy whom he already knew well and who would henceforth be able to demand that right of personal accessibility which was denied to ministers. The new Ambassador had used this argument effectively with Congress to explain why, so long as he remained a minister, it was almost impossible to obtain satisfaction for our claims. It was therefore not a little embarrassing to come back with a higher rank and find the Sultan unwilling to receive him. No reason was given for this, but Leishman, worried by the protracted delay which was hard to explain at Washington, looked around for recognition from the other embassies. We concocted together some not very subtle schemes to induce this, and as an excuse wrote to ask them for their governments' archaeological publications. When answers came addressed to the American Ambassador, my chief felt that an important diplomatic success had been gained. But for mysterious reasons Abdul Hamid continued to keep Leishman in suspense, and only after more delay did His Majesty, for reasons equally mysterious, suddenly fix the time for the audience. The customary state coaches, with a cavalry escort, were sent to convey the new Ambassador and his staff to the Palace of Yildiz. While we waited for the Sultan to enter the reception hall, coffee was served in diamond-studded gold cups used only on the greatest occasions ever since one of these cups, as a chamberlain related to us, had been carried away by an English lord for a souvenir. A few minutes later, Abdul Hamid entered the audience chamber. I was struck by his unhealthy colour and his curious shuffling walk. The audience ceremony was simple and brief. The Sultan exchanged a few commonplace remarks with the Ambassador and graciously held out to me two fingers of his limp and waxy hand.

For the next three years I was to be closely associated with Leishman and grew to be very fond of my new chief. He was a self-made man who had been reared in the world of Pittsburgh steel and was not without displaying certain weaknesses, due to his upbringing, which to superficial critics obscured his real qualities. He had a disconcerting habit of pressing his twitching thumbs into his sides on the not infrequent occasions when he would laugh at his own jokes, and his English was often atrocious. But I found him able and patriotic, with that passionate love for their country which many Americans have although they live abroad. He was kindly and tactful and possessed the rare merit of making his Secretaries feel that they really belonged to his official family. More than any chief I had known, Leishman regarded it as his duty to shape their diplomatic education and would take infinite pains to explain the different angles from which every affair required to be treated in the light of its possible political reactions in the United States. No communication received by the Embassy was too insignificant to have his personal attention. There is a type of official who puts himself out to oblige people only when these are of sufficient importance, and pays little attention to the request of humbler individuals, but in Leishman's time everyone who addressed himself to the Embassy would receive the same courteous consideration. As a chief he possessed the gift of persuading others to share his views while they believed these to be their own, and no one took a keener interest in diplomacy or possessed a more penetrating insight into the tortuous workings of the Oriental mind.

His wife and daughters used to twit him with what they described as his Turkish diplomacy, for in private, as in public, he was not averse to the procrastinating inertia which was a characteristic of the Sublime Porte. Leishman felt at home in Constantinople far more than he did later in Rome and Berlin. He liked Eastern ways, he was immensely proud of his Embassy, which he regarded as his child, and he infused this same pride in his staff. Work under him ran at times into the early morning hours, but I never found it tedious like my former routine when a junior Secretary in Paris and London. At Constantinople I was to learn how the most trifling incident became significant as soon as it was attached to any question of precedent or principle, for diplomacy still possessed a meaning in Turkey which it had lost in more civilised countries.

Seven cities claimed Homer's birthplace, but for the game of bridge Constantinople disputes a similar honour only with Teheran. Leishman's love for cards was somewhat greater than his skill, but every day after lunch at the Embassy, to which his Secretaries were always invited, he would summon the staff, before they returned to the Chancery, to play three rubbers—never more, never less—and every day at five he would go to the Club for his game, and woe betide any Secretary whose duty it might be to interrupt him at the card table. The bridge played at the Cercle d'Orient was of a brand peculiar to the Near East, and not unlike its diplomacy, for it was generally based on the principle of never declaring the hand one held in the hope of alluring an opponent into an ambush. Like other Oriental devices it was so subtle that it was transparent.

My new chief's principle obsession was a violent hatred of the missionaries who provided the Embassy with three quarters of its work. Their affairs led to many difficulties, for American missions owned or rented much valuable property in Turkey, and irritating questions about taxation, leaseholds, and transfers were continually cropping up. Mission houses were often partly rented for commercial purposes, and Leishman, who always suspected the worst, felt convinced that certain missionaries asked for tax relief while conducting their own little private businesses. Disputes unending dragged along about such questions, for facts were hard to establish, statements were contradictory, and the Turks were always refractory. Every morning, after the Ambassador had read the incoming mail, which was principally taken up by these incessant controversies, he would hand over the correspondence to me, invariably using the same oath, which expressed a theological condemnation of missionary ancestry, and ending by announcing his firm intention to "flay them alive." The repeated expression of this fierce hatred would have been more impressive if it had been less humorous. The joke was that no man worked more conscientiously than the Ambassador to defend missionary rights, and his violent invective was merely a harmless safety valve for duties which he performed admirably. Ten years later, when during the war I was once more at Constantinople, and Leishman, long retired, could be of no further use to the missionaries, it gave me real satisfaction to hear from Mr. Peet, one of their leaders, that my former chief was still most appreciatively remembered and that no other ambassador at Constantinople had ever accomplished so much for them.

The missionaries, in their black frock coats, white lawn ties, and heavy boots, brought to the Near East the Sunday atmosphere of an American small town. Certain of them, like Dr. Bliss of Beirut and Drs. Washburn and Gates of Robert College, were worthy of the highest respect and deeply imbued with the dignity of their task. Others more commonplace found existence in Turkey pleasanter than the farm life they would have led in America, and turned religion into something of a business. They never converted any Moslem nor would they have been allowed to remain in Turkey if they had done so. I heard of only one Mohammedan who, many years before, had become a Christian and had to be sent to England, though his son, who was a poor creature, returned to Constantinople. Apart from some excellent schools and the useful American medical missions, much missionary work went to convert Gregorian Armenians to Protestantism. The native sects, who for a thousand years had suffered persecution for their faith, would complacently be called nominal Christians by many of the missionaries. Tolerance was not among their most conspicuous virtues, and I heard a Mormon complain bitterly at the Embassy that when his wife fell seriously ill in a remote locality where the only decent abode belonged to an American missionary, the latter refused to have his house polluted by any member of that sect although the Mormon husband offered to sleep in the barn.

In troubled times the missionaries stationed in the interior became a source of anxiety. Their relatives would deluge the State Department with requests for help, and excited telegrams asking for American soldiers to be immediately despatched to their rescue would arrive from localities often hundreds of miles distant from the nearest railroad. One became sceptical of such alarms. Washington always passed responsibility to the Embassy, and the Embassy would pass it to the Porte and to the nearest consul, but before anything could be done the missionaries had nearly always extricated themselves even from the most difficult situations.

I learned how ingenious they could be after one related to me his experiences during a drought. As the crops were withering in the parched fields, the peasants gathered in their places of worship and begged their Imams and priests to pray for rain. The American missionary alone refused to join in any such entreaties. In spite of the intercession of Moslem, Orthodox, Gregorian, and Catholic clergy, no rain fell, and the peasants despaired as they watched their wasting harvest. My missionary friend however possessed a barometer, and one day he noticed that the mercury was rapidly falling. That day when all hope had been abandoned by the other religious communities, he summoned his congregation to pray with him for rain. Solemnly they fell on their knees and even as they prayed the sky suddenly darkened, the clouds broke, rain fell in torrents, and the parched crops were saved.

Shortly before my arrival the kidnapping of Miss Ellen Stone, an American missionary lady, had become an incident of international celebrity. The supposed perils which this middle-aged and somewhat obese virgin had been exposed to while she was a captive in the hands of the desperate brigands in Macedonia had been widely and almost hourly featured by the entire press of the United States. The danger to her life and virtue, and the anxious and protracted suspense caused by her confinement as a prisoner, aroused the sympathy of the warm-hearted American public, who subscribed generously for her ransom. To negotiate her release the Embassy dragoman,* Mr. Gargiulo, a gentleman of Neapolitan extraction and possessing a temperament which would have been no disgrace to Casanova, had gone into the wilds of Macedonia with bags of gold coin, accompanied by Mr. Peet, a prominent and highly respectable missionary. Since Don Quixote and Sancho Panza, no odder pair could be imagined than our Neapolitan dragoman and the black-coated missionary of stern virtue. Saint and sinner scaled Balkan fastnesses, faced the kidnappers, and after encountering innumerable delays, difficulties, and adventures, at last succeeded in arranging with the bandits for the virgin's freedom, paid the ransom

* A dragoman was a clerk in a legation or embassy in Turkey whose principal function was to serve as interpreter. Customarily the only permanent member of the Embassy staff, the dragoman tended to become an important official.

subscribed by sentimental small-town Americans, and returned in triumph with the rescued Miss Stone.

In private, Mr. Leishman always maintained that this expensive lady had virtually been kidnapped by her own Sunday School, although she herself was innocent of any collusion. It is certain that she was never exposed to the slightest danger, and instead of being hidden in those remote fastnesses of the Balkans, which the Embassy dragoman had reluctantly been forced to scale, she had passed her entire confinement in a house near Sofia. The Bulgar *Comitadjis** who captured her had devised the ingenious scheme of a "kidnapping" with all necessary publicity at a time when they badly needed money in order to buy arms to continue their savagery. In this way they were able to finance their next Macedonian campaign with the help of kindly middle western Americans who had subscribed liberally for Miss Stone's release. The process employed for obtaining funds, although not original, was highly successful. In much the same way the late ruler of a European nation who is greatly revered as a patriot and a statesman had in the course of his adventurous career rifled an express train for a similar patriotic purpose.†

The Macedonian problem came up like a hardy annual every spring when the atrocity season opened, to agitate Europe with the fear of international complications. This unhappy province had been ravaged for many years by rival bands of hired ruffians who, in the name of a supposed religious zeal for a Greek Patriarch or for a Bulgarian Exarch, had cut their victims' throats and committed many less mentionable refinements of cruelty. The most gruesome photographs of mutilated corpses would periodically be sent to the embassies of the great powers at Constantinople by all the diplomatic representatives of the Balkan states, each of whom would profess a most humane indignation at their neighbours' savagery. Murders were committed supposedly because of an excess of religious faith. Actually this nationalist fanaticism aroused in the name of creed extended even to the most unexpected persons. A sedate Greek banker whom I had never before seen excited, trembled with rage as he related to me how a Bulgar band had broken into an Orthodox church and burned the sacred books. I

* Generally speaking, this refers to a body of men attached to a monarch or nobleman by the obligation of military service.

† Einstein alludes here to Josef Pilsudski, Polish Statesman.

mentioned having lately heard a similar tale about a Greek band's behaviour in a Bulgar church. He shut me up, saying, "Those were heretical."

It was common knowledge that from Sofia and Athens, from Belgrade and Bucharest, armed bands were continuously despatched into Macedonia. The powerful Bulgarian terrorist organization was built up in cells which were kept so small that no one, even under torture, would be able to betray more than the very few who belonged to his immediate group. It worked on the principle that any member ordered to kill someone would himself be slain if he dared to disobey. Balkan diplomats have since boasted to me that when they were consuls at Salonika one of their duties was to arrange for their enemies to be handed a *"boutonnière,"* which was the euphemism employed for a knife stab in the back. Those who were engaged in criminal activity justified themselves on patriotic grounds. They wished to eliminate rivals in order to extend their national influence in Macedonia and so to stake their claims for the eventual break-up of Turkey, which everyone anticipated. The great powers were not directly concerned in this murderous rivalry but felt occasional qualms and some apprehension about its consequences. Vienna was then petting the Bulgars, and St. Petersburg, the Serbs, whom they hoped to use as pawns, although in the Great War it was the Serbs who used the Russians. In England, the influential Macedonian Committee existed as a relic of Gladstonian liberalism and was headed by the Buxton brothers, whose name could never be mentioned at the British Embassy in Constantinople without an imprecation. Formidable because of their votes in nonconformist constituencies, this committee agitated widely and kept harassing a reluctant Foreign Office to press for reforms in Macedonia so as to stop Turkish iniquities.

Diplomatic questions are like bacteria, for they live peacefully in a healthy body but multiply, usually with fatal results, in one which is weakened or diseased. A country like Turkey, notoriously in a hopeless mess, could continue its disorder providing only that the old familiar abuses went on, but it was certain to collapse as soon as any real attempt was made to introduce reforms. Yet for several different reasons the great powers felt called upon to put a stop to the annual crop of atrocities. Out of this somewhat confused fatherhood of reform there issued an ominous offspring. From the dark cesspool of Balkan crime,

Austro-Russian rivalry, German indifference, British nonconformist agitation, and Turkish corrupt helplessness there was born in Macedonia a monster who from a puny infancy grew to be the giant that caused the Great War. Out of a simple and seemingly innocuous plan for reform demanded by credulous humanitarians and carried out by incredulous diplomats was born the Turkish Revolution, which brought about the Austrian annexation of the Duchies, was the cause of a European crisis, and then led by huge strides to two Balkan wars. The fury of the Serbs, who found that the fruits of victory were denied them by the Habsburg Empire, finished by provoking an Archduke's murder at Serajevo and thus brought on the First World War. All these events took place within eight years, yet no one could humanly have foreseen how or when the great tragedy would occur.

When the programme of Macedonian reforms was first introduced, it seemed to be neither more nor less consequential than many other similar plans which, during the last half-century, had periodically been advanced, ostensibly to regenerate the decaying Ottoman Empire. Such programmes always bore a family likeness and always provided for Christian officials who, when these were natives, would be called *Evetjis* or "Yes-makers" by the Turks. All reforms had a double objective, which was to satisfy Western European opinion and to do this in the way least likely to rouse a too open Turkish obstruction. In Macedonia the programme agreed to by the powers provided for an international police commanded by the Italian General de Robilant, who was a competent soldier and was to have under him a number of European officers recruited from different armies. Macedonian reforms however did not concern the United States. American diplomatic interest in this Balkan question, entirely unsuspected by American opinion, arose in a far more curious way.

It was natural for a British Foreign Office, with a wish to placate the nonconformist conscience at no cost to its own taxpayer, to offer some sound advice to the Sultan, but reforms in Turkey always boiled down to a question of finding the money, a process which meant clapping more taxes on an already impoverished peasantry. The Sultan invariably pleaded good will but scanty means, and argued with some reason that there was no fairness in taxing the population of an empire for the sake of improving conditions in two provinces which he knew he was anyhow likely to lose. The only easy means left for a bankrupt state to obtain money for Macedonia was therefore to raise the eight per cent customs duties levied on all Turkish imports by an additional three per cent. The reforms could then be paid for out of this additional revenue and the Sultan appeased with the expected margin left over. Because of the ancient Capitulations,* Turkey was however obliged to ask for the consent of other nations before any such surtax could be imposed, and although the great powers expressed an immense sympathy for reform, all took occasion to remind the Porte that they also possessed certain claims which hitherto they had vainly tried to settle. Before they were prepared to consider any customs increase, they invited the Sultan's attention to these ancient disputes. Tacitly, Macedonian reforms were to be used to clean up old slates.

The treaty position of the United States in one respect was very different in Turkey from that of the great European powers. The latter possessed "Capitulations," or charters, which had been freely granted by the sultans centuries before at a time when the Turks were at the height of their power, in order to encourage foreign trade; among other matters these fixed the customs dues. The first treaty of the United States with Turkey dated however from 1830, when the Porte no longer granted Capitulations but accorded only a "most-favoured-nation" treatment by which American citizens were placed on the same footing as Europeans in the Ottoman Empire.

It had never been possible to agree on what the term "most-favoured-nation" treatment really meant, but the influential German Ambassador, Baron Marschall, advised the Porte that the states represented at Constantinople could be divided into three classes. The first of these were powers like Germany and France that possessed Capitulations and were able to enforce them. In a second class he put smaller nations like Holland and Sweden that had the same rights but not the power of enforcement. In last resort he placed countries like the United States on the ground that a most-favoured-nation clause signified only that Americans would be entitled to receive the same treatment which was accorded to others. The practical effect of this argument was to relegate the United States to an inferior position, as the Turks, who were obliged to negotiate for the consent of the great Euro-

* Treaties made by the Sultan with the great powers that conferred rights of extraterritoriality and other privileges on nationals of the countries involved.

pean powers before making any changes in their customs, would have had no need to ask for authorization from Washington.

Leishman therefore took the view that, if the permission of other states was asked, it would also be necessary to ask that of America, and he announced that he would refuse to recognise any tariff increase until the approval of the United States had been obtained. In taking this stand he was able to secure the valuable support of the friendly British Ambassador, Sir Nicholas O'Conor, who, apart from the satisfaction which he felt in throwing a spoke into the German wheel, disliked seeing a tariff raised, the burden of which would fall mostly on English trade, and who was therefore pleased to discover so good a reason for delay. The smaller Western European powers that possessed Capitulations which they could not enforce all rallied gladly under American leadership.

Apart from establishing an important principle, there were several practical considerations behind Leishman's position. Like every mission at Constantinople, the American Embassy had its troubles with the Porte, which dragged on year after year without ever approaching a settlement. The Sultan's refusal to recognise our missionary institutions, which would have enabled these to obtain legalized exemption from certain taxes, had on two occasions brought an American fleet into Turkish waters, once at Beirut and again at Smyrna. In both instances the ships had been despatched with Rooseveltian impetuousness against the Ambassador's wishes, and the latter had felt apprehensive of the possible complications arising from this demonstration. Nor could Leishman forget that on the second occasion the fleet had been ordered to sail by the President without consulting either his envoy at Constantinople or his Secretary of State, John Hay, and after it arrived at Smyrna it had been ordered to depart before a settlement could be concluded, thus leaving the American representative powerless to extract from the Sultan more than a worthless verbal promise. The "three per cents," as the customs increase was called, now dropped like manna from the sky to help the Embassy gain by diplomacy what two visits of the fleet had failed to accomplish and obtain an unexpected satisfaction for further claims which would otherwise have been impossible to settle. I shall describe only one of these, not because of its importance but to illustrate the nature of the questions which came up for diplomatic handling.

An Armenian by the name of Azarian, who was a naturalized citizen of the United States, some time before had died intestate at Constantinople, and the American Consular Court decreed that his property should revert to his only son. The deceased however had in his employ a cook who, after her master's death, found means to introduce a forged marriage entry into the register kept at the Armenian Patriarcate. As his supposed widow, she then arranged to have herself sued for a trifling amount which was alleged to have been owed by the deceased. As she admitted this debt, she was condemned to pay this by the Turkish court before which the suit was brought. Then, armed with a certified copy of the fraudulent marriage entry and a transcript of the judgment decree against herself as the deceased's widow, she went before the Ecclesiastical "Sheri" Court of Constantinople, which decided all questions of Ottoman inheritance. This court, having no reason to enquire into the validity of the documents submitted, without more ado awarded her the lawful share of her supposed husband's estate, both in ignorance of and indifference to the Embassy's contention that only an American court was competent to decide questions of inheritance for American citizens. In this manner the fraud of an Armenian cook arrayed Washington against Mohammed, as there was a direct conflict of law between the United States and the Turkish government. From the point of view of the Porte, it was impossible to disavow the competence of a Mohammedan religious court. From the point of view of the American government it was impossible to disavow the competence of the Consular Court. So in the usual fashion of Constantinople, this question had dragged on for years without approaching a solution and might never have been settled without the "three per cents." But justice to the rightful heir became part of the price which the Embassy exacted before consenting to the customs surtax, and the fraud of an Armenian cook ceased to obstruct the path of Macedonian reforms.

Rome in the days before Nero was less of a pathological despotism than was Constantinople under Abdul Hamid. Every Turkish regulation and law which had not been devised to extract money was designed to increase the supposed security of the Sultan, and the most incredible measures were taken for his safety and health as primary considerations of state policy. Thus the importation and use of telephones, of typewriters, and of all electrical machinery was strictly forbidden lest such dangerous modern appliances should be utilized by conspirators for their plots. The Sultan's fixed purpose was also to keep his Mohammedan subjects from being contaminated by any contact with Western ideas, and the few Turks who were bold enough to call on diplomats and who were not spies would often be summoned by the police and be obliged to explain their visit. In the native press, foreign news was usually suppressed or else deliberately falsified. When for instance the King of Portugal was assassinated, I saw his death announced at Constantinople as being the result of an accident. A well-known missionary told me that once he had ordered Voltaire's tragedies for the use of his class at Robert College, but the book was seized by the Customs. He went to expostulate, and after a heated argument carried on in Turkish with an official who, as he supposed, knew not a word of any foreign language, the latter suddenly exclaimed to him in perfect English, "Why can't you let us go to hell in our own way?"

The more intelligent Turks viewed their country's future with unfeigned dismay. The nervous and timorous Sultan lived at Yildiz, far from his subjects, surrounded by an Albanian bodyguard, and the set of ruffians who were his chamberlains and secretaries. I knew that these men ought to have been behind bars, but instead they appeared at state ceremonies in splendid gold-braided uniforms, their chests covered with high decorations conferred on them by the rulers of Europe. Under guise of devotion to the Padishah,* the Court officials furthered their rascally ends by preying on his most abject fears.

Abdul Hamid was no ordinary sovereign. Already as a boy when his uncle, the Sultan Abdul Aziz, had taken him to London, Lionel Moore, the English aide who accompanied the young prince, had discovered him one night with his brother hidden under a bed at Buckingham Palace, jibbering with terror. Perhaps the remembrance of how his uncle, whom he succeeded, had been bled to death in his bath in a so-called suicide added to that fear of assassination which never left him. The dread that any Western innovations might lead to demands for liberty and that these could lead to revolution grew more marked with the Sultan till it became an obsession and a disease.

In physical appearance Abdul Hamid was shifty, with a long thin nose and hollow eyes which were sunk deep in fleshy pockets. His

* A title designating the Sultan.

colour was waxy, his fingers thin and limp, his walk shuffling, and he stooped badly. He wore a simple military uniform when he received diplomats and his conversation was affable on these occasions, but the impression he made was the reverse of soldier-like and failed pitiably to suggest the martial origin of his race. Constantinople gossip has lost nothing of its venom since the "Secret History" of Procopius* was written, and some professed to detect certain Armenian features in the Sultan, but this explanation must have been pure slander for in looks he was not unlike many of his predecessors. For the traits of the House of Othman are characteristic like the Habsburg lip, as anyone can see from their portraits in colour in that splendid art book, Young's *Emperors of Turkey,* which was published in the year of Waterloo.

The Sultan felt neither the ability nor any wish to introduce reforms, for the first effect would have been to lessen his authority and perhaps to sweep him off his tottering throne. Also any reforms would have turned to the advantage of the Christian minorities, and he justified his objection to these on national and religious grounds, though in common with the majority of the Turks, Abdul Hamid felt little concern for the future nor cared much about what happened to his Empire after he had gone. As a ruler he was industrious, with much low cunning, but contrary to an often heard opinion, he possessed little statesmanship or any real diplomatic skill. The reputed craft with which he was supposed to keep greedy diplomats at bay by sowing dissensions among them was largely a legend that rested on a complete misconception of the famous "Eastern Question"† and ignored the powers' inability to reach any agreement and their unwillingness to precipitate a conflict. The rough and bloody settlement effected since his downfall has come only after the havoc and destruction caused by four wars and a series of wholesale massacres.

Abdul Hamid knew that the great powers preferred to maintain

* Procopius was a Byzantine historian of the late fifth century A.D. His Secret History, the *Anecdota,* supposedly a supplement to the *Histories,* ca. 550, was a harsh commentary on the governing bureaucracy of the Empire, describing corruption, debauchery, etc.

† The perennial diplomatic problem that confronted the European powers throughout most of the nineteenth century, namely, the disposition of the Turkish Empire, including the Straits. There was a tacit assumption that the "Sick Man of Europe" (Turkey) was doomed to extinction, and each of the powers wanted to be in a position to exploit Turkey's weakness and to prevent rival powers from doing the same.

the hollow shell of a weak Ottoman Empire and pursue only trade advantages rather than to risk the perils of a division. Among the powers there existed at this time a kind of gentleman's agreement, carried out by methods that had little in common with gentlemen and which divided Turkey into spheres of economic influence. Germany was then engaged in developing Anatolia and building the Bagdad Railway,* France maintained an ancient claim over Syria which began in religion and ended in rails, Italy looked hopefully to Libya for her future expansion, Great Britain was commercially interested in the Aidin Valley† and politically in the Persian Gulf, and lastly Russia watched jealously that no power should enter the Black Sea provinces. Everyone knew that the Czar's ultimate aim was Constantinople, but after the defeat in Manchuria this ambition was for the time impossible to achieve, and the Russians preferred to see a weak Turkey continue rather than to encourage a break-up from which at that time they could not hope to benefit.

The Sultan was aware of this balance of pressure and his diplomacy rested principally on inertia and a marked reluctance to yield anything. Invariably he procrastinated, not always successfully, and occasionally, as in Crete,‡ he would be obliged in the end to abandon far more than timely concessions would have made necessary. The old Turkish paternal administration formerly possessed many merits, but during his reign a terrible deterioration had taken place in the personnel of the officials and no one was more responsible for this lowered standard than Abdul Hamid. No sovereign ever more wilfully corrupted the character of his subjects or availed himself more deliber-

* In 1902, German businessmen won concessions from the Sultan to construct a railroad connecting Constantinople to Bagdad and thence to Basra on the Persian Gulf. Constantinople was already linked by rail to Berlin. The Germans expected that this new rail tie would result in important trade relations and political influences binding Germany more closely to the Near East. By the beginning of the First World War, the railway was still far from completion.

† In Western Anatolia along the Büyük Menderes River, with the town of Aidin (or Aydin) about 100 miles upstream from Miletus. It was the terminus of the oldest and most important railway in Anatolia, completed in 1866, connecting with Smyrna.

‡ Einstein refers to the fact that the Sultan made concessions to Greece in 1878, in the wake of the Russo-Turkish War, and during subsequent years further concessions were made so that by 1914 Crete was virtually incorporated into the Greek kingdom.

ately of venality as a method of rule. The Sultan was perfectly aware that the men around him were thieves, yet he connived at their thefts in order to attach their interests to his person while holding them in his power by the knowledge of their misdeeds. Many were the crimes committed in his name. On one occasion his agents wanted to rob a Turkish friend of mine of a valuable estate which the latter owned near Aleppo. To keep up appearances they brought a fraudulent action against him before the courts. My friend knew that he did not have a chance to establish his rights and so took the bold course of telegraphing to the Sultan to say that he offered his property as a gift in order to prevent a miscarriage of justice from being committed in His Majesty's name. Between the fear of being sent into distant exile as a punishment for this piece of insolent audacity and the hope of receiving a proper compensation, my friend waited anxiously, but no answer ever came from Yildiz and the Sultan's agents without more ado took possession of the estate.

Spies and secret accusations are characteristic of all despotisms but nowhere was the system of espionage more developed than at Constantinople. Beginning with an outer fringe of small informers like Embassy servants who reported every visitor to the police and tried to overhear our conversations, the system permeated through every class of society and innumerable spies' reports were daily despatched to the Palace where they formed the Sultan's principal reading. After the Revolution thousands of sacks containing such information were discovered at Yildiz and became of great political use to the new government.

The contact with foreign embassies was left principally to a few native Christians in the Ottoman service on whose not disinterested loyalty the Sultan felt that he could rely. One in particular was a picturesque and far from unattractive Syrian adventurer who, to extort money from his brother, who was a Cabinet officer, had once opened a bootblack's stand outside his Ministry. Since then he had been given the rank of an Under Secretary, though his real importance came from being the head of one of several secret services which were supposed to watch over His Majesty's security and not infrequently quarrelled among themselves. This man had convinced Abdul Hamid of his zeal by causing the arrest of a few hundred Armenians after a bomb had been thrown at the Sultan's carriage during the ceremony of the Selamlik.* Most of these innocent Armenians had later been released and the Under Secretary took immense credit on himself for having saved so many lives. But he gave them their liberty after an effective "third degree," and one unfortunate victim subsequently testified that clad only in his shirt he had been forced to sit on an open barrel over an alcohol lamp. Yet the Sultan, to show gratitude for the thorough manner in which this investigation was conducted, authorised the Under Secretary as a reward to handle the lucrative tramway concession at Beirut. The latter peddled this about Paris where he entertained lavishly at the Ritz, and few of his fashionable guests supposed that this well-dressed and flashily good-looking Pasha had only recently been engaged in torturing innocent people. The inquisitor found means to ingratiate himself still further on his return by bringing back some expensive trinkets from Cartier which Abdul Hamid was delighted to distribute among his harem favourites.

A considerable part of the Sultan's time was passed in the harem where he liked to play the dandy and to wear fancy waistcoats. No one had access to him in his privacy except the Chief Eunuch, who enjoyed the rank of Highness and as the third dignitary of the Empire came immediately after the Grand Vizier and the Sheikh-ul-Islam.† In every absolutism the power of individuals rests on the degree of their nearness to the ruler far more than on the office they hold, a circumstance which explains the great importance of eunuchs in Eastern lands. One saw these unpleasant beardless creatures at every ceremonial occasion, wearing the regulation "Stamboulin," which was a frock coat buttoned up to the neck. In Turkey only the Sultan kept white eunuchs but, black or white, all save one honourable exception at Yildiz bore the reputation for delighting in malicious intrigue.

Occasionally Abdul Hamid would relate to certain ambassadors intimate details of his private life of a kind not generally divulged. Yet he regarded himself as a model of domestic virtue. The harem was a state institution, for any child born within its walls was legitimate and stood in line of succession. At the ceremony of the Selamlik, visitors caught

* A ceremonial visit by the Sultan to a mosque.

† The chief mufti, the office having been created by Sultan Mohammed II in 1453. He was in effect the head of the ecclesiastical side of the state while the Grand Vizier directed the secular side. A *fatwā* issued by the Sheikh-ul-Islam became law immediately. Sultan Abdul Hamid was deposed by a *fatwā* in 1908.

glimpses of his favourite ladies when these, in closed carriages, fol lowed the Commander of the Faithful to mosque. It was not easy on such occasions to see much more than their eyes, which are usually the best features of Orientals. The half-transparent veils they wore enhanced their mystery. Abdul Hamid, as a moralist, frowned severely on any greater exposure and a woman's *décolleté* offered in his eyes an unholy temptation. When for instance the wife of a German general arrived in a low-necked dress to attend a banquet at the Palace, the Sultan was so shocked that he ordered a chamberlain to bring a shawl which he was ordered to wrap around her buxom shoulders. The tactful official pleaded with the unwilling *Frau general* that he did this because His Majesty was fearful lest she should catch cold. The lady vigorously assured him of the contrary and never understood the real motive behind the Caliph's solicitude.

Abdul Hamid had deliberately plotted the murder of hundreds of thousands of his Armenian subjects, yet in personal intercourse he was mild mannered, kindly, and considerate to those around him. He demanded only one virtue—loyalty—and as is usual in absolute states, professions of the most servile devotion to the ruler were pushed to the point of absurdity. In the Palace of Yildiz for instance a private opera was maintained. Many years before, one of those third-rate Italian troupes which formerly toured the seaports of the Levant had arrived at Constantinople. After they had given a performance at the palace an attractive offer was made to the artists to enter the Sultan's service. In order not to burden the Civil List unnecessarily the tenor was directed to draw a general's pay from the Minister of War and the soprano was given the remuneration and rank of a colonel, a procedure which was not unusual, for I knew some Turkish vice admirals who had never been aboard a ship. Diplomats occasionally would be invited to the Palace to see the wretched performance of an Italian opera, and on these occasions the Master of Ceremonies would enter an ambassador's box and praise the domestic virtues of the artists. Thus he would offer a long explanation of how when the tenor kissed the leading lady he was really embracing his own wife and that after the performance instead of going to revel at late suppers which the Sultan understood to be the custom in Western capitals, both artists would return together to their home and look after their children. The Master of Ceremonies remarked that His Majesty appreciated that etter singers in the world, but there could be none e was so pure and who moreover had the great merit of ely devoted in their attachment to His Majesty's person.

these performances Mrs. Leishman took with her a fan, of which were covered with the autographs of many celebri- was seated next to the Sultan and asked him if he would not onor her with his signature. Abdul Hamid wrote his name on a of the fan without any intimation that the request had been other- e than agreeable but next day an aide-de-camp from the Palace alled to see the Ambassadress. The officer explained that he came on behalf of His Majesty who desired once more to see a fan which bore so many famous signatures. A few days later the official returned with her fan bearing Abdul Hamid's name set in brilliants over the former signature, which had disappeared. The Sultan also understood the art of rebuking others in the most polite manner. On one occasion when cigarettes were passed at the palace to a Texan diplomat the latter refused these and asserted his own manly preference for chewing, which he followed with an unexpected exhibition of that practice on a valuable carpet. With perfect equanimity Abdul Hamid remarked that he also took pleasure in chewing but restricted its delights to when he walked in his own garden.

An ancient custom handed down from the days when the Turks were a warlike tribe and needed a man to be their ruler demanded that the succession to the throne should pass to the eldest male member of the House of Othman. The amiable practise of having all their brothers murdered was formerly adopted by Sultans on their accession, but the thoroughness of this drastic method had fallen into disuse at the same time as the Turkish Empire decayed. It was generally believed that Abdul Hamid would have wished to change the order of succession in favour of his son, the pasty-faced Prince Burhan-Eddin, who usually accompanied his father to mosque on Fridays, but the Sultan never attempted to carry out this innovation, restrained probably by fear of upsetting the ancient family law.

A curious instance of the respect Abdul Hamid felt for another sage of his House happened to a young prince I knew who was the tan's nephew and who had been bold enough without asking con- o marry a charming girl of one of the best Turkish families. The llow was in despair, for Abdul Hamid had sent for him and after rebuking the young man for violating every family tradition had forced him to divorce. All princes of the imperial blood, like the Sultan himself, were only allowed by an unwritten law to marry slaves. The reason for this practise was that family relationships, which are based on a kind of clan system, count for much in the East and it was regarded as impolitic to have the Sultan or any of the princes open the door to outside influences through a father-in-law. Doubtless for the same reason Byzantine emperors not infrequently married beautiful peasant girls.

The domestic happiness of the imperial princesses was provided for by a different device. When these attained to marriageable age they would be conducted to a latticed gallery, from which they could look out on a kind of mannequins' procession of good-looking young men who were paraded for their inspection. I knew one of these who after the war became Grand Vizier, but finished his life on the gallows. The lot of the husband of a princess was not enviable, and it was popularly said that court etiquette required the consort to crawl from the foot into the conjugal bed.

Outside the Palace, polygamy had fallen into disuse except among the peasants who found it agreeable to smoke a *narghileh** while they made their wives till the fields. The position of women was often misjudged by foreigners, and in higher Turkish circles the relations between the sexes were at times conducted with feelings of great delicacy. The son of a famous Grand Vizier related to me a story about Sultan Abdul Medjid, who was greatly beloved by his subjects and whose worst misdeed was to have been the father of Abdul Hamid. To curry favour, a Pasha had sent to him as a gift a Circassian slave girl of ravishing beauty. The delighted Sultan assigned to her the finest apartment in the palace and gave orders that the wishes of the new favourite were to be treated as though they were his own commands. But whenever he knocked at her door he found it shut and no answer came to his call. Day after day he returned but the lock of the door was always bolted. From afar the eunuchs gazed with amazement at the sight of the Sultan on his knees, and overheard him imploring the slave girl to open, saying that it was her servant Abdul Medjid who knelt before her door as an expectant lover. Yet she continued deaf to all his entreaties and would send him away with harsh words, nor could he

* A water pipe.

ever bring himself to do violence to her consent. The Sultan, famous for his generosity, daily lavished rich gifts on the Circassian, but she continued to remain indifferent to his attentions. At last he discovered that the reason for her coldness was because this beautiful slave loved a common soldier who was stationed in a distant frontier garrison. Touched by this devotion, the Sultan dowered her generously and gave her freedom to marry the lover of her choice.

According to the Turkish view, marriage was only a civil ceremony which permitted the husband to begin a courtship that might lead to further intimacies although the latter were often long delayed. A prominent Turkish lady I knew had waited for three months after the ceremony before she would consent to become a wife and expressed the wish that her daughter, who had just married, would also follow her example. Divorce, although extremely easy for it needed merely a declaration, was restrained by the husband's obligation to return his wife's property. The only further restriction was one prohibiting a man from divorcing the same woman more than three times. After the third separation it became necessary for her to marry someone else before the couple could again be lawfully reunited. This legal restraint led to a curious occupation, for in every Turkish town there existed a profession for aged men, who might have impersonated Joseph the Carpenter in the medieval drama and who hired themselves out to act as temporary husbands in order to permit couples to be remarried after their third divorce.

Palace influence had little to do with official position and the most powerful personages generally stayed in the background or held only lowly rank. One of these was the Sultan's astrologer, Eboul Houda, who afterwards was killed during the Revolution. But by far the most influential man in Turkey after the Sultan was then his Second Secretary, a grasping and venal Arab named Izzet Pasha. His methods were always suave, but no one was more brazenly dishonest and no one was more universally hated for his rapacity. As a liar he was unblushing. On one occasion he had sent for a French banker to assure him that the Sultan held the financier in such particular esteem that he proposed to confer on him, as a mark of special favour, the signal honour of asking for a loan. When the banker hazarded an enquiry about the security for the money, Izzet remarked with a smile that he would have the finest guaranty in the world, which was His Majesty's sacred word of honour. The loan was made, for the French Embassy regarded it as diplomatically desirable, but when the time came for it to be repaid Izzet repeatedly put off the banker. The latter pleaded that he had only advanced the money on the strength of the assurances he had received about the Sultan's word of honour. "Did I say that?" was Izzet's disarming explanation. "Then I lied."

In one matter only the Second Secretary was scrupulous. He personally directed the construction of the Hedjaz railroad which was then being built across the desert to Mecca to serve as a kind of political religious propaganda for the Sultan. This line was to be a purely Mohammedan enterprise in order to exalt Abdul Hamid's prestige as Caliph of the Moslem world.

So much nonsense has been written about the Caliphate that a few words on this subject may not be amiss. The claim to the title which was made by the Ottoman Sultans dated from the days of Selim the Grim who, when he conquered Egypt early in the sixteenth century, bought the right from an old beggar in Cairo who could trace his descent from a former Commander of the Faithful. Thereafter Turkish Sultans styled themselves Caliphs, a title which they bundled together along with innumerable others but to which they attached about the same importance as did formerly the Kings of England when they called themselves Kings of France. Outside the Ottoman Empire a greatly divided Moslem world regarded the Sultan of Turkey merely with the respect due to the most powerful of Mohammedan rulers.

Not until after the Crimean War did the idea of the Caliphate begin to assume any modern importance. English suggestion may at first have had something to do with this, for at that time Stratford de Redcliffe was all-powerful at Constantinople and it seemed desirable to exalt the prestige of a Sultan whose influence might be useful among Indian Moslems. It was left however for the Germans methodically to expand the doctrine of Pan-Islamism. When the Kaiser declared himself to be the great friend of the Turks he aimed to utilize this idea as a potential weapon which he could direct against Russia, France, and Great Britain, for each of these states had millions of Mohammedan subjects. Abdul Hamid was therefore encouraged by Berlin to despatch his emissaries among Moslems throughout the world. They carried gifts from the Sultan, and as they asked for no more than lip service they were welcome wherever they went. Later in Peking I saw a few of these agents. Their real importance was slight, but their presence often led to gross exaggeration on the part of ill-informed statesmen who refused to apply common sense to unfamiliar phenomena. That Pan-Islamism was principally an article of German manufacture became apparent by its complete failure during the Great War. Owing to quite different reasons, it exercised a considerable influence for some time over British policy in India. Today it is admittedly dead, replaced in Turkey by a Turanian* brand of Balkan nationalism.

In a characteristically Oriental way the Sultan believed that his imperial glory was exalted by keeping around him a staff of foreign aide-de-camps, principally German, certain of whom held the rank of field marshal in the Turkish Army. Their duty was to run behind His Majesty's carriage every Friday, at the ceremony of the Selamlik, where they looked rather like the jaded kings of Asia in Marlowe's "Tamerlane." These overdecorated officers, several of whom had grown old and enormously fat after years of idleness and rich Oriental food, had nothing more important to do than cast a tinsel glamour on an Eastern potentate's tinsel grandeur. Oddly enough, among these officers of various nations was a Maine Yankee aide-de-camp whose appointment had come about in a curious way.

An old dispute between Turkey and America concerned certain missionary claims that dated back from the first Armenian massacres. The Sultan had always refused to admit these but at last, to show good will, was induced to order a cruiser to be built in the United States and offered to pay a little more than its actual cost, the balance to be unofficially used for the satisfaction of these claims. Only a trifling difficulty remained, which was that no available funds existed to pay either for the cruiser or the claims. One day Leishman learned accidentally while playing bridge at the club that the sheep tax of two provinces, hitherto assigned to cover interest charges on some former loan, was about to be released. By quick action he succeeded in having this tax earmarked to guarantee payment for the cruiser, which some years later in due course arrived at Constantinople. The Sultan gazed at his new warship from the safe distance of a palace window, felt pleased at this instrument of his power, and as a mark of favour expressed the wish to appoint an American officer to his suite. The Navy Department at Washington evinced no enthusiasm for Abdul Hamid's offer,

* That is, Turkish.

but Leishman did not like to reject it and obtained the position for Bucknam, the stumpy Yankee sailor of the merchant marine who had navigated the vessel to Turkish waters. Bucknam was made a Pasha, donned a fez, ran behind the Sultan's carriage every Friday, and had assigned as his aide a young naval officer named Raouf, who during the Balkan War commanded this cruiser and became for a short time a Turkish national hero and even a Grand Vizier, and later ambassador in London.

Presently the American Pasha found his opportunity. A forty-year-old completely obsolete battleship had been refitted at enormous cost in Kiel. The scandal was so great, even for a hardened Constantinople, that a commission of enquiry was appointed, but the admiral in charge died suddenly under mysterious circumstances and the investigation was not further pursued. When this prehistoric craft was ready to sail, a German firm had the impudence to ask forty thousand pounds for navigating so dangerous an antiquity to Constantinople. Bucknam learned this and offered to undertake the job with a Turkish crew for one tenth of the sum. The Sultan was delighted and still more pleased when later he learned that Bucknam, carrying the money to pay the coal bill, was attacked by some roughs on the docks at Kiel and single-handed had knocked out five of these whom he then turned over to the police. The next time that Abdul Hamid saw Leishman the Sultan held up his fists like a boxer to illustrate his aide-de-camp's pugilism, in which he took a vicarious pride. Bucknam returned in triumph and the Sultan presented him with a thousand pounds. For the first time in over a century a Turkish crew had sailed the Atlantic. They made only one stop at Algiers, where the Moslem sailors' sole dissipation was to ride in trams and visit mosques.

During his long reign Abdul Hamid had concentrated the authority of an Empire in his person, for he made use of the officials of the Sublime Porte only as convenient buffers. Thus the Minister for Foreign Affairs, Tewfik Pasha, was a courteous gentleman of the old school, whose wooden appearance and still more woodeny character made him a useful intermediary. His principal duty was to receive the diplomatic kicks administered by foreign ambassadors, who not infrequently would address him in almost insulting terms. There was never any hard feeling on either side because of these, and amenities of this order were a recognised procedure with diplomats who liked Tewfik personally even when they wrote him the most offensive notes. Leishman for instance would pretend to blame the Minister for his audacity in presuming not to carry out the Sultan's solemn promises, knowing perfectly well that Tewfik was merely obeying Palace orders. The latter was too accustomed to this solemn farce to care about insults, and our personal relations always remained on a most friendly footing. Tewfik's strength, like that of his country, lay in inertia.

It is said that Orientals are only susceptible to force, to flattery, or bribery, but the Sultan could occasionally be moved by information on condition that he had obtained this surreptitiously. Experience had taught him that a blast of threatening notes, which in any other country would have led to a rupture of relations, need not disturb him. But once, most mysteriously in the midst of a controversy of this nature with the Embassy, all Turkish obstruction to American demands suddenly caved in and an unexpected satisfaction was received. Long afterwards Tewfik frankly explained what had happened. The Sultan had read a private letter written by Leishman to his daughter, who was then on her wedding journey, advising her not to come to Constantinople as the situation was so serious that the Ambassador might be obliged to leave at any moment. This letter opened in the Turkish post office had convinced the Sultan that the United States was this time really in earnest.

Like many more Turkish officials than is commonly supposed, Tewfik was an honest man. Until Abdul Hamid debauched his official caste, there had been a class of excellent administrators among the Turks. Their courtly manners and dignity, a rough justice, and a sense of humour made these officials of the old school most sympathetic to foreigners. One of these was Saïd the Kurd, a former Grand Vizier. He was an old man and had retired from office when I knew him, but he was fond of relating the experiences of his early career. His first post had been that of Governor of Mytilene, an island inhabited solely by a Greek population. Shortly after his arrival, not feeling well, he had sent for the local doctor who, after an examination, suggested that the trouble with the Pasha came from overindulgence in the pleasures of the harem. Saïd replied that this was impossible as he had left his family behind at Constantinople. The Greek doctor then suggested that the contrary might be true and proposed that he should show his favour to some lady of the island, for no one would dare to resist the

Governor. Saïd, keeping silent a moment, then said to the physician, "Send me your wife tonight." The doctor laughed at his sally, treating it as a joke. The Governor insisted. After he had reduced the Greek doctor to despair, Saïd spoke. The women of Mytilene, he declared, were his daughters when they were maidens, his sisters in their womanhood, his mother in old age, and never would he as the Governor bring dishonour among them.

Easy generalizations about corrupt practises caused foreigners to give insufficient credit to the Turks who were decent. Few of these held high office, but many in private life were most honourable men. I have in mind Hamdi Bey, formerly Master of Ceremonies, who left the Palace to become director of the great Archaeological Museum which was entirely his work, aided by his brother, Halil Bey. Hamdi's love of art was most unusual among the Turks, few of whom have any aesthetic feeling, and perhaps could be explained by his origin. Although he was the son of a former Grand Vizier, his father had been born a Greek child and was saved from the massacre of Chios and brought up as a Turk. A personal experience I had with Hamdi was greatly to his credit. The late art collector Charles L. Freer had called on me in much distress. He had just purchased at Damascus a number of Nabbatean antiquities which with his customary enthusiasm he described as being treasures that were as priceless as they were unique. While attempting to smuggle these out—for the export of antiquities was strictly forbidden in Turkey—the statuary had been seized at Haifa. Mr. Freer's anxiety was all the greater because of the fear that the exposure of this illegality would reflect on the remainder of his collections, which he intended to bequeath to the United States after his death and which are now exhibited at Washington in the Museum that bears his name. I could only suggest to him to make a clean breast to Hamdi and offered to introduce him. The latter was kindness itself. Far from being censorious he remarked that the Museum already possessed a good deal of Nabbatean art and offered to make a friendly exception and authorise the export of these statues. Incidentally they turned out to be forgeries, the work of some Italians in Damascus, but at the time none of us were aware of this. Hamdi then invited Freer to visit the store-rooms of the Museum and pointed out seven recently discovered Parthian sarcophagi, all of the same blue vitreous stoneware and all precisely alike. Freer became wildly enthusiastic and

Hamdi remarked that if he liked them so much he would sell him one. The collector could no longer restrain himself. Freer wanted to sign a contract at once to buy every duplicate in the Museum and asked me to act as his agent and help enrich a collection which was to go to the nation. No price which Hamdi asked was too great and Freer would not hear of any limit. The collector was obliged to leave Constantinople next day and he placed the matter of the sarcophagus in my hands with an embarrassing discretion. Time and again I talked with Hamdi, but I was never able to get any further with him in this affair. At last he admitted that after discussing the matter with his brother they agreed that as a principle it would be unwise to sell any duplicates, for after they had gone such practices might lead to abuses.

# 3. *Diplomatic Life and the Turkish Revolution*

## I

Diplomats are nomads by profession who feel the same need for rugs as Bedouins who live in tents. It was the fashion to take advantage of one's stay in Constantinople to lay in a stock of these after prolonged bargaining at the bazaar. I used to go there frequently, for I enjoyed my talks with Persian boothkeepers who, as they offered me Oriental tea, would caress their objects, for they found in them something more than articles to sell. They felt immensely proud of the ancient culture of their race, and they regarded the Turks as barbarians and looked on them with a contempt which was cordially reciprocated by the more virile Ottomans.

I had one Turkish friend, named Reshad Fuad, who was a gentleman of the old school and a real collector. His house in Stamboul contained great numbers of old Vienna jam pots which were made for the East and which he placed on a few fine pieces of French eighteenth-century furniture that had strayed to Constantinople, sent perhaps as gifts from the Court of Versailles. My friend was enormously fat, but his charming manners made one forget this physical infirmity. He was a lay brother of the Mevlevi sect of dervishes. Tourists used to be taken to their monastery to see the inmates whirling about in a dance which symbolized the course of the planets through the firmament. As they did this, they attained an ecstasy in which they lost all consciousness. It would have been difficult to picture my obese friend as a whirling dervish, although his movements were never ungraceful and his conversation always delightfully light, enlivened with a natural wit which he inherited from an ancestor who had been a famous Grand Vizier. Every educated Turk held some office, and my friend was a Counsellor of State with only nominal duties. He kept aloof from officials, most of whom he despised, and his principal pleasures were chatting with his friends and adding to his collections.

Below the Suleymanieh Mosque in Stamboul a network of lanes

runs between ancient walls of cut stone that date from Byzantine times. These would be decked in May with purple trellises of wisteria. This was my favourite quarter to browse in with Reshad, but he was no great walker and as soon as he began to pant we would stop to sip coffee in the courtyard of a small mosque under the shade of a giant sycamore. The "Gate of Felicity" was a Turkish name for Constantinople, and much of my friend's happiness came from his enjoyment of the city's charm. He felt it was part of his own blood, but he was enough of a Westerner to view its beauty with an artist's eye and to deprecate the false appreciation that he found in Pierre Loti's *Désenchantés.** Reshad always insisted that the French novelist had never understood the true Orient and to convince me of this he would draw a picture of an East which was filled with his own kindly tolerance, his courtliness, and his scorn for material success. No such East had ever existed, but Reshad saw the old Turkey with a lover's eye. He would describe to me with romantic enthusiasm a past that had nothing in common with the realm of Abdul Hamid and still less with the new Balkanized state which was shortly to destroy this. My friend could hardly admit that the world he depicted was only an illusion, though I suspect that in his heart he knew this and that it saddened him to think that he was the last of his kind. In the tradition of his fathers he used to go regularly to the cemetery to pray at his parents' grave, but he foresaw that his sons would not do the same for him after he had gone.

Half furtively, Turkey was being Westernized. Its culture, after having been for centuries a plant of Persian growth, was already following the literary fashions of Paris and had left Hafiz for Mallarmé. On the Bosporus a French architect had built a graceful abode for the Oriental muses in a lovely rose garden that overlooked the ruined castle of Roumeli Hissar. I never saw a more beautiful site, for the library was shaded by tall cypresses and approached between hedges of Bengal roses which fringed carpets of blue iris. In this paradise the architect, who had in him the soul of an artist, created a dream of beauty for a Turkish friend, for whom he built an airy pavilion in the Persian style worthy of the great shahs at Ispahan. Here was housed a unique private collection, that exists no more, which contained several thou-

* Loti was the pseudonym of Louis Marie Julien Vand (1850–1923), who wrote almost forty novels, mainly about nature and the sea. *Les Désenchantés* was published in 1906.

sand ancient Oriental manuscripts with many rare specimens of calligraphy, an art highly prized throughout the East. Certain of these manuscripts were written by famous scribes and illuminated by great miniaturists, and among these books I saw some finely chiselled fifteenth-century bindings to convince me that the Venetian craftsmen of the Renaissance had borrowed their art from Persia.

Close by at Bebek the Khedive* passed his summers. There one entered into a very different world. The ruler of Egypt had built an ultramodern palace in which he maintained royal pomp, and when the Ambassador called on him the stairs were lined by innumerable officials in brilliant uniform whose rank increased with every step. I followed Mr. Leishman into the Viceregal presence where a Nubian brought us coffee in cups which were of equal size for the Khedive and his guest, but slightly smaller for me, as befitted my lower rank. Our host's talk to my chief was patronizingly informative and dwelt on the merits of certain Confederates who after our Civil War had entered the Egyptian service. Solemnly the Khedive assured Mr. Leishman that in all his future campaigns he would place reliance on the officers who had been trained by our Southerners.

In Turkey the Khedive was treated like the governor of a province. The Sultan did not encourage expressions of nationalism, and Turks themselves were still as careless regarding their conquering past as they felt unconcerned over their alarming future. Mohammed's capture of Constantinople is now I believe celebrated as an anniversary, but at that time the Turks, with unconscious humour, had borrowed a superstition from the Greeks and regarded Tuesday, the day on which the city fell, as unlucky. They showed as yet no interest in their past, for the prevailing look of neglect and the crumbling walls overgrown by weeds, which one saw everywhere, seemed an appropriate counterpart to the Sultan's ramshackle empire. There was no need at Constantinople to create that deliberate picturesqueness which formerly induced Georgian architects to build artificial ruins in English parks.

Only exceptionally are diplomats in Oriental countries able to break through the crust of the native mind, for their relations are usually restricted to officialdom or confined to inferiors long accustomed to foreign ways. Every chancery is filled with the dead records of the

* The title of the Viceroy in Egypt, conferred by the Sultan of Turkey in 1867. It was abolished by the British in 1914.

past, where these are reduced to a kind of common denominator of lifeless notes and despatches which hardly penetrate into the soul of the country. Within embassy walls life tends to be recast into a legal and statistical mould which goes far to explain the limitations of the official intellect. This frigid aloofness from the awkward stresses and bulges of a shifting humanity once helped to preserve diplomatic prestige. Envoys and indeed all diplomats in the Levant discovered to their pleasurable satisfaction that they were raised on an invisible pedestal, but they sometimes failed to discover that they were enveloped in an atmosphere of deliberate flattery. The absence of a Court or the framework of any real society in Constantinople left the way open to the foreign ambassadors to fill the vacuum with some magnificence. Old traditions of diplomacy in fact were better preserved in the Golden Horn than in any other capital. The representatives of the great powers lived in huge palaces at Pera and had splendid summer residences on the Bosporus that lay in beautiful parks. Armed guards attended them when they went out; launches and a steam yacht were always at their disposal. Even the wily ladies of Pera to whom certain diplomats showed an ostentatious devotion felt honoured by this intimacy. In no other capital was the position of an ambassador so exalted, and nowhere else as in that mixed population was a knowledge of the practical workings of diplomacy so widely diffused. The precise meaning of every official move was shrewdly judged and the text of every note carefully scrutinized not only by the Turkish officials at the Sublime Porte but by the Levantines who would read into it all and more than was left unsaid. Underneath a Byzantine tradition of effusive compliment and much servile flattery, the worth of every envoy was quickly and shrewdly appraised.

The British Embassy was housed in a great Roman palace built on a commanding site at Pera which dated from the period after the Crimean War when English influence was paramount. The Foreign Office then used architectural splendour to glorify its agents at a time when people spoke nervously of the Eastern Question, and the Sick Man of Europe still looked to Englishmen for advice. The British Ambassador, Sir Nicholas O'Conor, was an old-school diplomat, intelligent and resourceful, who resided in the same palace as his masterful predecessors, but did not enjoy their prestige, since the protector of the Ottoman Empire was no longer a widow at Windsor, but a Kaiser at

Potsdam. Certain illogicalities had contributed to make the greatness of Britain's position in the world, but they also made O'Conor's position as Ambassador difficult and often contradictory. English influence had been built in Turkey on substantial interests and an inherited prestige. Critics might remark that the Ambassador stood for no clear policy but would have found it much harder to state how any clear policy could possibly have fitted into a welter of so many conflicting interests. O'Conor had to press for reforms in the Ottoman Empire and yet to deter the Sultan from touching near to any region that was of special concern to England. The Ambassador had to insist on a kind of open door and yet to maintain certain exclusive rights at Bassorah and in the Aidin Valley. He had to consider English merchants in Smyrna and British bankers in Threadneedle Street whose interests were not always the same. He had alternately to flatter and frown on the Turk and administer occasional platonic pats of good will to the Armenians. And always he had to think of the Ottoman Empire as being a great milestone in the European game. If ever he entertained any doubts as to the wisdom or consistency of a most intricate and tangled policy, he kept these hidden under a grave countenance, an old-fashioned courtesy, and some rather mangy Dundrearys* which made him faintly resemble Palmerston.

Suavity and deportment are commonly associated with the diplomatic profession, but the appearance and manner of the dean of the corps, the German Ambassador, Baron Marschall von Bieberstein, was not unlike that of a great bear. Further resemblance stopped at this point, for his want of social grace was more than made up for by a sense of authority and an ability which commanded respect and was independent of his office. Intrigues had removed Marschall from the Wilhelmstrasse, but in spite of the semi-exile of his appointment to Turkey, he was a leading figure at Constantinople, and German influence owed much to the impressive personality of its energetic representative. When for instance a Hamburg merchantman had been improperly detained in the Golden Horn the Ambassador, instead of writing notes of protest and beginning a legal discussion with the Porte which would have dragged on indefinitely, went himself on board, ordered away the Turkish guards, and refused to leave until the ship had been released.

* Long, flowing side whiskers.

During the summer months while Baron Marschall was away, his place would be temporarily filled by his former friend and later enemy, Herr von Kiderlen-Wächter, who at that time was German Minister at Bucharest. Kiderlen was a jovial man who enjoyed his rubber of bridge and whose respect for the proprieties was never excessive. He exuded a somewhat coarse good fellowship in that South German way which reeks of the beer *Keller* and endeared him to the Kaiser, whose boon yachting companion he had been. This surface *bonhomie* concealed a real talent for intrigue which had helped to oust Marschall from the Wilhelmstrasse, but which went also with a capacity for hard work. When later Kiderlen became Foreign Minister, he showed much good sense in settling the Moroccan dispute with France. Like Marschall, he died suddenly before the war and is hardly remembered today except for a cigar which perpetuates his name.

German influence was then paramount at Constantinople. When Western Europe had been horrified by the Armenian massacres, only the Kaiser had smiled on Abdul Hamid. But it was Turkish fear of the Russians which made the Germans seem natural allies. The older generation with memories that dated from the Crimea still looked up to England, but the younger men, particularly the soldiers, were under the influence of German military prestige, which was then at its height. Berlin sent von der Goltz to reorganize the Ottoman army, and numerous Turkish officers received their training in Prussian regiments. German enterprise was then engaged in building the Bagdad Railway with money largely borrowed from Paris bankers, and German princelings wore decorations given by the Sultan. The Turks knew that they could not escape from being exploited by some Western power and chose the one which seemed to offer them the greatest advantage.

The interest of France in Turkey was primarily a financial one. The French Ambassador, M. Constans, was a vigorous old gentleman of considerable ability and a dictatorial touch which came down as a Napoleonic tradition and is often associated with French radicals. He was a newcomer in diplomacy and his past had been anticlerical, but by virtue of his office in Turkey he became the protector of the Catholic Church and his position made him take his seat on the throne in the cathedral. No one more than Constans enjoyed the humour of this situation.

His reputation as a strong man came to him from the time when he was Minister of the Interior and had pricked the Boulanger bubble* by making out a fictitious warrant for the General's arrest. The would-be dictator, summoned by Constans, caught sight of this warrant prepared and signed on the Minister's desk, left there accidentally so it seemed by the latter who had previously arranged to be momentarily called away. Constans enjoyed relating his part in this affair with some modesty, much humour, and more cynicism; he frankly admitted that he had Boulanger followed all day and that if the General, instead of bolting to Brussels, had ridden to the Elysée, he would have been the first one there to receive him.

Many were the strange tales told about Constans' career, not all of which were credible. The Ambassador possessed a keen sense of humour and enjoyed relating stories of the most doubtful propriety even against himself, but there was one which he never told. When he was Governor of Indochina, Constans had greatly admired a jewelled belt of immense value which belonged to the Emperor of Annam. His admiration became so insistent that at last the harassed monarch presented the Governor with his girdle. The gift provoked sufficient criticism for Constans to be summoned to Paris. The explanation he offered was most unsatisfactory, but when the belt was shown to the experts for a valuation, the precious stones of the Emperor's gift were all found to have been paste.

Mr. Leishman's relations with M. Constans were extremely cordial and on one occasion the French Ambassador showed a readiness to oblige which might have been embarrassing. An American minister, stationed in a neighbouring country, had his cipher code stolen and telegraphed asking the Embassy to arrest his former butler who was on the point of arriving at Constantinople; the wire stated that the proof of the theft would be forwarded by the next post. The supposed offender was a Frenchman, and Leishman sent me to request Constans' assistance. The French Ambassador was most eager to oblige a friendly

* The reference is to the attempt by George Boulanger, a military hero and political figure, in 1889 to modify the French Constitution aribitrarily to accord with his political inclinations. He had much public support, but the new government led by Pierre Tirard and his Minister of the Interior, Ernest Constans, decided to bring Boulanger to trial on charges of treason. Boulanger fled the country, however, and his trial and conviction occurred in his absence. Public support for Boulanger quickly subsided, and he committed suicide in 1891.

colleague, but as his own power was limited to offences committed in Turkey, he suggested that something trivial might be trumped up against the culprit on his arrival and he would then have him arrested and confined at our pleasure. One of our vice consuls in fact offered to start a brawl with the man as soon as he landed, but fortunately Leishman entertained certain misgivings as to the wisdom of doing this, for the butler turned out to be innocent. The Minister who had sent the telegram had been as unpardonably careless in announcing the despatch of proof which was never forwarded as in guarding the code entrusted to his care and which soon afterwards was offered to the Japanese Embassy at St. Petersburg.

The traditions of diplomatic life at Constantinople had been handed down from a more leisurely age, and certain diplomats still retained the flavour of the past. One in particular was His Catholic Majesty's Minister, the Marquis of Campo Sagrado. Official duties never oppressed the Spanish envoy and on the rare occasions when he felt it desirable to communicate anything to Madrid he would borrow his colleagues' despatches, which would later be returned with three quarters of the text struck out after having been marked by him as "superfluous." The Marquis once explained to me that his own dream of happiness was to be a king in exile, to be rich and live in Paris. If he had been able to realise this dream he would have been its uncrowned king, for this old-world Spaniard—short, fat, and ungainly in appearance—possessed a grand manner and an incomparable charm which made him loved by everyone and left him with no enemy other than himself. Not even Franklin Roosevelt could smile more winningly, and I have never known any man who gave the impression of being so great a gentleman. The graces and gallantry of life meant infinitely more to him than did its sordid economic problems. He had notoriously ruined his family by the wildest extravagance. Yet when he left Spain for a diplomatic post at St. Petersburg his first act on arriving had been to purchase a magnificent sable coat in which he had himself photographed and sent the likeness to his brother in Madrid, writing on it, "Behold how I am." The latter then had his own picture taken naked and despatched to the impenitent spendthrift with the inscription, "This is how you have left us." The Czar more than once paid the Marquis' debts in Russia, but in the end he was transferred to Constantinople, where the opportunities for a lavish extravagance were fewer. At his death Campo Sagrado still possessed property worth several million pesetas, but his ignorance of money matters was so great that he did not suspect this, or nothing would have remained of it, as his nephew who inherited this legacy told me.

A chronicle of diplomats is not unlike Homer's calendar of ships, except that it requires a satirist's pen. No ordinary writer for instance could do justice to the Persian Ambassador, who enjoyed the double title of Prince of Peace and Generalissimo of the Persian Army. These honours were alleged to have been self-decreed, and there was little to suggest that the Prince's military duties went beyond repeated changes of his always resplendent uniform. I knew him principally as a host, for the Ambassador delighted in extending invitations for a "five o'clock tea *à trois heures*." At his banquets, the Prince's seat at table would be marked by a card bearing the inscription "My Highness." His inseparable companion at all these ceremonies was an oily Armenian dragoman who enjoyed the pacific rank of "Civilian General," and had been honoured by the more suggestive title of "Seed of the State."

Persian ambassadors in Constantinople, in lieu of salary, were then in the habit of levying taxes on some twenty thousand of their countrymen who resided in that capital mainly earning a livelihood as donkey boys and porters. The rumour that the collection of these taxes was not unremunerative must have reached the ear of the Shah, for one day the Prince found himself summoned to Teheran. An invitation of this kind was never welcome, and a lurid tale was current about a predecessor who, after having been called back in similar circumstances, was reported to have been strangled aboard the imperial yacht. On this occasion the Prince of Peace showed his skill as a diplomat by addressing a telegram to the foot of the Peacock Throne. He explained that if he had to follow only his personal inclination he would abandon public life in order to devote himself to the many literary and scientific academies which, in every country of the world, were clamouring for his presence. It was only the devotion he felt for his master that caused him to understand how impossible it was to absent himself for a single day from his post.

The Prince's interest in letters was as a poet who needed little encouragement to recite his own verse. Once started, it was difficult to arrest a flow of Persian rhymes in which listeners ignorant of the language of Firdausi* would hear the same syllable always repeated at the end of every line. It is hard to criticise the merit of verse in an unknown tongue, but after an hour's recital, when the Ambassador stopped for a second to catch his breath, my wife tactfully attempted to dissuade him from going on by suggesting that so great a work of genius deserved a decoration. The Prince gave her a look of benevolent pity for the ignorance she had displayed and remarked, "They can't—I have them all."

## II

The summer of 1908 was the third that I had passed at Therapia. It began uneventfully and pleasantly, for we enjoyed the usual picnics in the Forest of Belgrade and the delicious pilaffs of quail cooked in vast kettles under the great oaks. A particularly pleasant party was given there by Selim Pasha, a sympathetic Syrian who was at that time Minister of Mines and Forests. After lunch I walked with Selim through a clearing in the wood and asked him about the methods of forestry which he utilised. The Minister explained that there were two systems, each of which had its merits; one called for annual planting and regular cutting by rotation, but the second, which was the one he had adopted for Turkey, left nature to replenish itself. Selim administered his forests and mines with practices which were current under Abdul Hamid, but unlike most of his associates he had been wise enough to retain the considerable fortune he had made and wiser still to keep most of this in London. That day as we chatted in the forest everything seemed at peace, yet hardly a week later, at a moment's notice, Selim Pasha was obliged to flee for his life.

Some reports had from time to time filtered through about recent disturbances in Macedonia, but they conveyed something so chronic and so remote that no one at Constantinople paid much attention to them. Only one novelty that one heard seemed like a joke. This was a rumour about certain Turkish bands who demanded a constitution, which was still an unfamiliar word. Everyone knew that a group of

* A Persian writer (940–1020) who assumed the great literary labor of completing the rendering of the Zoroastrian Khoda'ināma, or Book of Kings, into Persian verse. After 35 years of intensive work, he finished his magnum opus, the *Shāhnama,* as it was entitled, with magnificent success. Critics have long acclaimed the power and beauty of his language.

political refugees had lived for years in Paris and in Geneva, but most of them were believed to have long ago made their peace with the Sultan and the others hardly counted. Their unreconciled leader was Ahmed Riza, an honest but naïve visionary whose ambition it was to remodel Turkey into a kind of Victorian England. This small group, living in exile, favoured Western reforms, but did not exercise the slightest influence, and it was difficult to discover any connection between the feeble expression of their liberal ideas and the activity of the revolutionary bands in Macedonia.

The supposed omniscience of diplomacy is a current fallacy. Particularly in states where the free expression of opinion is driven underground, members of the profession are often remarkably badly informed, for they dare not enquire too closely into dangerous matters or frequent men who are under suspicion lest they also should seem unfriendly to the government to which they are accredited. Few of us moreover had any real contact with the military. In Constantinople this was very difficult for several reasons, one of which was that the officers of the Army Corps stationed in the capital were promoted from the ranks on the theory that illiterates would be less likely to listen to subversive ideas. Diplomats were still less in touch with the Masonic lodges at Salonika or the military circles in Macedonia, where the insurrection had started. Everyone was therefore amazed to learn that the army, after fighting *Comitadjis* for years, had itself begun a revolution. They were still more astonished by its instantaneous and overwhelming success. Until the very last moment the Sultan's rule had given the impression of great strength. But when a despotism loses its vitality it collapses without any warning. That is why diplomats in their blindness foresaw nothing, and the downfall of Abdul Hamid, as soon as a few soldiers turned against him, came to everyone as a complete surprise. Without a sign of resistance, without a protest or a blow, the Sultan's authority, which for thirty years had remained unchallenged in its despotism, crumbled and vanished overnight.

Never was a change more complete in so short a time. Of bloodshed there was virtually none, for there was no opposition, but every Turk instantly expressed his horror for "reactionaries" and his attachment to the new order. Absolutism seemed to have perished overnight, and constitutional liberty was proclaimed amid immense enthusiasm throughout the Empire. Most remarkable of all was the temporary disappearance of old racial hatreds. The backwash of the French Revolution at last had reached the Near East, and liberty and fraternity were shouted to the sound of a new constitutional march which was played and sung everywhere. Spontaneously Turks went to Armenian cemeteries, to make speeches praising their martyrs who had fallen in the common cause of freedom and to declare that all races within the Empire were henceforth brother Ottomans. Bulgar *Comitadjis* and Greek archbishops, who only the day before would gladly have cut each other's throats, publicly embraced. For a moment everyone believed in the permanence of this new fraternity of races and creeds. Turkish officers spoke in the streets to urge Ottomans to join together and dig a common grave in which all their former hatreds should be buried. And they were sincere when they exhorted their listeners to engrave on the tombstone, "There shall be no Resurrection."

The more unpopular members of the Hamidian régime made their escape by a hurried flight from Constantinople. Izzet, the Sultan's Secretary and the most hated man in Turkey, bolted to safety in Egypt. Selim Pasha rushed on board an Italian ship, escorted by the Ambassador, the Marquis Imperiali. Eboul Houda, the Sultan's astrologer, was murdered, and a few spies of the late régime who were not sufficiently clever to join the new one in time found themselves savagely pursued. Tales were current about the discovery of entire rooms at the Palace which were filled with sacks containing their denunciations.

Strikes had up to then been forbidden in Turkey, but with the new liberty of the Revolution everyone struck, down to the small boys who were employed by the embassies at Therapia to pick up tennis balls. The usual anecdotes, told also in the Russian Revolution, were circulated about peasants who wondered whether the Constitution was a man or a woman. It was soon apparent that as a field for Western democratic institutions, the Ottoman Empire was not particularly promising. Yet a Turkish Constitution had been drawn up more than a quarter of a century before, at a time when the Sultan was still under British influence. This charter, suspended almost at once, had never been formally abrogated. It was now taken out of the drawer, early elections were decreed, and a Parliament was convoked by the Sultan. Once more the oldest subscriber of the London *Times,* the blue-eyed octogenarian Kiamil Pasha, an official of Cypriot-Jewish origin, mild mannered and with liberal sympathies, became Grand Vizier. The Sultan accepted his new rôle of a constitutional monarch with seeming good grace—far too frightened to act otherwise. He talked to everyone as if he understood the error of his former ways, and as if constitutional rule was really most welcome to him. He flattered the young Turks, offered their leaders a banquet at Yildiz, drank to the nation, and publicly kissed the forehead of his great enemy, the respectable Ahmed Riza, who was elected President of the new Parliament. The Revolutionary era in Turkey began with a delightful honeymoon, and the Sultan gracefully acted his novel part as an enlightened Western ruler. Reform was in the wind and the catch-words of liberty filled the air. The German Ambassador, who had been a notorious pillar of the old régime, voluntarily effaced himself. The British were once more in the ascendant. I went to greet the new English envoy, Sir Gerard Lowther, on his arrival at Constantinople and found it difficult to make my way to the station through a crowd of thousands of cheering Turks who received him with the wildest enthusiasm and followed his carriage in a triumphal march through the streets to the British Embassy.

Hitherto unknown men now became the heroes of the hour and many exiles returned, some from abroad, others from distant provinces. The Revolutionaries, amazed by their own success, behaved at first with exemplary moderation. Enver Bey, fresh from Macedonia, appeared for the first time at Constantinople, enjoying his new celebrity as a professional hero of liberty. Along with another officer, Niazi Bey, Enver had taken the regimental cash box, fled to the mountains, proclaimed the Constitution, and started the revolution. Niazi had no taste for applause, but his new-found popularity delighted Enver after the years of obscurity which he had passed as a subaltern in the wilds of Macedonia. He was young, good-looking in a flashy hairdresser way, loved the favour of the crowd, and a success which went beyond his most extravagant dreams soon turned his head. As a man he was wanting in any clear political ideas or convictions beyond personal ambition. The position in the army of an officer of junior rank who monopolized attention would have been difficult for anybody, and Enver was induced to accept the post of military attaché in Berlin. No one could then foresee that this would expose him to new influences which in the World War helped to bring Turkey on the German side.

The most interesting member of the new Cabinet to me was Talaat, the Minister of the Interior, who later became Grand Vizier. Strange tales circulated about his origin, but there is good reason to believe that he was a Turk, born of a gypsy mother in a village of Pomaks, who are Bulgarian Mohammedans. From a small telegraph clerk at Salonika he had become the moving spirit in the Committee of "Union and Progress," which until the end of the war, except for one interval, ruled Turkey with an iron hand. When I first met Talaat in 1909 he was as slim as he afterwards became obese. He was still new at this time to official life, but his intelligent eyes, a certain directness of phrase, and a sympathetic manner, which later disappeared, produced an impression of Western frankness that contrasted favourably with the mellifluous equivocations of old régime officials. I had an example of this not long afterwards over the Adana massacres in which some twenty thousand Armenians and Greeks were butchered, amid circumstances that have never been properly explained. This piece of devilry was I believe the deliberate work of reactionary officials who had been retained in office and who tried in this way to discredit the new régime, in order to provoke foreign intervention.

Atrocities never occurred spontaneously in Turkey, but always by command, and not a few accused the new government of having secretly ordered these massacres. It is hard to see the advantage which the Adana butchery could have brought to a revolutionary administration still struggling to win credit abroad, but a circumstance which lent colour to this charge was the part taken by several Hamidian officials who had kept their posts and the conduct of Turkish regiments despatched to Adana supposedly to restore order. Particularly disgraceful was the rôle of the governor, who remained hidden in his *Konak** during the killings while the British Vice-Consul, a splendid fellow named Doughty Wylie, later awarded a posthumous Victoria Cross at the Dardanelles, was wounded as he gallantly rode through the streets of Adana while attempting to stop the massacre.

Two American missionaries were killed there by accident. I was then in charge of the Embassy, and when attempting to secure redress for these victims I pressed for the punishment of the guilty parties. Several times I approached the Grand Vizier, Hilmy Pasha, on this subject, and invariably he would put me off with the customary eva-

* A large house in Turkey, especially one used as an official residence.

siveness of the Sublime Porte. On the other hand I always found Talaat responsive and seemingly frank. He was lavish in his praise of Doughty Wylie, who had risked his life, and outspoken in condemning the cowardly governor who hid while twenty thousand people, for whose safety he was responsible, had been murdered. Talaat declared to me that if he had anything to say the latter would swing for his disgraceful neglect of duty. I was convinced at the time of his sincerity and he impressed me as being a far franker type of man than any Hamidian official I had known. The governor of Adana was not executed, but for the first time in Turkish history a number of Mohammedans, who were of doubtful guilt but of obscure station, were hanged for the murder of native Christians.

For many years the powers had preached reforms in Turkey without any expectation or particular wish that these should really be carried out. They were now to prove how little any true reform was to their taste. Every government in Europe had been waiting for Abdul Hamid to die, without knowing what would then take place or having any real plan of how to make stability issue from chaos. The ambition which now seized the Turks to try to set their own house in order by adopting parliamentary institutions upset every calculation and began by precipitating a European crisis. This developed rapidly and most alarmingly after Bulgaria, in collusion with Vienna, threw off the Sultan's sovereignty over Eastern Roumelia.* Simultaneously Austria, by annexing Bosnia and Herzegovina, nearly caused the World War to break out in 1909. Instead of meeting with sympathy in their efforts to reform, the Young Turks unexpectedly received two sharp raps to their prestige which aroused their fury and stopped any further attempts at fraternization with Christian Ottomans. Cynics will probably say that the blissful harmony of different races could never have lasted, yet the bitter disillusion met with on this point was to hasten the transformation of Turkey into a Balkanized Asiatic power.

The new rulers of Constantinople cared nothing about religious practices and were quite indifferent to Abdul Hamid's Pan-Islamism. Their ideal was nationalist and Turanian, and like the German dis-

* The European portion of Turkey, which became an autonomous province of Turkey under a provision of the Berlin Treaty of 1878, but was incorporated into Bulgaria in 1885.

ciples of the Frenchman Gobineau,* they discovered a novel racial philosophy in the books of another Frenchman, which in a curious way came to exercise a great influence over their political ideas. A learned librarian of the Arsenal in Paris, named Leon Cahun, had written a remarkably interesting history of Central Asia, in which he described the martial exploits of the Turks and their kindred Mongols in the early Middle Ages. Centuries before the present Turks had settled in Asia Minor, conquering Turkish tribes had made cavalry raids all the way from China to the heart of Europe, and had ruled an empire which stretched from the Yellow Sea to the Baltic. The peaceful librarian in Paris could never have suspected that his history was to exercise later a political influence in the Near East. The discovery of an unsuspected pedigree of military greatness was to be honey to the Turkish nationalists. A newly found Turanianism filled the younger soldiers with a new pride, and simultaneously a literary movement was started to purge the Turkish tongue of those Persian and Arabic excrescences which had been used to enrich a simple language with the exotic hyperbolism of the Court, and to replace this latter with the popular speech. It became a fashion, particularly among army men, to study Tchagatai, the primitive Turkish dialect of Central Asia, and certain officers even began to trim their beards square in the manner they supposed of their early conquering ancestors.

The leaven of the West at first spreads slowly in Eastern lands. Before it penetrates the masses and gathers momentum, nearly always a reaction takes place which finds its strength in the roots of old religious practises and leads to an easily aroused fanaticism. Unexpectedly this was now to rise to the surface in an almost absurd way. The general in command of the Army Corps at Constantinople was Mahmoud Moukhtar, a gallant but headstrong officer whose military education had been acquired in the Prussian Guard. The headgear of Turkish soldiers was at this time the fez, which although inconvenient in a warm climate allows Moslem worshippers to touch their heads to the ground while saying their prayers in accordance with the Koranic prescriptions. Mahmoud Moukhtar was bold enough to attempt to add to the fez a kind of movable vizor which he had designed in order to protect the soldiers' eyes from the sun. Instead, he had to protect himself

* Joseph Arthur de Gobineau, whose most important work, *Essai sur l'inégalité des races humaines* (1854) propounded a theory of Teutonic racial superiority.

by preciptious flight from his own soldiers who wanted to kill him for committing what they regarded as sacrilege.

Until this storm broke, the city had never seemed more quiet. Orientals because they are usually docile give shallow observers an impression of placid submissiveness. The very ease with which popular obedience is obtained by any firm authority tends to mislead opinion. Whenever Asiatics are stirred to violence by some emotional impulse, which in the Near East generally takes a religious form, their apparent passiveness changes with unexpected terrifying speed to a fury which can become capable of any excess and is then heedless of any consequence. The secret workings which bring about this change nearly always occur below the surface and until the storm breaks they may be hidden under an apparent outward calm. Certainly the most amazing feature of the Counter-Revolution which on April 13th, 1909, broke out at Constantinople was its unexpectedness. No rumblings from below the surface had even been faintly audible. The night before it occurred no diplomat, no dragoman, no Levantine entertained the slightest suspicion that anything in the city was unusual or amiss. Everything seemed quiet and normal. There was no warning of any kind to heed, no signal to observe. The Young Turks themselves were taken just as much by surprise as we were.

I had at that time a Montenegrin servant who had been recommended to me by his former employer, who was an Italian diplomat, with the assurance that he was extremely courageous and ready to kill anyone on his master's order. I had not yet tested his obedience in this respect, but when on April 13th, 1909, he entered my room to wake me, he announced with a smile that the soldiers of the garrison early that morning had murdered their officers. Without any warning, thirty thousand mutineers rose in the name of the Sacred Law, killed a number of their superiors, routed out the Young Turk government which only the day before seemed firmly established but now was in full flight, and affirmed their loyalty to a greatly frightened Sultan.

The same regiment of fusiliers which had started the Revolution now started the Counter-Revolution ten months later. All this happened because, partly as a reward, partly because it was believed that special reliance could be placed on its loyalty, this regiment had been moved from Macedonia to the capital to act as the trusted guardians of the Constitution and the Young Turk régime. Once in Constantinople, the officers, after years passed chasing Balkan bands, had spent their time talking politics in the cafés and lost touch with their men who, unaccustomed to the attractions of the capital, fell an easy prey to the agitation of the Softas, or theological students. The soldiers, who were corrupted by gold alleged to have come from the Palace, were persuaded by the reactionaries to perform another patriotic task and save their country, this time by making an end to the pig-eating impiety of the Young Turks. The mutineers raised the green flag of Islam, murdered some officers in their beds, and put the rest to flight. A few civilian officials of the new régime were also killed. One poor fellow, Emin Arslan, a Druse deputy who claimed direct descent from the Virgin Mary and whom the night before I had seen play bridge at the Club, was murdered by mistake owing to his unfortunate resemblance to a Young Turk minister.* Colonel Cloman, our Military Attaché in London, arrived at Constantinople the morning of the mutiny bearing a letter of introduction to the Emir. He wanted to call on him at once, and I had to break the news that he had come just three hours too late to present this.

With Cloman I drove to Stamboul to see the mutineers. The city was perfectly quiet, and except for a few barricades hastily thrown up near St. Sophia the soldiers seemed peaceable enough and appeared puzzled by the extent of their victory. Beyond demanding the fall of the Cabinet, which had bolted, beyond waving the green flag and shouting vaguely for the Sacred Law, of which none of the mutineers knew anything, the men seemed to have neither plan, direction, nor leadership. All day I watched the rebellious soldiers, many of them walking hand in hand, wandering aimlessly through the streets. The authority of the Young Turks apparently had collapsed quite as suddenly as that of the Sultan the year before, but the outcome was still uncertain, for there were two loyal cavalry regiments at Adrianople and it was believed that these would be sent for by Mahmoud Moukhtar in an effort to repress the mutiny.

That night as the guests at the Embassy sat around the bridge table, Mr. Leishman's servant entered to announce that he heard the sound of gun fire in Stamboul. We were convinced that the loyal regiments had arrived from Adrianople and we rushed to the terrace where the

* He was mistaken for the deputy and journalist Hussein Djahid Yalchin, editor of the *Tanin,* whose printing press was wrecked by the counter-revolutionaries.

sound of firing, although far away, was unmistakeable. Before long the noise became much louder, and soon the valley below us rang with the call of bugles, the crackle of rifles, and occasional piercing screams. We were all convinced that Mahmoud Moukhtar's reinforcements had attacked the mutineers and that under cover of the night a great battle was being fought, but we could not yet tell which side was victorious. It seemed incredible to be standing in our evening clothes on the Embassy terrace watching a struggle which was to decide the fate of Turkey while only a few hundred yards below us men were dying. Colonel Cloman and an English officer whose experience dated from the Boer War were already estimating that with fighting at such close quarters there could be not less than fifteen hundred dead. The shrieks became wilder and the firing drew nearer, till suddenly a few bullets whizzed by our heads to flatten against the Embassy wall. Watching a battle in evening clothes seemed foolish as soon as it became dangerous, and after this brief experience of warfare we took refuge indoors, thrilled by the excitement of the great fight which we had just witnessed.

Presently there came a lull, and the firing began to die down. The Ambassador asked us all to stay for the night, but I preferred to return to my own rooms, which were above the Orient Club less than a mile away. In the street I discovered a solitary *Araba* to drive me back and was almost home when I found my carriage unexpectedly sandwiched in by a regiment of soldiers marching in the same direction, who suddenly began to fire off their rifles all around me. I thought that they were being attacked, and as safety was only a few steps off I jumped out and ran in a zigzag to the shelter of the Club doorway. As I did so the soldiers shouted at me not to be afraid, though only afterwards did I understand their words. My head was filled with the impression of the great battle that I had just witnessed. So strong was this feeling that it took me a long time before I could bring myself to believe the story which I heard only then at the Club, that there had been no battle and that the soldiers were only firing off their guns as a sign of rejoicing.

During the next twenty-four hours happy mutineers walked through the streets of Constantinople, letting off their rifles in the air and wasting over a million rounds of ammunition to the imminent danger of people who gazed at them from their windows, a few of whom were accidentally killed. Some soldiers went to the Ottoman Bank, in the vaults of which millions of gold were stored, but they only asked for a few rifles that they knew were kept there in order to fire these off to show their joy, promising to return them later. When at last to our relief this noisy demonstration finished, the city settled down again to a surface quiet. During the next thirteen days, in no other capital in the world would a mutinous soldiery have behaved with so much moderation. There was neither pillage, robbery, nor violence, nor were any further excesses committed. These Turkish soldiers who had murdered their officers and carried out a seemingly successful revolution acted like lambs with their new-found power. In some mysterious way the city seemed to run itself, for nowhere was there visible the sign of an officer or a policeman. Authority remained nonexistent, for the mutineers created none of their own and the Young Turks had all bolted or were in hiding. One of these, Raouf Bey, the future Grand Vizier, came to seek refuge at our Embassy until, skilfully disguised by the Ambassador's valet, he was able to escape by boat to Salonika.

Once more the Turks were supposed to be living under the sacred law of Islam, and nominally at least the Sultan's authority had been restored. Abdul Hamid granted at once a general amnesty for acts which not unlikely the Palace instigated, though I cannot think that the Sultan personally directed these and I believe that he merely acquiesced in a daring plot engineered by others. The puzzle was to find a leader for the Counter-Revolution; since no one claimed this honour it was natural to look for him at Yildiz. At the British Embassy the influential first dragoman was Fitzmaurice, who possessed the stuff of a great agent. No one knew Turkey better or had a more penetrating insight into the Oriental mind, but he had little sympathy for the Young Turks. An official of the Porte once described him to me as caring only for such Turks as said their prayers five times a day and turned to an Englishman for all advice. There was some truth in this criticism, for Fitzmaurice had an exceptional personal acquaintance in reactionary circles which were unknown to other diplomats. But as often happens with experts, the excess of his local knowledge led also to a mistaken opinion which overestimated the strength of the reaction and professed to believe that the Sultan was once more safely seated on his throne.

At the British Embassy it was given out that the Padishah had understood the error of his former ways and now desired to govern his empire in the manner of an enlightened constitutional monarch. The wish may have been father to the thought, but Abdul Hamid, to carry out this solemn farce, now appointed Tewfik Pasha as Grand Vizier. It was unfortunate that the powers held by that respectable and woodeny official were nonexistent and those of the Sultan were probably no greater at this time. The touching picture of the Caliph's sudden conversion to Western liberal ideas which certain English supporters now tried to draw rested on a complete miscalculation and minimized the fact that Abdul Hamid, aware of his weakness and far too frightened to act, was yet frightened enough to promise anything to anyone. All this time, while Baron Marschall astutely kept himself effaced in the dim background, Sir Gerard Lowther made a gallant eleventh-hour attempt to give a safe direction to the chaos by using the Sultan at the only moment of his reign when he could no longer be of the slightest use. For Abdul Hamid showed no sign of even wishing to react to his new opportunity.

A ruler with less timidity and with greater decision than the Sultan in a country which was always ready to respond to any firm authority might then have done something with thirty thousand men at his back who had acclaimed him as their Padishah while they waited for his lead. The Young Turks had made plenty of enemies during their brief term of office, and the opposition which they aroused had assumed a peculiarly dangerous religious form when it exploded in the Counter-Revolution, but the leadership and the courage needed to take advantage of this circumstance were precisely the qualities which Abdul Hamid could not give. The Sultan could intrigue and corrupt as skilfully as anyone, so long as he worked in the dark, but he was not enough of a man to dare to show himself at a critical moment before his own subjects. Already a quarter of a century before, when disturbances broke out in Alexandria, Abdul Hamid had asked the advice of the American Minister, who was then General Lew Wallace, the author of *Ben Hur.* Wallace possessed a fine soldierly appearance and drew himself up to his full height before the little man, bawling at him, "If I were your Majesty I would place myself at the head of my troops and charge the rascals," an advice he repeated with so much emphasis that the Sultan, frightened, ran out of the room. Age had not added to Abdul Hamid's courage. At the very moment when the Counter-Revolution brought him a seeming momentary triumph, he lived in the most abject fear, unwilling to do anything. This indecision, and the fact that there was no one in authority at Constantinople, made it impossible to foresee from hour to hour what would happen in this city of mutiny. We were living on a volcano which at any moment might erupt.

I had been studying Turkish for some time, having as my master a young scholar steeped in French decadent poetry, who made me painfully aware of the difficulty of learning an Oriental alphabet in which the writing of each letter varied according to its position in the word. My teacher had just declared to me that he was so saddened by his country's misfortunes that he could no longer continue to give me lessons. I asked him on which side his sympathies lay, and he replied that both were "des canailles." Later he became an important official.

Forty-eight hours before the fighting began I was dining with Marling, the British Counsellor. At table I ventured to express the opinion that the Sultan would shortly be deposed, whereupon he offered to bet me four to one that Abdul Hamid would still be on his throne the following year. As only an hour before I had been tipped off by a Turkish friend of what was going to happen, I could neither accept the bet nor explain the reason why. The Young Turks, when they escaped from the capital, gathered at Salonika where the military direction was assumed by General Mahmoud Shevket, a grizzled soldier who commanded the Macedonian army corps. He accomplished the march on Constantinople by the simple process of having his men take the train to San Stefano, which was at the gates of the city. In a few days he had collected a considerable military force in that suburb of the capital without encountering the slightest opposition. I went out to visit the camp and met with no difficulty from either side going or returning.

Meanwhile the rumours usual in the East announced alarming things and impending dangers. Nine times out of ten such rumours are unfounded, but recent events had been astonishing enough to make one sceptical of scepticism. We heard at one moment that the army at San Stefano would enter Constantinople peacefully and the next that there would be first a massacre of foreigners, deliberately provoked by the mutineers in order to force the powers to intervene. If the tension had been prolonged much longer this might have occurred. It was not altogether an idle fear and the well-informed M. Huguenin, the Swiss head of the Anatolian Railroad and President of the Orient Club, where I was living, felt apprehensive enough to ask me for an American flag to fly with that of the other great powers in order to show the international character of the Club. The rumour of massacre, whether true or not, was supposed to have precipitated the march of the Salonika army on the capital.

Precisely thirteen days after the Counter-Revolution broke out, I was awakened by a clatter of hoofs on the cobbles below and, looking out from my window, I saw a number of riderless cavalry mounts galloping by. The iron shutters of the shops in the Grande Rue were suddenly lowered, and from not far off came the report of rifles and the crackle of machine guns. The excitement of the imaginary battle lived through a fortnight before had left me extremely sceptical. I was determined not to be fooled again and was only convinced that this was a real fight after I saw some badly wounded men brought in on stretchers. I then joined the crowd which was watching the soldiers step from behind the cover of houses and fire down the street. A battle was in progress, and the population of Constantinople has never been noted for its temerity. Yet the dominant instinct was far more one of curiosity than of fear. Only the soldiers dispelled my belief in Oriental fatalism, for they seemed much more interested than the crowd in finding cover. A slight bend in the street, which until that day I had never noticed, although I must have passed it a thousand times, made the position of spectators fairly safe from the storm of bullets at the further end of the Grande Rue. I watched some baker boys make their regular deliveries within a few yards of the firing line, quite unconcerned by the shooting. More than anything this impressed me, for until that day I had never realised how the daily drudgery of life goes on unchanged close behind the actual fighting.

That morning at dawn the Salonika army had entered the capital after a surprise night march. The mutinous soldiers were quartered in their barracks or else stationed at small posts without having prepared any concerted plan of defence. The engagements, in progress at different points, were less a battle than a series of sharp isolated fights. Certain early attacks had been beaten off and at the Taxim barracks, not far from where I lived, it was necessary to bring up artillery against an enemy that was sheltered behind thick walls. In the afternoon, except for some occasional sniping, the battle was over and the Salonika army was everywhere victorious. I was delighted to see several Turkish officer friends who had previously been reported as murdered by their men. Instead of their usual smart soldierly appearance, they looked dirty and begrimed, but all of them seemed happy after the day's hard fighting. That evening I too felt as irrationally happy as any Young Turk.

The punishment then began. The Salonika troops showed themselves merciless towards the mutinous fusiliers. In the courtyard of the Taxim barracks the survivors of this famous regiment were that night exterminated to a man, and in other quarters of the city great numbers of theological students who had instigated the mutiny were massacred. I felt almost a personal satisfaction when on April 27th the National Assembly met to decide Abdul Hamid's fate. After the Sheikh-ul-Islam had read an impressive indictment of his crimes, Parliament unanimously voted to depose him, probably for the only misdeed of his reign of which he was not guilty. The Sultan was the first to go of the great hereditary autocrats in Europe and was to be the last real sovereign of his House, for his successor was only a shadowy figurehead.

From Yildiz shortly after, there took place an exodus of the thousands of servants and slaves who had formed part of the Sultan's immense household. One day I watched a long procession of closed landaus and saw women's faces, which were hardly veiled, peer out curiously from the carriage windows on a world which they had not gazed upon for years. These were the ladies of the imperial harem which was being dispersed, for its inmates were sent back to their former homes in Georgia and other parts of the Caucasus. More than anything else in the Revolution, this procession seemed to mark the end of an era.

The last days at Yildiz were tragic. The victors wisely made no attempt to force the Palace and merely cut off light and water. Like the Czar, eight years later, the Sultan suddenly found himself abandoned by his attendants, who only a few days before had been obsequious in their servile professions of devotion. The Commander of the Faithful, the once despotic ruler of a vast Empire, whose word was law and before whose whim millions had trembled, was now a poor miserable creature. Accompanied by four remaining wives, Abdul Hamid, without a protest, allowed himself to be quietly removed, at first to a villa at Salonika, where he passed out of history, never again to take part in the affairs of his country. He gave his gaolers no trouble, and in fact they were said to have become very attached to him. During the remaining years of his life, which were spent as a prisoner in a palace on the Bosporus, the Sultan impressed his captors by his submissive kindliness.

Soon afterwards the Palace of Yildiz was thrown open to the public. Abdul Hamid's pet pigeons were sold for a few piastres to any visitor, as well as many of his rugs, all of which had been made at the Imperial factory of Hereké and were in the worst possible taste. I went to visit the little kiosks that until a few days before had served to house the ladies of the harem. They were built on one model and stood behind a diminutive artificial brook. Each one had before it a small lawn with coloured glass balls as ornaments. These kiosks seemed more like summer cottages of some retired French grocer than dwellings for the favourites of the greatest of Oriental potentates. An atmosphere of tawdriness pervaded Yildiz, and even the formal gardening was a bad imitation of flower beds near the Casino at Monte Carlo. The taste of the Sultan, who had ordered the death of hundreds of thousands of his subjects and reduced his Empire to a reeking nest of spies and torturers, had been one of hopeless vulgarity.

Abdul Hamid's brother Mehmet, a harmless and kindly creature, now mounted the Imperial throne. For thirty years the new Sultan had lived as a prisoner in the palace of Dolma Bagtché, on the European side of the Bosporus, and whenever the ferry boat passed his residence Turks of any standing would gaze fixedly towards the Asiatic shore, lest spies should denounce them at Yildiz for having signalled to the heir. One act of this Sultan however deserves to be recorded. On the Friday after his accession, as he was going to mosque, a beggar shouted out to him, "Any country can find a Padishah but not every Padishah can find a country." Mehmet related that he had stopped his carriage to reward the mendicant for pronouncing these wise words. At the coronation the Commander of the Faithful girded the sword of Osman, received the diplomats, and left on us all the impression of being a benevolent half-wit.

The new military government at Constantinople instituted courts martial to try their enemies and sentenced the mutineers found guilty of the murder of officers to be hanged on the Galata Bridge at the very spot where certain of their victims had been assassinated. The executions were carried out at dawn and the bodies left on the gallows until they were cut down in the early afternoon. That day I had some pressing business at the Porte which obliged me to cross the bridge. As I wished to avoid this gruesome sight, I delayed my visit until the latest possible moment. Just as I was congratulating myself on having escaped the execution, my carriage had to pass through a vast crowd which unexpectedly congested the Stamboul end of the bridge. Suddenly I was struck by the spectacle of three pale men, seemingly of gigantic stature with long distended necks, whose heads towered above the throng around them. It took me a little time to realise that these were the hanged men who just at that moment were being cut down from the tripod gallows on which they had dangled since dawn, with their feet only a few inches above the ground.

The new Turkish government was headed by Mahmoud Shevket, the grizzly, bearded general in command of the victorious Salonika army. He was an honest soldier, who disliked politics, but he died suddenly soon afterwards. Other military men, hitherto unknown, many of whom had spent their lives in exile or else fighting in the Yemen and in Macedonia, came to Constantinople to bring with them a more virile impression of the Turk. One of the most sympathetic of these was Nazim Pasha. As a prisoner, he had broken stones on the road and now, by a turn of the wheel, he became Minister of War. He had some of the woodiness of the old Turks, which inspired so much more confidence than the younger men's flashy intelligence. He also had some of their chivalry. During the Balkan War it was Nazim who saved Enver from disgrace, after one of the latter's hair-brained schemes had failed, which did not prevent that hero of liberty, a few days later, from foully shooting down his benefactor.

It has been said that the only thing one could feel certain of in Turkey was that no forecast, however carefully made, would ever come true. After the Counter-Revolution, a new chapter of the Eastern Question opened. The Balkan states understood that if the Turks were able to reform themselves the factor of time, which until then had worked in their favour, would henceforth be against them. The great powers felt perplexed and uncertain. They professed friendship, but their policy was tied to too many special interests to convince the Turks of their sincerity. They wanted peace, but jealousies among themselves, particularly between Russia and Austria, made it difficult for them to cooperate or to agree about anything. Everyone knew that sooner or later the gangrened limbs of the old Turkish Empire would have to be amputated, but no one knew how this could be effected without a war. The need for a fresh policy was obvious, but as no nation could decide on one the great powers merely changed their ambassadors.

A new Russian envoy, Mr. Tcharykoff, arrived who took a considerable interest in higher mathematics and professed an unexpected benevolence for the Turks. He came, so he declared, to inaugurate a novel policy of friendly neighbourliness towards the old hereditary enemy. Nor was this altogether insincere, for Russia, weakened by revolution and the war with Japan, was in no condition to benefit by any adventure and preferred to see a moderately strong Turkey rather than to watch its division among other states. There was no need to change the German ambassador, for he had already changed himself. After the Revolution, when German influence sank to its lowest ebb, Baron Marschall remained hidden in the background. During the Counter-Revolution, the German envoy had wisely kept aloof from his former friend at Yildiz, but soon after the latter's deposition the Baron became as intimate with the Young Turk leaders as he had formerly been with the Sultan, and German influence once more reigned supreme.

My own stay at Constantinople was drawing to a close, for I left in September 1909. During the summer months at Therapia, after the recent excitements, there came a welcome lull. Our last party was a picnic given in a cove of the Black Sea, and I recall with gratitude a few unknown Turkish soldiers who saved it from ending in a diplomatic incident. Foreseeing that we would return late, I had asked the Porte's permission for our launch to enter the Bosporus after sunset, but they refused this in order not to create a precedent. I therefore had no excuse, except that the party was a success, no one wanted to go back, and as host I did not like to hurry my guests. After the happy day we had spent together, when at last everyone was reluctantly ready to return I saw the hour with terror, knowing that we could never hope to pass the forts at the mouth of the Bosporus before sunset and that orders were strict to fire on any craft which might attempt this. A Russian ambassador had even been obliged to spend the night outside the Straits for disregarding the regulations, and at best I saw the same fate awaiting us. We steamed back as fast as we could, anxiously watching the sun sink slowly below the horizon and unable to understand why for some mysterious reason the Turkish Crescent still waved over the fort long after the sun had disappeared from the skyline. With immense relief, we passed the battery at the entrance of the Bosporus without the warning shot being fired. Another second and the flag was hauled down. Every military regulation had been observed, no precedent had been created, but like Joshua that day we had made the official Turkish sun set long after its time.

# 4. *Peking Days*

The almost forgotten "Crane Incident" came as the first cloud over the Taft Administration and also contributed to my going to Peking. When Mr. Taft asked Mr. Knox as a favour to step down from a safe seat in the Senate in order to become his Secretary of State, the latter accepted the premier position in the Cabinet with the understanding that he was to run his own department. The President assured him of this but soon afterwards, in a mood of absent-minded geniality, meeting Mr. Charles R. Crane, offered the latter the Legation at Peking. Like Napoleon and several other eminent men of small stature, Mr. Knox possessed a far from unjustified sense of his own authority and resented the fact of not having been consulted regarding a diplomatic appointment to a capital in which he took a strong personal interest. Yet he said nothing and bided his time. In due course Mr. Crane went to Washington to ask for the customary official instructions before sailing for his post. At the State Department he found no one to whom he could talk, except the permanent Assistant Secretary, Mr. Adee, who was afflicted by deafness. His deafness was particularly bad that day for he failed to hear any of Mr. Crane's searching questions about China and merely recommended the new envoy to take up photography and perhaps also the use of a microscope to help pass his time as a diplomat in Peking.

Mr. Crane, feeling that he had been insufficiently enlightened about the Administration's Chinese policy, called on the President to ask his advice as to the nature of the speeches he was expected to make at the numerous banquets which were to be held in his honour before he sailed for his new post. Mr. Taft's stimulating suggestion to let them have it "red hot" may have been somewhat vague, but Mr. Crane regarded it as illuminating. After this interesting piece of Presidential advice the new Minister felt free to make a series of speeches which received an embarrassing attention from the American and a resentful one from the Japanese press. Mr. Crane was just on the point of sailing from San Francisco and his baggage was already aboard the ship when he was handed a telegram which recalled him instantly to Washington. His resignation as Minister to China promptly followed and brought about what was known as the "Crane Incident," which proved very hurtful to Mr. Taft. No one more than the President regretted being obliged to take a decision for which his own inadvertence had been responsible, but after Mr. Crane's "undiplomatic speeches" Mr. Knox insisted on the latter's recall. In vain, Taft entreated his masterful Secretary of State to reconsider his demand for Crane's recall. The latter was adamant, and the President knew that unless he yielded he would lose the leading officer of his Cabinet at the very beginning of his administration. Between two evils he sadly chose the lesser and dismissed his own appointee, but American opinion found that Mr. Crane had been somewhat shabbily treated.

The late Minister came from Chicago, and political expediency made it desirable to select his successor from the same city. A new envoy was discovered in a highly estimable lawyer, Mr. William C. Calhoun, who was a close friend of Mr. Taft's Secretary of War, Mr. Dickinson. Mr. Calhoun possessed no previous training in foreign affairs although he was appointed to succeed the experienced W. W. Rockhill, a diplomat of remarkable ability who had accomplished a great work in China but whom the new Administration was to scrap with that light-heartedness which so often characterises the waste of human resources in America. The first Secretary of the Legation, Henry P. Fletcher, had just been promoted Minister to Chile. Mr. Knox knew me from Constantinople, appointed me to succeed Fletcher at Peking, and asked me to write to him personally from my new post.

American Secretaries of State at this time found it desirable to display a particular interest in certain regions of the world. The policy of the United States towards Europe was then only platonically amorous; their range was therefore somewhat limited and used to alternate with the regularity of a pendulum between Latin America and the Far East. Secretary Root having discovered the novel merits of Latin America, it was inevitable for Secretary Knox to turn his attention to the Far East, and he did this with considerable zeal. If Knox's experience of diplomacy had equalled his ability and his fine courage, he would have made a great Secretary of State, but his previous career had been little occupied by foreign affairs, and this want of familiarity was responsible for his making certain initial mistakes which a diplomat of far less talent would have avoided. Knox suffered moreover from an ambition common to politicians who, when they take up world affairs, try to impress on these the stamp of their own vigorous personality during a brief tenure of office and are unwilling to allow time to do its work also. He made an unfortunate beginning in the Far East by being overstrenuous. With insufficient understanding of the difficulties inherent in the situation Knox, like the business lawyer he had been, tried to push forward too rapidly and left to his subordinates the routine affairs which merely bored him. Yet after the chastening effect of an early misadventure, the new Secretary's general policy towards China later became far wiser.

In 1909 the untapped resources of the Chinese Empire were believed to be on the eve of a vast economic development. The wealth of Manchuria was currently reported to hold out the prospect of another Eldorado, with soya beans taking the place of gold. A British construction company had then secured a railroad concession in that region but, unable to obtain any backing from its Foreign Office, it was attempting with the aid of American capital and the support of Washington to build a line intended to compete with the Manchurian Railways, which were in Russian and Japanese hands. The Chinese, seeing a possibility to recover Manchuria with American assistance, had therefore offered some attractive inducements to a group in Wall Street who enjoyed the State Department's support and were prepared to finance this road. And Knox, after having encouraged the bankers to accept these proposals, found himself unexpectedly and simultaneously opposed by Tokyo and St. Petersburg. After having been enemies, the two countries had united to resist this piece of diplomatic poaching on territory which they regarded as their preserve.

At the same time as this occurred, the Secretary of State was attacked at home by the Democrats for his "dollar diplomacy," as if he had invented something new and unholy, even though the Democratic President Buchanan's forgotten Mexican policy fifty years earlier had offered a far worse example of this.* Mr. Knox's real error had been to exaggerate the importance of the Manchurian provinces as an indis-

* Einstein has described a nineteenth-century version of "dollar diplomacy" in his essay on Lewis Cass in *American Secretaries of State and Their Diplomacy,* ed. Samuel Flagg Bemis (New York, Knopf, 1927–29), *6,* 338.

pensable element for the salvation of China. This belief led him to approach the Far Eastern problem from its most difficult angle. Even if he had been successful, an American railroad built in that region would have been of little benefit to the Middle Kingdom and far more dangerous to the peace of the United States than was ever understood at this time.

Washington had then more to gain from cooperation with the European powers, whose interest in the Far East, like our own, was economic, than by playing a lone hand. It was not long before Knox understood the advantage of encouraging American financiers to work together in China with those of Great Britain, France, and Germany. For in spite of all that his critics alleged, the Secretary of State cared little about the bankers, but thought that he had discovered in their resources the easiest means to extend American influence and to place the United States on the same footing as other nations in the Far East. This policy had been suggested to Knox by Willard Straight, the son of an American missionary in Korea, whose proselytism had taken a financial turn and whose attractive presentation of his ideas was responsible both for the highly questionable plan of selling Manchuria to Wall Street and the sounder one of bringing together the great banking houses in New York to form the so-called American group in China.

I cannot leave Knox without mentioning an example of his caustic humour which went along with much personal kindliness. Ten years later, when the Treaty of Versailles was being discussed and President Wilson lay ill, the Senator, whom I used frequently to see, read me a reservation which he proposed to offer as a substitute for the famous Article X. After he had finished I said jestingly, "If you put that in, Senator, you will break the heart of humanity." Knox drawled, "You mean swell its prostate gland."

On my way to Peking in March 1909, a trifling incident occurred at Moscow. At the Kremlin I met by accident an old friend, the Swedish art critic Dr. Martin, who accompanied us to the station where we were to leave at midnight by the Siberian express. My wife had with her a little Belgian griffin, and when I tried to purchase a ticket for it the official was emphatic that the dog would not be allowed on the train. Dr. Martin spoke Russian fluently, and on the strength of a personal friendship with Prince Khilkoff, who was then Minister of Railways, he asked to see the station master, to whom he explained that he felt certain the Prince would find no objection to an American diplomat travelling with this pet dog in transit through Russia. The official drew himself up and remarked stiffly that Prince Khilkoff himself would not be allowed to take a dog on a train unless authorised to do so by a special ukase of the Czar countersigned by all the ministers.

The Siberian express was leaving in another few minutes, and crestfallen I returned to my wife, who calmly declared that she proposed to take the griffin with her, ukase or no ukase. She hid the dog when she stepped on the train, but no concealment was possible during the long journey across the Russian Empire. I tried to tip the conductor, but he refused my bribe, which added to my offence. In any case Siberia was before us: I wondered how I would be able to communicate with my Embassy after the arrest, but an international incident was averted, for during the ten days that we passed on this train no official again raised the question of the dog.

At Peking the little griffin was the first that had been seen of his breed. Orientals love pets and many Chinese would try to fondle him, but for some instinctive reason the dog hated the yellow race and barked at every coolie. I never saw an animal more bewildered than the day a Chinese friend lunched at my table and the griffin's anxious expression showed all too plainly his astonishment. Racial prejudice was reciprocated in kind by Mongol horses, many of which will not allow Europeans to ride them—for the Chinese say that the odour of whites in their nostrils is like that of corpses.

The American Legation at Peking was built somewhat on the model of a Middle Western educational institution. A largish central building contained the Minister's residence. This was symmetrically flanked by smaller ones which served for the Chancery and the Secretaries. All were built in a so-called colonial style, which is monotonous and commonplace. The Legation architect desired to be economical as well as classical and had ornamented the front of the more important residences with imitation granite pillars made out of painted tin, the seams of which had split open. Except at the French Legation, no attempt had then been made at Peking to bridge over the gulf which separated occidental from Eastern styles. Chinese building is curiously inadequate in different respects, but it is so rich in accessory and ornament that its decorative features, suitably adapted, would have helped to relieve the drab monotony of the so-called Western buildings. Yet nearly all the new construction which was then being erected in China was as hideously incongruous as were the coolies who wore bowler hats. Chinese styles can be successfully grafted on those of the West, as was done from the time of Queen Anne to the Regency. But though there is far more talk about taste today than was ever heard in the eighteenth century, its feeling is much less diffused. Nor were foreign builders in the Far East helped by the young Chinese who, only keen to learn Western technical methods, were inclined to turn their backs on whatever reminded them of their own past. Native and foreign architects alike made little attempt to marry the East with the West and merely produced a hideous spate of modern edifices which have brought new ugliness into the Orient.

Next to the American was the Dutch Legation, which was built in the style of a manor house in Gelderland. There Jonkheer Beelaerts von Blokland, with smiling and genuine bonhomie, was beginning his distinguished career as the Minister of the Netherlands. Not far away a lofty Venetian campanile overtopped the Italian Mission and on the other side of the road a Flemish château housed the Belgian envoy, Baron Cartier de Marchienne, who was as popular in Peking as he later became as Ambassador in Washington and in London. All the legations had been built with funds obtained from the Boxer Indemnity, and they reminded one of those sample specimens of different national architectures which serve as restaurants and beer gardens at world's fairs. The diplomatic quarter was also a fortified city, and since the siege it was guarded by an international garrison of soldiers, sailors, and marines. We were protected on three sides by a low rampart beyond which stretched a wide glacis serving at one end for a polo field. On the fourth side rose the great Wall of the Tartar City between the Hatamen and Chienmen gates. These two magnificent examples of ancient military architecture formed part of our plan of defence in case of another siege, but protected us much less effectively from the odour of garlic and of rancid oil which rose every evening above the Chinese city.

My new chief, Mr. Calhoun, whom I had already met at the State Department, was a man of transparent honesty and much kindliness, with the simple direct speech of our Middle West. His passage from a law office in Chicago to the Legation in Peking was perhaps too abrupt for a man who had hitherto been without diplomatic experience, and he found it somewhat trying to adjust himself at once to his new surroundings. At first the unfamiliarity of life and conditions left him ill at ease and unhappy. Periodically his thoughts would run back to all he was missing at home, and the arrival of the Chicago newspapers stood between the Minister and a longing homesickness which made him not infrequently regret that he had accepted the post. Apart from the usual routine of missionaries, oil and tobacco interests, our principal work consisted in pushing railroad and currency loans in the self-approving belief that we were making history. We tried to help American interests and also China by helping the bankers. Calhoun, Straight, and myself were all very much in earnest, and we firmly believed in the immense importance of our mission. Willard Straight in particular was moving heaven and earth to overcome Chinese official inertia, behind which there was also Japanese and Russian obstruction to our Manchurian railway schemes. If there had been no Chinese Revolution impending, no Wilson Administration at Washington, and finally no European War, we might perhaps have built the first arch in that long bridge over which we expected China to travel with our guidance. The combination of all three difficulties was too great to overcome, and as soon as Bryan became Secretary of State he put an end to the so-called iniquities of "dollar diplomacy," much I suspect to the relief of the Wall Street bankers, who had been unjustly vilified without obtaining much profit for their pains. I saw little evidence of iniquity but considerable futility, which in the long run was probably much less disadvantageous to the United States than success would have been, as an American forward policy in Manchuria could have exposed us to many unnecessary risks.

China was engaged at this time in one of its periodical anti-opium crusades, which was marked by destroying the crops of small farmers, incidentally keeping the monopoly of secret sales in the hands of the higher officials. The scandal of this traffic rarely came out publicly, but when a newly appointed governor to Turkestan died on his way to that distant province an enormous quantity of opium was discovered in his baggage. The State Department was however doing its best to suppress an evil which was among the few international movements to which the United States could then safely adhere. Not long after my arrival it happened that one of the staff at the Legation complained of being in very great pain. A navy surgeon was called in. Doctors in the fleet who look after able-bodied seamen usually have only a limited range of diseases to treat, but this one had used his service in China to make a special study of opium. When the sick man asked for relief from his pain the surgeon promptly diagnosed his case as indicating a craving for drugs, urged the sufferer to confess, and offered to cure him if only he would admit his failing. The poor fellow stoutly denied the charge, but as he continued to ask for anything so long as his agony could be relieved, the surgeon was more than ever convinced of the truth of his diagnosis and insisted that the sufferer's denial was only the habitual lie of an addict. He expressed this opinion with considerable force to Mr. Calhoun, who felt perplexed. The Minister was the kindest of men and had every wish to be just, but he had also a definite duty to perform, and he feared that it might be necessary to report the case to Washington. All this time the sufferer remained in complete ignorance of the suspicions he had aroused and went on imploring relief, only to corroborate the surgeon's opinion. His fate was still in suspense when I called in a French physician who treated the sick man for a painful inflammatory rheumatism which he fortunately was able to cure.

I must mention another French doctor who died a hero. In the middle of winter, bubonic plague, brought by fox-bitten rats, broke out in northern Manchuria, near the Siberian border. The epidemic crept from town to town with a grim march which daily brought death nearer to us. At Harbin its ravages were terrifying. There was then a well-known French physician at Tientsin who was regarded as at the top of his profession in North China and had been through several plague campaigns. When he learned about the shortage of doctors at Harbin, he gallantly left at once for that city. Three days later we were horrified to hear of his death. He had caught the disease immediately on arrival and, knowing that there was no remedy, had locked himself up in his room and given orders that his wife should only be told after he was dead.

The plague kept drawing closer and at Tientsin, three hours from Peking, it raged with violence. The authorities threatened drastic punishment for all unreported cases, but the only effect of these penalties was to make the Chinese secrete their dead, and at the height of the epidemic the official death rate in that great port became negligible. At Peking the diplomats took the few precautions that were possible. The German Minister barricaded himself in his house, and outside the Japanese Legation the sentries on duty wore plague masks. Fortunately the force of the disease was spent by the time it reached the capital, and sunshine remedied what doctors had failed to cure. The bacillus which during the arctic winter of North China had wrought such deadly havoc in the wretched unaired hovels of the coolies suddenly lost its virulence with the approach of spring.

At the Legation as Second Secretary I found Leland Harrison to be the most helpful and loyal of companions. At first he would solemly ask me to instruct him regarding matters of which he knew far more than I, and he did this with a composed expression which under a grave official exterior hid an inward smile and a warm heart. I can think of no earthquake, cosmic or human, from which Leland would not emerge placid and efficient. As Commandant of the Legation guard we had also an excellent man in John Russell, who later ruled Haiti and the Marines and whose wife's Southern charm made her an immediate favourite with everyone in our small group. The isolation of our surroundings in Peking threw diplomats together in conditions of intimacy which would have been impossible in greater centres. With little of the pomp of the large capitals, our life in China could not have been pleasanter. Everything was absurdly easy and abundant, and there was a daily round of gaieties. All who knew Peking in 1910 and 1911 still look back pleasurably to the enduring friendships recalled by the memories of those years.

At the Japanese Legation the Minister, Mr. Ijuin, came from a generation which still believed in being courteous to the Chinese. His staff was more inclined to truculence, and the Japanese Counsellor, Mr. Honda, sighed for battleships while his wife sighed for Paris. The Third Secretary, Matsuoka, who since has tried to play the Bismarck,* was then still a pleasant youngster with a sprightly mind, who professed to regret the good old days when men in Japan with nothing to say kept silent instead of indulging in the foolish chatter that they had learned in Western countries called small talk. Only rarely is it possible to jest with a Japanese, or for that matter with a German—the

* The reference is to Matsuoka's grand design and his attempt to further it by negotiation of the Soviet-Japanese Non-Aggression Pact and the Tripartite Axis Alliance with Germany and Italy during the 1930s, in the manner of Bismarck's diplomacy in the 1870s and 1880s.

Western-educated Chinese understand our sense of humour better. Matsuoka was ready to jest with us, but he was a fierce nationalist at heart.

The real centre of our circle was Madame de Margerie, the wife of the French Minister whom we knew from Algesiras. Her husband was the type of able and conscientious official who for centuries has been the mainstay of every French administration. She was a sister of the poet Rostand, and she added to beauty and a rare charm those qualities of grace, tact, and sympathy which will always make me associate her memory with that of the great Frenchwomen of the eighteenth century. She possessed intelligence and cultivation, but she also had something more that is less definable and which gave her an unequalled attraction for those who were privileged with her friendship. Jeanne de Margerie was the beloved leader of our little circle in many excursions to the temples in the hills, where Buddhist priests clad in yellow silk would welcome us with their chattering laughter.

We would often go in parties to the Temple of Heaven without realising our unintentional sacrilege, which fortunately did not offend the Chinese, whose hypersensitiveness concerned far more mundane matters. I recall one picnic to the Princess' tomb, which is some miles out of Peking by a road that led across the dry bed of a stream. The Princess buried there was the sister of the first Manchu emperor. She had lived as a nun and she was still reverenced as a saint. The pagoda in which she lies stands in the middle of a fine grove of trees at the end of an avenue which is flanked, like the tombs of the Mings, with statues of camels and elephants. We had hardly arrived there before a storm of tropical violence forced us to take refuge under the shelter of the pagoda, where we watched flashes of lightning with Wagnerian effect illuminating the sacred grove. After the tempest had subsided, we started our return in a somewhat drenched condition, to discover that the stream which only a few hours before had been quite dry was now swollen into a rushing torrent. Madame de Margerie and my wife were together in the same carriage and their coachman tried to find the ford, but in the darkness his horses took a false step and tottered over the brink, below which ran a surging mill race. Luckily the ladies were near enough to be carried safely to the bank in the very nick of time, for a moment later the carriage, hood down, toppled into the roaring stream. Dora Brambilla, the sister of the Italian Chargé d'Affaires, saw it fall and fearing lest her friends were pinned underneath, gallantly dived into that dark flood, from which she emerged fortunately none the worse for her wetting.

Peking was then a most agreeable capital for diplomats. In spite of the outrageous "squeezes" of our "boys," who levied toll on every object their masters bought and made us resort to furtive but vain devices to circumvent their piracy, life was absurdly cheap, and poor men experienced the pleasant sensation of living magnificently for nothing. The servants in the Legation quarter were in the habit of assessing every household at a secret figure. Any economies attempted below the line which they established in hidden conclave were always frustrated, but they gave us excellent value for our money.

Cooking for foreigners is of two schools in China. At hotels and on trains one is served with a flavourless imitation of an already flavourless English cooking which finds its triumph in an Irish stew and boils its vegetables in tepid water. But many years ago a French Minister arrived in Peking bringing with him his own chef, who was to educate a few Chinese in the august traditions of the Gallic art. His talented disciples were rare and much sought after by diplomats who were ready to condone their banditry. We had discovered such a phoenix who, worthy of his teacher, was always addressed as the "Great Master," though even his greatness had to yield in his own home to his mother's unquestioned authority. Every morning, attired in spotless black silk, he came for orders. My wife, who wished to prove her familiarity with the local market, once mentioned to him the price of eggs, a hundred of which cost a quarter of a dollar. He agreed, but at the end of the month two thousand eggs were charged in his book. My wife remonstrated that our diet was not exclusively one of eggs. "Perhaps too many," he readily admitted. The following month he only charged for fifteen hundred. Comparing notes we found that a French friend who had accused his cook of being the greatest robber in Peking was calmly assured that the greatest thief of all was the Russian Minister's chef and that he came only second. But when the Italian envoy tried to cut down his cook's brigandage, the latter waited for revenge till the next official dinner. Every dish came up perfect until the dessert was reached. There was none. The cook, summoned to explain, merely said, "No money, no sweet." Deliberately he had wanted his master to lose face before his guests.

The question of "face" is paramount with the Chinese, and the source of many of our troubles came from the inability of Westerners to understand its finer distinctions. Nominally "face" signifies that ideal portrait which every Celestial delights to draw of himself and which goes with an instinctive fondness for acting a part. There was a wide gulf between the lofty standard proclaimed and actual practice, but it was unwise for foreigners to assume that there could possibly be any lapse from perfection on the part of Orientals. Chinese contempt for Western barbarous manners was largely based on our ignorance of the significance of "face" in forming part of the complicated deportment of an ancient etiquette which made that of the Habsburgs seem crude. In such matters, self-denial provides the greatest of all tests, and the rigid code of "face" led at times even to this. Certain Manchu princes who had been invited to dine at the Italian Legation smilingly pointed out to their host a number of pieces of furniture which had formerly embellished their palaces but had been looted after the siege. The Minister, who was unaware of this, felt so embarrassed that he wrote at once to Rome and obtained permission from his government to restore the articles to their rightful owners. The princes however refused to receive them back as this would have meant a loss of face. The observance of similar practices descended into every class. To accuse a servant of "squeezing" meant that he would be obliged to leave his master's employ in order not to lose face. As his successor was unlikely to be more honest and probably less well trained, it was usually better to avoid such extreme language and accomplish the same purpose by informing a domestic that as trades people were great cheats he should be more careful. For Chinese servants were not unlike the card sharper who, caught cheating, had punched his accuser's face and remarked that even if the charge was true he allowed no one to tell him so.

In other respects the Legation servants were always honest. It was a common practise for the "boys" in diplomatic families to borrow from each other what their masters needed without ever asking the owner's consent. At dinners in friends' houses I would often recognise my silver, and later discover at my own table some object which belonged to a neighbour. Nor did these borrowed articles ever go astray. Our coolies received the standard wages of eight Mexican dollars a month on which they fed and lodged themselves, but this was so munificent that they would frequently sublet their jobs. Yet servants took a real pride in their house. Certain of them possessed a discriminating taste in art which made even the humblest coolie wish to have a painted scroll or a porcelain vase holding a flower to adorn his cubicle.

The Chinese call the peony the King of Flowers and the triumph of Celestial gardening is to have it blossom for their New Year, which comes in February. The intense cold of the Peking winter makes this no easy performance, for the windows of their greenhouses are only covered with oil paper and much of their forcing is carried out in dark cellars. Far Eastern gardeners cultivate fruit trees for their blossom and train plums and cherries to grow on a flat plane which they induce to flower in mid-winter. Next to the peony in general esteem is the chrysanthemum, but to a Chinese eye the gigantic specimens that are prized in the West are monstrous. They discover an equal beauty in flower, leaf, and stem, and desire that a definite relation should be kept among the three. The Oriental theory of gardening aims moreover to create nature in miniature while preserving its proportions. Celestial taste finds a further delight in artificial rocks which they pile up in gardens in order to simulate diminutive crags and miniature precipices. Yet where a wider expanse permits, trees will be planted with a bold irregularity, as one sees in the groves of the Forbidden City or on the temple terraces in the Western hills. Chinese gardening, like their taste, felt more at home in eighteenth-century Europe than it does in the Western world of today. It is hard to say why this is true except that Oriental serenity is nearer to the contemplative ideal of the Vicar of Wakefield than it is to the modern outlook. The Chinese garden was in fact the immediate ancestor of the English garden and the forerunner of the return to nature which succeeded to the earlier formalism that had been imported from Flanders and Italy. At Dropmore, near Windsor, which Lord Grenville planned at the end of the eighteenth century, there can still be seen the remains of a Chinese garden and an aviary built of porcelain tiles with flowers grown in lustred pots and artificial rocks that have been piled up in Celestial taste.

One of the great pleasures of life in Peking was the peddlers who called every day with their wares done up in blue cotton from which would issue a spate of silks and sables, jades and rubbish. In the fashion of the East, everything would first be stretched on the floor, and when an object of particular interest was produced the peddler would whisper as a special inducement that it had been stolen from the Palace. Anyone interested in Oriental art found in the curio shops of the Luli Chang an unfailing delight. The windows in that street contained little of merit, but there was always a small court at the back of every shop after which came a second pavilion full of better wares. Whatever was really good was left for a room behind the second court, where foreigners were somewhat grudgingly admitted, for dealers tried to sell them only trash, disliking the idea of seeing their better objects leave the country.

I was treated with a little more indulgence because I had the good fortune to make friends with Mr. King, a Chinese gentleman of taste, with whom I often visited the curio shops. By profession my friend was a judge of the newly established Supreme Court, the duties of which did not seem to be particularly arduous. I knew him principally as a judge of porcelain, and I remain grateful to him for having trained my eye to a better understanding of the Chinese appreciation of colour, which is far more delicate than our own. Once he urged me to purchase a small cup, which owing to a slight flaw was unsuitable for his collection but would be useful, he insisted, in order to educate me to a proper understanding of white. He compared its hue to the complexion of a girl of twelve and then contrasted this with the shade of a neighbouring vase which was like that of a woman of forty; and after he had pointed out these differences, the value of white possessed a new significance to me.

When I first went shopping with my friend, having no cash with me I offered to pay a curio dealer with a cheque. The latter brought me a brush, for he did not possess a pen, and half jokingly I painted my signature and then repeated this performance at other shops. Next day my painted cheques were all refused by my bank, where the manager thought I had gone native, but instead of coming to me the dealers went in a body to dun Mr. King. Like most Chinese my magistrate friend was an inveterate collector. It was at that time illegal to possess an Emperor's portrait, and only with the greatest secrecy did he show me in his house a likeness of the Emperor Kien Lung on horseback, painted on a scroll in European style by Castiglione, the Italian eighteenth-century Jesuit, although the landscape of this picture was by a native brush.

By far the greatest collector at Peking was the former Viceroy, Tuan

Fang. The Chinese feel tolerant towards most kinds of official delinquency, but they accused Tuan of having abused his viceregal position in order to obtain some unique archaic bronzes that were his special pride. Except for these vessels, which were displayed conspicuously on a table in his great gallery, the rest of his vast collection of porcelains was kept Chinese fashion in innumerable wooden boxes piled up like barricades which reached to the ceiling. He received me between two rows of cases, and after the inevitable bad champagne had been served, our host, clad in very soiled silk robes and hardly distinguishable from the menials surrounding him, displayed his treasures, opening box after box, but so rapidly that there was little leisure for real enjoyment. Perhaps he thought that as barbarians we were more curious than appreciative, though the Chinese are usually at their best as hosts. Poor Tuan Fang did not live long to enjoy his collection. During the Revolution, which broke out the following year, his head was cut off and I heard that it was phototographed on a table in the midst of his prized treasures. Several of his unique sacrificial bronzes have since found a permanent home in the Metropolitan Museum in New York.

Celestial taste in porcelain differs greatly from our own. Orientals prize above all the delicate Yung Ching and take delight in a more finicky decoration than we relish. But in painting the Chinese incline to a bolder style. When I called on Earl Li, son of the great Li Hung Chang, who had inherited some of his father's collections, the latter unrolled for me a number of airy landscapes with backgrounds of green blue mountains like the Dolomite rocks in the paintings of Leonardo, and which dated from the Sung dynasty. "We Chinese call these pictures American taste," my host remarked after I had expressed my enthusiasm. I was not displeased to mention the fortunate coincidence of American taste being the same as that of the Chinese during one of their greatest ages.

The merits of Eastern painting were just beginning to be understood in the West, and Peking dealers related with a smile the story of a German lady who, after having disdained the pictures offered her because they were not ancient enough, afterwards bought the same ones at a higher price when the signatures of the painters had been replaced by others of an earlier date. The Chinese were delighted with their joke, but the lady had the last laugh for she sold her treasures with good profit to a famous museum.

Pictures were not yet a luxury, and until foreign collectors put up their price no one paid more than a few dollars for excellent scrolls. I saw two well-known American collectors in Peking blandly go from shop to shop exhibiting a letter which a Japanese dealer in New York had written for them in Chinese, to say that they were searching for pictures of the Sung and T'ang dynasties, which needless to say were at once forthcoming. I was glad to find at Peking my friend Charles L. Freer, who had got over his interest in the Nabbatean forgeries which brought him to Constantinople. He was then in quest of a picture by Li Lung Mien, who had been Prime Minister in the Sung dynasty but had left the Emperor's service in order to become a painter. Authentic specimens of a talent which flourished nearly a thousand years ago are rarer than Giorgiones, and although many works have been claimed for his brush few undisputed examples of his art exist except among the treasures of the Emperor of Japan. Freer however felt convinced that he was on the track of one in Peking. The picture was not for sale nor was he allowed even to see it; but the knowledge of its existence excited his pursuit, and when he asked for a suggestion of how it could be obtained the intermediary advised him to return in twelve months, as the family might then be in need of money.

After the year had elapsed Freer arrived once more in Peking and related to me with immense pride that he had been able to purchase not one, but seven of this artist's masterpieces, which most unexpectedly had come to light in the interval! Nonetheless, American collections owe Freer a debt of real gratitude. His taste was not always discriminating and often he allowed his enthusiasm to run away with a judgment which he believed to be infallible, but he explored fields of art which at that time were still novel, and he accumulated the immense number of objects, many of great value, that now enrich the museum in Washington which bears his name. I tried in vain to persuade him to buy an ancient Chinese pavilion with exquisite stone work in order to house his works of art in an appropriate setting but, like many collectors, Freer was more interested in accumulating objects than in the manner in which they were to be displayed.

My first impression of the beauty of Chinese buildings came at a memorial service for King Edward, held in an open pavilion at the British Legation, which was formerly the palace of a Chinese prince. The diplomats present were covered with the usual gold braid and the soldiers and the sailors of every nation wore their ceremonial uniforms, but the Manchu princes and dignitaries in their simple fur-lined robes looked as a body far more distinguished. I found their faces refined and their raiment as elegant as it was sober. How luxurious it could be I understood when a Chinese marquis showed me four of his dressing gowns lined entirely with sable. Soon after this ceremony, we went on the customary round of visits paid by diplomats to members of the Imperial family. Our first call was on Prince and Princess Púlun. The Prince, many Chinese thought, should have been the rightful Emperor, but he had been passed over in the succession by the Dowager Empress. We were received with great politeness in a so-called Louis Sixteenth boudoir, filled with gimcrack European furniture, for the artistic refinement of the Chinese stops short of any appreciation of Western taste. Among the less pleasant forms of Oriental hospitality is the practise of offering foreigners bad champagne at the most unseasonable hours, presumably under the impression that this is our customary beverage. After the glasses had been emptied with many appropriate smiles, Princess Púlun opened the conversation by touching my wife's sleeve and muttering *Howw!* "Her Highness says it is beautiful," the interpreter translated. My wife, to be no less polite, touched the Princess' skirt, exclaimed *Howw!* and admired the blooms of fresh double jasmine arranged as bangles in her hair. After more touchings of apparel and more exchanges of *Howw,* the audience was over. The Prince had remained silent, and in fact the only English word I ever heard him utter was "dry" over a glass of champagne. Unlike other members of the dynasty, he seemed for some odd reason to be genuinely fond of foreign society and spent much of his time at the Wagons Lits Hotel playing billiards with a former warrant officer in the German navy. Also, the Princess often visited the wife of a Danish shopkeeper, much to the horror of certain diplomats who deplored the inability displayed by members of the Imperial family to appreciate Western class distinctions.

This conversation was typical of many others exchanged with Manchu princes. To talk through an interpreter rarely elicits more than the expression of some awkwardly worded commonplaces, but there were not many points of sympathy between the reigning family and ourselves, and something beside linguistic difficulties stood in the way of any closer intercourse. We could never expect to penetrate those hidden recesses in the Oriental mind where East and West cannot be bridged. If these differences are instinctive or derived by their training I cannot say. I suspect the latter, for when talking to foreign-educated Chinese one had a very different impression, and time and again I was struck by the seeming nearness of their mental processes to our own, particularly in the conversation of those who had studied in America.

Orientals sought our society for several different reasons. A Mongol princess who owned many of the gambling houses in Peking enjoyed frequenting the legations and took more pleasure in attending our dances than did the diplomats in seeing her arrive, for the presence of Chinese royalty dampened any party. Yet when she was not asked she would send word to enquire if her invitation had not miscarried. Everyone was aware that the enjoyment she felt on these occasions was of a scandalous kind, for Western dancing seemed peculiarly immoral to Chinese eyes. Once at a ball at the French Legation I watched a eunuch kneel before his mistress, the Princess Yulang, and implore her to flee with him from that scene of iniquity. The Princess refused to go, but later during a waltz she told my wife that she could not understand "how mothers allowed their daughters to take part in such love dances."

In all capitals, official banquets are among the minor tortures of diplomatic life. Usually they mean a stuffy atmosphere, boring neighbours, messy food, and tedious toasts. In China, where three quarters of the population can hardly feel sure of having a meal every day, state banquets were also a severe punishment because of their exaggerated length. The obligation of having to sit between two high dignitaries who spoke no foreign language, belched and clucked their food through fifty courses, since any host who offered fewer was considered parsimonious, became no more pleasurable because of the costly rarity of the dishes served. Duck's tongue and deer's tendons convey ecstatic delights to Celestial appetites which were wasted on our grosser palates. The tediousness of sitting through successions of courses was only alleviated by guests being allowed to leave the table for an indefinite time without causing any unfavourable comment. During the Peking season, a fashionable young man might even attend two or three banquets on the same evening. The briefer repasts which diplomats offered were regarded by the Chinese as proof of Western niggardliness in contrast to their own greater generosity.

Invitations for these banquets were always gracefully worded. When a host asked me to dinner he would write that "We have cleansed the wine cups and await your instructful conversation." Politeness demanded that a guest should arrive at a party holding out his invitation, which he would vainly attempt to return to his host on the ground that he was unworthy to receive so great an honour; a similar etiquette obliged a Chinese gentleman who passed a friend in the street to hide his face behind his fan when he had no time to stop and talk to him. A certain ostentation was displayed over many trifling details which assumed much grave importance in Celestial eyes. When a high official offered me a cup of tea, he remarked that the water with which it was made came from a fountain in Szechuan over a thousand miles away. Other forms of social intercourse I found more trying. Certain Manchu princes had a regrettable fondness for fixing seven in the morning as an appropriate hour to receive an official visit, and the vile champagne, mostly manufactured in Antwerp and known among diplomats as the Taotai brand, which was invariably served at these visits, does not count among the pleasanter recollections I retain of Peking.

Chinese life was already beginning the rapid transition which was affecting its ancient structure. I had instances of this during the visit of the Secretary of War, Mr. Dickinson, which provided a simultaneous illustration of the old Palace arrogance and the new desire for Western innovations. Placed in charge of the Legation end of the arrangements, I suggested to the Chinese officials with whom I conferred that it would be appropriate for the Regent* to invite an important American Cabinet Minister to dinner. This proposal was curtly dismissed as if I had demanded something preposterous, but as a concession it was intimated that perhaps Prince Tsai Tao, who was the Regent's brother, might do this. To my remark that the Emperor of Japan had personally entertained Secretary Dickinson during his recent visit to Tokyo there came a reply that was still more contemptuous. "In Japan anyone can see the Emperor." I retorted that the Japanese did not seem to be worse off because of their sovereign's accessibility to dis-

* Prince Ch'un.

tinguished strangers. The answer again was illuminating. "The best friend of China in the West was James Gordon Bennett. He had visited Tokyo and the Japanese had showered attentions on him till they made him feel a great man, but when he went to China no one took the slightest notice of his presence, and he left with the conviction that China must be a great country for there he was a nobody. Since then he had always shown himself to be the greatest friend of the Celestial Empire."

Prompted probably by the Wai Wu Pu, or Foreign Office, the Palace extended a splendid welcome to the Secretary of War, who arrived accompanied by General Edwards and a party of friends. A programme of entertainment was mapped out for every hour of their day, and Prince Tsai Tao, the most sympathetic of the Manchus, showed himself to be an excellent host. He escorted the Secretary to the Great Wall, and I recall the Prince's remark as we stood on the top, that a work of this character could never have been carried out in a constitutional country. Valuable gifts from the Palace to Mrs. Dickinson and Mrs. Edwards caused some unfortunate heartburnings, but the crowning ceremony of the visit was the *Regent's* formal reception. Imperial sedan chairs were sent to the Legation to convey the Secretary, the Minister, and the Legation staff through the ceremonial courts of the Palace to the Audience Pavilion. There, in solemn state, the Regent, surrounded by all the great dignitaries of the Court, received us. The Secretary of War read a speech oozing over with conventional expressions of good will, but Mr. Dickinson's purposely colourless remarks greatly disappointed the Chinese who, for some unknown reason, had persuaded themselves that this tourist visit to Peking meant a new departure in American policy, which would henceforth support them against the Japanese. After his speech, the echoes of their disillusion were loud enough to leave me in some doubt if the Chinese did not regret the honours that they had lavished on their visitor.

The Palace maintained much of its old arrogance, but the Western-educated officials of the Wai Wu Pu had expressed a wish for Chinese ladies to be invited to the Legation reception held in honour of the Secretary of War. This innocent request meant a revolution in the social history of China, for never before had any such innovation been heard of at Peking. I asked for a list of the ladies whom they desired to have invited and noted that this was headed by the Princess of Ch'ing.

The Prince was, after the Regent, then the greatest dignitary of the Empire, but I was under the impression that he was a widower. It is not good form to enquire too closely into Oriental family relations, and not unnaturally I supposed that the Foreign Office knew more about these particulars than I did. At the Legation reception the first ladies announced were the Princesses of Ch'ing. Two indifferent-looking Manchu women were ushered in and advanced smilingly side by side, talking only Chinese and followed by a number of female attendants. Half at a loss to know which one to pick and half as a joke, I offered an arm to each, which they gravely accepted, but something else than my buffoonery caused social Peking to flutter next day. The Prince was a widower, and the so-called Princesses were what the Chinese styled his number two and three wives, who were his concubines and were never supposed to be seen in public. The lady who ought to have been asked was the wife of his eldest son, and she was furious at her omission. Yet the Foreign Office officials who had prepared the list of guests were solely responsible for this blunder.

The Walls of the Forbidden City in which the Boy Emperor* lived were on the other side of the street, barely a stone's throw from the Legation. The Imperial residence might well have been in Mars for all we knew of what went on inside, beyond the fact that the Dowager Empress Lung Yü ruled there from a palace which was still the center of the most populous empire in the world. In the ancestral hierarchy of the Chinese, she owed her position to the late Dowager Empress Tzu Hsi, but she did not possess her aunt's dominating personality. Peking gossip related that she imitated her mainly by leaning on a handsome, so-called eunuch, who had previously been married and had fathered two children. A Manchu censor even showed himself courageous enough to memorialize the throne regarding this eunuch's peculations, which were said to have run into millions of taels. The censor produced case after case to prove his charge. He showed that the repairs of the Palace drains, for which Chang the Eunuch had drawn eighty thousand taels from the Board of Finance, called for a real outlay of seven thousand, but the Empress suppressed the memorial and administered a sharp rebuke to the censor.

Some five thousand eunuchs resided within the Forbidden City, but

* P'u-i (Hsuan Y'ung).

according to the confidences of one Manchu princess many of these were not true ones. Whatever their condition may have been, the influence which they exercised behind the scenes was enormous. Orientals live in a much closer intimacy with their attendants than do Westerners, and the intriguing eunuchs penetrated into every secret and made themselves the intermediaries for every audience and had a finger in the bestowal of every office. They shaped Court life to suit their own pilfering instincts. It is said that the eunuchs brought about the fall of the Mings, and they contributed not a little to bring down the reigning Ch'ing dynasty.

The Dowager Empress, far less occupied by affairs of state than was her aunt, the "Old Buddha," left these to the well-intentioned but weak Regent, Prince Ch'un. While Japanese militarism and Western finance were knocking at the door, the Regent was ineffectually attempting to reform the ancient pattern of a patriarchal state in which the priests of the Temple of Agriculture kept the plough, the farmer's hat, and the rustic garments that the Emperor used when twice a year he went there to worship and sow seed for the next harvest. These venerable ceremonies were symbols of religious practises admirably suited to a static civilization which was based on the soil. A worship that exalted the permanence of the family and revered the Emperor as the Son of Heaven formed part of a philosophy of statecraft out of touch with the modern world but that would have been easily understood by another imperial race. For the Roman idea of family and of religion was not dissimilar to the Chinese. The Divine Augustus would have sympathised with the Regent if he could have read as I did in the Official Gazette an Imperial decree by which Prince Ch'un had cancelled the divinity of the God of War and reduced that fallen deity to the humbleness of an ordinary mortal.

The Regent earnestly wished to preserve ancient practices which already had lost much of their meaning. But he also understood that reforms were unavoidable, nor was he opposed to these, for he had approved a programme which aimed at their gradual introduction. On paper, his three-year plan was reasonable and moderate, but it needed an iron hand to carry out its execution and the Regent, who was far from possessing this, was destined to fall between two stools. Instead of maintaining patriarchal virtues he found himself enmeshed in patriarchal abuses and unable to cut loose from the vested interests of an ancient inherited corruption. At the Palace no one wanted the reforms which he tried to launch, and outside the Palace as soon as the Revolution broke out no one of the younger generation wanted the Regent or any more Manchu rule. The confusion into which China was fast falling was in this way precipitated by the absence of a pyramid of authority to direct the difficult transition between old and new.

When a state is built on the primitive economic structure of Old China with hardly any intermediate class between the gentry and the coolies and peasants, the process of disintegration as soon as it begins is rapid and halts only when new forces arise after the irreducible unit of life has again been reached. The collapse of Imperial authority which took place developed suddenly in the Celestial Empire because, unlike Japan where the reigning family was native, the Manchus were regarded as foreigners, however much they had identified themselves during the past three centuries with China. While they were blamed as aliens, their real sin was weakness, for even their iron-capped princes* had lost the virility once associated with that proud title.

When the last Ming emperor was about to fall, a courtier tried to commiserate with his master's sad fate. The Son of Heaven replied that his personal affairs caused him little concern, but all his sadness came from the thought that his reign had not been illuminated by a single actor of talent. Then next day, after removing the Imperial cap and with his hair carefully dishevelled, he wrote on the lapel of his robe that as one feeble, of small virtue, and ashamed to face his ancestors, he died. He strangled himself in a pavilion of the Forbidden City, along with a faithful eunuch who did the same. Something of this spirit of flippancy coupled with Imperial pride lingered in the Manchu Court. The dynasty still clung obstinately to the shreds of past glory at a time when there was no one at the Palace who had either the authority, the will, or the ability to regenerate an empire which, undermined by the ferment of Western ideas, was visibly falling apart. The old governing class, with their power and prestige daily receding, hated to watch the advancing tide which they could not stem and which they foresaw was shortly to submerge them. Only the older offi-

* The phrase comes from the designation in 1778, by the Emperor Ch'ien-lung, of eight great families of the Manchu ruling house as Princes of the Iron Helmet. From this time all the descendants of these princes had pre-eminent rank at the court in Peking.

cials still delighted to parade a swank of empty arrogance which at times came out unexpectedly. At a Legation musicale I heard one dignitary, asked by a diplomat if the Chinese were familiar with the piano, reply that its use had been abandoned in the Middle Kingdom two thousand years ago! The former scholarly training had largely disappeared, and old-fashioned Chinese, who had nothing in common with those educated abroad, deplored the new Western education and pointed out that it had not yet produced a single statesman. In a land in which time and life have different meaning than in the West, a paradox of the situation lay in the high individual intelligence of the Chinese, which is almost greater than that of any other race, along with much collective foolishness. I can offer no explanation for this baffling paradox. Fresh from Constantinople, after having witnessed the Sultan's régime collapse without a struggle, it was easy to foretell that something similar was bound to happen before long in China. The prophecy which I wrote Secretary Knox—that a revolution would occur within the next two years—turned out to be correct.*

In 1910 the ferment of Westernization was fast progressing, but it had not yet touched the masses and at Peking we were more aware of its effects than of what was happening at the root. A wave of foreign-educated Chinese was already fast filtering into different branches of the administration. Not a few of these men had ability, some had charm, nearly all were intelligent, and all felt vast confidence in themselves with a persuasive eloquence and the most unlimited pretensions. I remarked to a youthful general of twenty-eight on the speed of his military advancement, and he reminded me that Napoleon had attained the same rank as he at twenty-six! A new generation of Chinese, largely from Canton, was claiming the right to speak in the name of four hundred million people when only a negligible fraction of this multitude was remotely aware of the existence of their would-be spokesmen. The professions made by these patriots would have sounded more convincing if they had been less intent to affirm their own position, and the fierce nationalism which they proclaimed was in itself an article of foreign inspiration useful for their self-advancement. The old Chinese nationalism, not unlike that of the ancient Greeks, prized its culture so highly that its votaries were almost indifferent to

* See Einstein's Letter to Secretary of State Knox, Oct. 17, 1910, Einstein Mss, University of Wyoming Library.

the political rule under which they lived. But the students who returned in increasing numbers from Western countries, usually feeling that they had acquired something vastly superior to their ancient civilization of which they knew but little, were far keener about their rights, for they anticipated the advantages to be obtained from asserting these. Probably the same remarks have been made in every revolution. Irritating as were these young nationalists, their actions were understandable, and it was hard to blame them for resenting the former arrogant assumptions of Western superiority. The British merchant class in particular, who had regarded China as a kind of colony, was far too prone to treat "natives" with undisguised contempt; in Shanghai at this time, although any drunken white loafer could walk in the public gardens, the entrance was strictly forbidden to Chinese gentlemen.

Orientals are more sensitive to good manners than are Westerners, and foreign claims to superiority were not always convincingly asserted. Nor were some missionaries free from blame, for they made it all too plain that equality before God in their eyes did not imply equality on earth. We passed the summer months at Pei-ta-Ho, where certain of these missionaries almost brought on a revolution by their high-handed attempt to levy a quite illegal tax on the donkey boys.

Yet Chinese reactions to white pretensions sometimes took a deliberately ludicrous form. Lanterns occupy an important place at Oriental festivals, and it was customary when one gave a dinner party to place outside the house large ceremonial lanterns on which would be inscribed the host's name and dignities. But the wife of a British secretary insisted on having her name and title painted on these. In vain the maker protested against this innovation, but in the end even a stubborn Chinaman had to yield to a stubborn Englishwoman. At her next dinner a guest who understood the Chinese characters was horrified to read the description of his hostess painted on these lanterns that stood before the door, for they described her as being the concubine of British Minister number two.

# 5. *Costa Rican Interlude*

Before setting out for my first legation in Costa Rica, I passed a few weeks in Washington. Justice and Mrs. Holmes, who were old friends,* maintained a pleasing custom of always having two seats laid at their dinner table ready for unexpected guests, so that one never felt importunate when calling at a late hour. Often I would find Mrs. Holmes knitting in her armchair, with her husband playing at patience beside her.

Before I left Washington, the Costa Rican Minister gave me a luncheon to which he had invited the envoys of the five neighbouring republics. The union of these republics was then a fond hope of the State Department, but this luncheon was the only example of Central American solidarity I saw, for the idea was unpopular, particularly in Costa Rica, whose white inhabitants regarded themselves with some cause as superior to the Indian majority of the population in the neighbouring countries. The only other guest invited to this repast, as being a friend of mine, was M. Jusserand. That day he was at his best, or rather at his worst, for the scholarly French Ambassador showed himself impishly humorous at the lunch table. M. Jusserand's puckishness was exercised at the expense of a small, swarthy gentleman who looked singularly ill at ease in a tight-fitting frock coat. Grandiloquent names when borne by certain people convey whimsical suggestions, and the circumstance of this diminutive Central American diplomat being called Belisarius proved too much for the French Ambassador's gravity. At the very moment when I was obliged to respond to a series of flamboyant toasts in a similar style, M. Jusserand whispered in my ear the libretto he was then improvising for an imaginary Offenbach operetta in which Belisarius figured as the agitated hero. All this time I had

* Lewis Einstein's correspondence with Oliver Wendell Holmes has been published: *The Holmes-Einstein Letters: Correspondence of Mr. Justice Holmes and Lewis Einstein, 1903–1935,* ed. James Bishop Peabody (New York, St. Martin's Press, 1964).

to keep a serious face to conceal inward laughter, but fortunately the other guests' knowledge of French was as small as the countries they represented.

Ten days later, with a glassy sea underneath and the cloudless sky of the tropics above, we arrived at dawn at Puerto Limon, the Caribbean port of Costa Rica. The first person to board the ship was the governor of the province, an amiable official who came to greet me with a grandiloquent address. He affirmed that Central America, as represented in his person, extended a welcome to North America, as represented in mine, and ended with the information that the President had sent his special train, which was waiting. I listened admiringly to a flow of eloquence measured in terms of continents. The hour was seven in the morning, and it was a little early to soar to the height of the governor's empyrean. That was my only excuse. I forgot Secretary Root's sage advice to diplomats who were leaving for Latin American posts, urging them to be sparing with comparatives and lavish with superlatives. The prospect of having to face a hungry railway journey made me lamentably prosaic. To my wife's horror, the only thing I found to say to the oratorical governor was that, before starting for the capital, I proposed to eat my breakfast.

The gentlemanly conductor of the special train sent for me was the President's nephew, but this circumstance did not affect the speed of the locomotive, which took six hours to perform a journey of a hundred miles. Trains are always slow in small countries, for this is a patriotic device to create the illusion that the territory is larger. The gorgeous scenery made me grateful for our snail's pace. We crawled through cuttings in the tropical forest of the lowland and then climbed over high trestles that spanned deep ravines in the Cordilleras, till we reached the beautiful valley which contains the coffee plantations and the inhabited portion of the Republic. At many of the stations I noticed pots of orchids hung by chains. From the car window I saw giant poinsettia trees in flower. The luxuriant vegetation of the country we traversed seemed like a magnificent horticultural exhibition which made one wonder why there was no glass roof.

The President had courteously sent his French landau to meet us at the station of San José. The well-sprung carriage rattled over streets paved with uneven cobbles along which flowed much of the town drainage. A short drive brought us to the door of an insignificant building which, like most of the other houses in the capital, was only of one storey. This was the American Legation. Two bare-footed servant girls, with uncombed hair flowing loose down their backs, gazed at us as if we were a fresh curiosity. Up to this point the novelty of a new country, the pleasure of my first independent mission, the grandiloquent speeches, a special presidential train, and the glorious scenery, had acted as a kind of opiate to sustain our spirits. With the excitement of arrival over, and left to ourselves, we now were faced by the prospect of having to spend an indefinite future inhabiting a squalid and most uncomfortable legation in a small town. The house itself was barely and badly furnished, with shabby horsehair sofas and chairs of the kind found in cheap auction rooms. On its dark walls I counted several varieties of spiders which I would have preferred to see behind the glass cases of a natural history museum. We were warned not to walk in our bedrooms with bare feet lest unpleasant ticks should burrow into our flesh. As night fell, our surroundings by the light of flickering lamps looked as shabby, dirty, damp, and desolate as any I have seen. Not even a cook awaited us, for none were available, since a bad earthquake the year before, which occurred while dinner was being prepared, had killed most of the cooks in their kitchens. My pompous title of Minister Plenipotentiary and Envoy Extraordinary seemed like a bad joke, for never in my life had I been so uncomfortable. Nor was there at that time at San José any possible hotel to go to. My wife sat down and cried; my stepdaughter sat down and cried; and both vowed that they would leave by the next boat. The Secretary of the Legation, who saw them in tears and wished to air his peculiar brand of French, remarked unsympathetically: "Est-ce que vous avez fini de beugler?"

The following morning a brilliant sunshine, balmy air, and great baskets of elaborately arranged cactus dahlias sent by unknown Costa Ricans greeted us with a very friendly welcome. People called at the Legation who were sympathetic, had pleasant manners, and behaved at once like old friends. They were kindly and amiable and ever so anxious to be of service. They sent us gifts of parrots and monkeys, although as soon as darkness fell, I would furtively help the latter to escape. Their children, whom they brought with them, were like Raphael's cherubs and had the most beautiful eyes I have ever seen. Already the dreary impression of the night seemed less sinister. We discovered a cook at the lunatic asylum. She knew little of gastronomic art but asked for the whisky bottle whenever she killed a turkey in order to make its flesh more tender, after which I would see an inebriated turkey run through the Legation. She offered to stay with us so long as my wife continued to teach her how to cook and would kiss her whenever she learned a new dish. We engaged as a waitress a fat Jamaican Negress who wore a bandanna, pilfered only moderately, and threatened to write personally to King George at Buckingham Palace whenever she was scolded. We might almost have lived on fruit, for in the Legation patio grew an orange, a mandarin, and a guava tree, which supplied abundantly all the wants of our household.

Soon afterwards I was able to rent a more suitable two-storey building which belonged to a German planter who was leaving for Europe and which was as clean and comfortable as it was devoid of taste. The house was said to be haunted, and every night one heard noises which sounded like a stampede, and every morning we discovered bits of paper torn into shreds and scattered over the floor. One evening in the billiards room, a strange animal darted almost from between my legs. The encounter startled me, but must have frightened the animal still more, for the ghost was henceforth laid. I learned that this was a *zorra,* a domestic fox which makes its nest in the eaves of the roof.

Formerly in Costa Rica, when a new Minister presented his letters of credence, an elaborate ceremony took place that required the presence of the entire army, who were then called out to line the streets through which the envoy passed. A German diplomat, who was described to me by the Minister of Foreign Affairs as dressed like Mars, had almost made an international incident out of some alleged imperfection in the military display attending his reception. After this had occurred, the ceremony was changed into a purely civilian affair, for the Republic was proud of having more schoolmasters than soldiers.

I was at a loss to know what to say to the President in my address, until suddenly I remembered a letter written by Victor Hugo to a friend in Lisbon, after Portugal had abolished capital punishment, and in which the poet declared that there were no longer any small countries but only small individuals. This gave me a cue for some grandiloquent remarks about the greatness of nations depending neither on numbers nor on size but only on the civilization of their inhabitants. I alluded to the oblivion which had befallen vast empires, when the memory of small cities like Athens and Florence kept green, and I finished my address by saying that the United States earnestly desired the preservation of the small republics' independence.

Until then I had not suspected that the Costa Ricans felt so acutely sensitive about their diminutive size, nor that they would discover certain pleasing implications in the comparisons I had hinted at of their country with Athens and Florence. This tiny republic possessed all the attributes of a sovereign state, for a population the whole of which might have been contained in any second-rate provincial town, though only one tenth of the then four hundred thousand inhabitants lived at San José. A Costa Rican politician later told me that, when asked by an American senator about the population of his country, he had drawn the long bow and doubled the number. He was therefore taken aback when the senator remarked that he meant the entire Republic and not merely the capital.

My address, which I had written on the spur of the moment, came in for unsuspected importance, for it was reproduced in the press of all the neighbouring republics and approvingly interpreted as inaugurating a brand new American policy. At San José, the newspapers solemnly assured their readers that the United States had, at last, understood Central America, and that they would no longer have to tremble before the great guns of our battleships or dread the gallop of our rough riders over their flowery fields. Fortunately I never detected any evidence of this fear, which was the last thing in the world I wished to instil. The Costa Ricans are eminently a peaceful people, and they were far more frightened of the neighbouring Nicaraguans than of the United States. Moreover, the lower classes were firmly convinced that they had already defeated the Gringos in battle. The origin of this singular belief had been handed down as a memory from the 'fifties of the last century, when that picturesque adventurer, Walker, invaded Central America with less than sixty men and was at last compelled to surrender with all his followers to a Costa Rican army. The greatness of this martial exploit, almost unique in their annals, has been commemorated in a public garden at San José, by a monument commonly referred to as that of the victory over the Americans.

There existed a pleasing Costa Rican custom of welcoming a new envoy by sending to serenade him the band of the Republic, which was composed of some ninety musicians, while at the same time the Minister of Foreign Affairs paid him an informal visit. On the night of this serenade a large crowd had gathered in the usually lifeless street outside the Legation to listen to the music. I knew that in another part of the town an anti-American meeting was being held that evening in order to offset this official welcome, and my heart sank at the silence of the crowd as the band struck up the "Star Spangled Banner." The polite assurances of the Minister failed to comfort me, and I only began to feel happier when the Costa Rican national anthem seemingly aroused no greater enthusiasm in the crowded street. Not until the band had played the waltz from the "Merry Widow" did I hear loud applause.

The Minister who had called on me that evening was Señor Brenes Mesen, who soon became a daily and always welcome visitor at the Legation. Like many other Latin American public men, he possessed a fine literary cultivation, for he was himself a poet of considerable distinction. Our daily walks in fact had far more to do with poetry than with diplomatic affairs. Business would be mentioned only casually, on the stairs, at the moment when he was taking his departure, and any request I made would invariably be attended to next day. No correspondence with the Foreign Office burdened my files, and I have often wondered if my successor was astonished not to find in the Legation archives the record of a single note addressed by me to the Costa Rican government. These conversations with the Minister were my greatest pleasure. Unlike the French and other continental countries, who took a fine pride in exhibiting their culture abroad, at that time we possessed few means to reveal our uncommercial sides. Yet nowhere more than in Latin American countries is literature appreciated as an art. Fortunately a new and wiser policy has now remedied our former negligence.

Not least among the charm of the older Spanish-American communities is the preference they have for a personal approach instead of an ungentlemanly insistence on the assertion of mere legal rights, which offends their sense of courtesy. In Central America I found friendly relations far more serviceable than any lawyer's argument. Henry Labouchère, who in his youth had been a Secretary in Mexico, used to say that one could get anything out of a Mexican providing that one had no legal claim to it. There was something of the same spirit in people as warmly generous as the Costa Ricans. For many years their government had refused to sign an extradition treaty with the United States (although one has since been negotiated) on the ground that many excellent citizens had settled in the Republic to escape from the penalties of the law. They might have added that the foundation of ancient Rome also took place in a similar way. The Costa Ricans were not Romans, but no one could have been more honourable than Ricardo Jiménez, the President of the Republic, and several other notables with whom I came into contact possessed a simple and worthy dignity that did credit to their country.

Spanish Americans have few greater pleasures than to act as hosts, but this wish is often restrained by an uncomfortable feeling that they cannot honour their guests sufficiently. Thus the consciousness of such limitations makes a hospitably inclined people appear less so to strangers who do not always understand the Latin reluctance to ask friends to partake of their own simple fare in the northern way. Central American hospitality was therefore an event that required an almost embarrassing attention. For example, at an afternoon tea given in our honour we found our host waiting at the sidewalk in order to offer his arm to my wife. The hostess received us at the front door, and arm in arm we marched solemnly into the drawing room while the band played the "Star Spangled Banner." The other guests had been asked to come earlier and were lined against the wall, waiting to be presented by our host, who conducted us in a kind of regal progress. After this ceremony, we were escorted into the dining-room to take our seats at a table decorated with intertwined Costa Rican and American flags, where we exchanged grandiloquent toasts over glasses of champagne.

This was an example of hospitality which many others would have liked to imitate. Yet literally the simplest entertaining at San José met with such enormous obstacles that it required heroic efforts. A new French Minister who had just arrived was enough of an optimist to attempt to give a dinner in a local hotel to which I was invited. I sat down, astonished to feast my eye on a Paris-printed menu worthy of an Elysée banquet, and wondered how this miracle had been achieved. All association with Paris stopped there, for the dinner was Central American at its worst. The cook had done her best to poison us in every way except by intention, and nothing was served hot except champagne. I saw one waiter, pointed out to me as a natural son of a former President, poking a dish under the nose of Señor Vergara, the testy

Chilean Dean of the Diplomatic Body and heard him shout to the latter "Ahi Vergara toma." The real tragedy of the dinner was not the execrable food, but my saddened and wiser host, who after it was over came to apologise abjectly and assure me that he had not intended his invitation as a bad practical joke. I tried to persuade him that the banquet was succulent even if at San José one could not expect the gastronomic perfection of Paris, but the poor man was too crushed to be comforted by any words of consolation. He swore to me on his word of honour that although he had paid for truffled turkeys, he had not been able to discover a single truffle in these birds. Worst of all he felt, as a French Minister, that he had disgraced France, for he reminded me that his country's cooking was the only superiority no one disputed. I never saw my French colleague again, for unable to bear this humiliation he left San José on the following day.

We gave a ball at the Legation which as a festivity was perfectly commonplace although it received an embarrassing attention in the local press. Next day to my horror I read an extravagantly coloured account of our party. A quite ordinary buffet was described as one of the most exquisite viands. Common crockery became embellished into Sèvres porcelain, vulgar glassware into *cristal de baccarat.* Hyperbolic praise was lavished on our persons and on our accomplishments till, as hosts, we felt that we had become supremely ridiculous. When the writers of these articles called next day, instead of the effusive thanks which they doubtless expected, I tried, as delicately as I knew how, to convey some inkling of my embarrassment and to suggest a personal preference for any future entertaining to be left unnoticed by the press. The words were hardly out of my mouth when I discovered that I had hurt their feelings to the quick. They assured me that they were *caballeros* and *hidalgos* who wrote from the heart with no other wish than to prove their affectionate esteem. There was nothing more to say.

Only one unpleasantness clouded many happy recollections of our stay in San José. A Secretary at the Legation, before my arrival, had managed to pick a quarrel with a popular young Yale-educated Costa Rican. I never knew what the quarrel was about, but it came to a head at a dinner given in our honour to which both men were invited. The Costa Rican, after having saluted the other guests, bowed to the Secretary, who rudely looked the other way. This had happened before we arrived, and all knowledge of the incident was considerately kept from me until the following day. Next morning, however, the Costa Rican went to give a piece of his mind to the Secretary. He described him as occupied in curling his moustaches. He walked down the principal street of San José and related to every passerby that he had insulted the American Secretary and called him a *hombre sucio,* but that the Secretary paid no attention to any insults and went on curling his moustaches. What could one do to such a fellow?

Not far from San José is a treeless plain, where formerly duels were fought, and many legends about these had come down from old days. The practice was then much less frequent, but it still existed. As an American official, naturally I could have nothing to do with a duel, but the honour of the Legation was at stake, and I did not like to see my Secretary branded as a cowardly boor, whatever were my personal feelings on the subject. An incident had occurred not long before in Mexico, when the chance remark of an American military attaché, overheard by a native officer in a railway carriage, was regarded as disparaging to the Mexican Army and had led to a challenge to a duel. The American could not fight and remain in the Army, but unless he fought he could not remain in Mexico. The Ambassador wisely solved the dilemma by telegraphing to the War Department at Washington and asking for the officer's instant recall, which was ordered the same day.

That morning I called on two notables of San José and submitted to these the draft of a letter which I had prepared. This letter was to be addressed to them by my Secretary who, as yet, knew nothing about it. The purpose was to place the entire affair in their hands, and though there was no mention of a duel there was enough suggestion of his readiness to fight to allow for hope that this subterfuge might do the trick. The Costa Rican notables agreed to give as their answer that the affair called for no further steps, and in this way honour would be satisfied. I returned to the Legation and summoned the Secretary who, thoroughly crestfallen, was prepared to fall in meekly with any suggestion. He even offered to fight a duel if I wanted him to, but I relieved his anxiety by saying that the duel was the only thing I did not want. He copied the letters which I then dictated to him and in due course received the replies that had been previously arranged. I suggested the advisability of his leaving at once on a prolonged holiday and he departed next day, to return no more.

My predecessor at San José had been a former sea captain who employed his daughter as a typist, his Chinese cook as a messenger, and boasted that he ran the cheapest legation in the world. After my secretary left, a considerable burden fell on me, and I felt like the crew of the *Nancy Bell*—Minister, Secretary, Clerk, and Messenger all rolled into one. I would go myself to the Post Office to carry or call for the diplomatic bag. In the benevolent atmosphere of San José even this was not taken amiss.

A worse inconvenience was the altitude of the capital. My wife found increasing difficulty in breathing, and it was painful to watch her drag herself anxiously from room to room carrying a bag of oxygen which had to be kept under her chair when she entertained at dinner. Our doctor, who was himself a former president of the Republic, advised me as a physician what he told me he deplored as a Costa Rican—that he felt it his duty to urge me to remove her as soon as possible. I wrote to Mr. Knox to explain the circumstances, and that kindly Secretary of State was considerate enough to consent to my taking her away, at once, on an unlimited leave. We left with a keen regret which only a few months before we could hardly have believed possible. During our short stay at San José, we had made many warm friends whose sympathetic remembrance we have never forgotten. All of these went to the station for our departure, several of them accompanying us to the coast. The President's car which took us down to Puerto Limon was turned into a bower of flowers.

As soon as my wife arrived at sea level she quickly recovered her health. A fortnight later, at a White House reception, where the usher had announced me to President Taft as the Minister from Porto Rico, we met Mr. Knox. The Secretary of State talked amiably to my wife and asked her how she felt. That evening she looked so well that my story about her recent ill-health could not have seemed very convincing. There certainly was a twinkle in Mr. Knox's eye.

# 6. *Constantinople in Wartime*

When war broke out I offered my services at Washington, but nothing came of this. Six months later, after we had taken a house in London to be near relatives during the anxieties of that period, the last thing in the world that I expected was to receive a telegram from Secretary Bryan asking me if I would go as Special Agent to Constantinople, and stating that I was greatly needed there. I learned afterwards that our Embassy in Turkey was overwhelmed at this time by having to protect nearly all the Allied interests. The staff was short-handed and certain missionaries, who had known me before, recommended me for the position. The appointment came inconveniently, but I could not refuse. The State Department directed me to go to my post at Varna, the Black Sea port of Bulgaria, which seemed strange, for the Bosporus was closed to navigation. This astonishing order turned out to be due to an error in the transmission of a cipher, which should have read "Vienna."

Before leaving London, I called on Sir Edward Grey. In the bureaucratic atmosphere of the Foreign Office, he wore country clothes and received me as if I had been his guest at Falloden. There was something quietly attractive in Grey's simple earnestness—a quality which he shared with other men who are close to nature. His refined traits that bordered on the ascetic gave him the appearance of being as detached from political events as from vulgar ambitions. I suspect that the diplomatic mistakes he made came principally from his virtues and that this nearness to nature caused him to live in a kind of moral isolation in which whatever was unfamiliar finished by conveying little to his mind. This mild-mannered lover of birds and trees, by a ludicrous distortion of the truth, had been travestied by the Germans, who represented him as a bloodthirsty ogre. The hatred that was wilfully created by the war was responsible for many lies, but never was there a grosser distortion of the truth. I spoke to Grey of events in the Near East, but I doubt if the Turks made any deeper impression on his mind than that of any other troublesome people who had gone mad. His own experience with them was limited to the Balkan Wars when he had helped to quiet down a crisis by sipping tea with European ambassadors who were his personal friends.

The success that Grey had obtained by applying a five o'clock method of solving a diplomatic tangle left him with the belief that no other panacea was quite so efficacious, and convinced him that the grave crisis which led to the World War could have been settled in much the same way. If he had any real understanding of the elements behind the Eastern situation, he kept this to himself, and there was some truth in Lord d'Abernon's epigram that Grey in the Balkans was like Parsifal sitting down to play poker with the devil. When later I saw him again after my return from Turkey, he was always charmingly courteous but did not seem to take any particular interest in that distressing part of the world. My most pressing concern, on the first occasion, was to propose a visit to the German prisoners in order that I should be able to say at Constantinople that from personal observation I had seen how well they were treated in England. Grey was of the same opinion, and a few days later he arranged to have me see a couple of hundred naval prisoners at Southend, where they were confined aboard a ship. I talked to them freely and found them well satisfied by their treatment, with no complaint to make. One sailor insisted on undressing to show me fifty-six wounds which he had lately received in action, apparently without otherwise injuring his health.

In a Europe at war, the journey across the Continent passed without any incident. At Vienna, we were handed our first bread cards and instead of the famous rolls were served with a sour-tasting brown substitute. The war was not yet six months old, but an atmosphere of gloom already hung over everything Austrian and the streets of the capital were dead. The isolation of the Central Powers had produced some queer opinions. We called on an old friend, Princess Windischgrätz, who repeated the current opinion held in Central Europe, that Calais would either be British or German, but was forever lost to the French. Like most Austrians, she felt no rancour towards her country's enemies and told me that she made a point of talking English in the trams. Yet, fearing that we might meet with some unpleasantness, she insisted on accompanying us next morning to the station, although our train left at seven. The following day, after passing the Roumanian frontier, we were once more in a land of plenty. From the car window I watched an endless procession of ox-carts climbing up the mountain roads, laden with food supplies for Hungary.

It was a very different Constantinople from the one I had left nearly six years before. Driving through Stamboul, one no longer heard the cries of the street vendors; even the wooden planks of the rickety old bridge had disappeared along with the lepers holding out their shrivelled hands. The chatter of the Levantine port had gone from a half-empty Galata. Only the dirt and smell of the Mediterranean, which is so different from any northern dirt and smell, still remained. The city was silent and dead, and one felt oppressed by the grimness of an atmosphere which was nearer to the Balkans than to Asia.

Many of my old Turkish friends I found visibly apprehensive. The impassive Turk showed his nervousness least, but the more voluble Greeks, and particularly those who were Hellenic subjects, felt anxious and did not know from day to day where they stood. The fate of thousands of the latter at Constantinople hung on the bitter struggle then going on at Athens between the King and Venizelos. Greek troops might soon be fighting on the Allied side, and this anticipation turned out to be an unexpected boon to neutral diplomats who were suddenly entreated by departing Hellenic friends to inhabit their houses before these should be occupied by the Turks. One American Secretary was begged to take over an entire hotel for his private use. As a great favour we were asked to move immediately into one of the finest houses in Pera, the owner leaving in it all his domestics and everything as before except for a photograph of Venizelos.

Soon after we had taken up our residence, an excited servant of my friend came to tell me that his master's country house at Therapia was about to be seized. We were unable to go there before some days, but I gave the retainer an American flag, which caused the Turkish mayor to express surprise that the well-known Greek banker, to whom the house belonged, should so suddenly have become a citizen of the United States. After this incident, we spent all our weekends at Therapia, which was empty except for the soldiers who occupied the hotels and passed their time digging trenches on the hills. The road along the waterfront, which formerly in summer had been gay with life, was now barred by a sentry who was stationed in front of the Italian Embassy and allowed only Turks to go beyond that point. Hardly any steamers were left on the Bosporus, and we used to drive out to the villa behind a good team of horses which another Greek friend had begged us to use in order to avoid their being seized by the military. The countryside was entirely deserted, and once I even saw a wolf stare at us, only a few yards from the road.

As I had come from London and took few pains to hide Entente sympathies, rumours were spread that I was the bearer of some secret peace overtures. Naturally this made me an object of suspicion to the Germans, and a wish to satisfy a personal curiosity about the *Goeben** did not help to allay this. When I left England there was considerable doubt as to what had become of this famous ship which brought Turkey into the war, and reports were current that she had recently been sunk. Borrowing the Embassy launch for an excursion up the Bosporus, I saw the *Goeben* snugly anchored in the harbour of Stenia, with a good deal of canvas around her, and protected from submarine attack by a string of barges. Next day, Baron Wangenheim, the German Ambassador, called to ask what my purpose had been, and shortly after this he accused me of circulating news hostile to the Germans. He even declared, with characteristic exaggeration, that he was having me watched day and night, as my house was supposed to be a gathering point for Germany's enemies. There were certainly no plots hatched under its roof, but the charge he made was not altogether untrue, for a bond of Allied sympathy united most of our visitors. In fact we felt like early Christians meeting to pray in the Catacombs, for we could do little more during these dreary days except to keep up our spirits by looking forward to victory and the longed-for intervention of Italy and of Roumania.

Usually diplomats of every nation meet on terms of easy familiarity, but our intercourse with the Germans at Constantinople was mainly of a formal nature. One saw them principally at the Dutch Legation, for they kept very much to themselves, resentful of the unfriendly atmosphere around them and mixing little even with the Austrians. The latter associated amicably with neutrals and were not indisposed to resent the assumptions of superiority that were advanced by their German allies. A few Turks also came to see me, like my old friend Reshad Fuad, the Counsellor of State, who would call, usually in the morning,

* See pp. 125–26 for further discussion of the *Goeben.*

when he knew that he would find me alone and could then pour out his heart. He would begin humorously at first by making some allusion to "our Little Vizier," and at once correct this intentional slip with an apology for not having called him "Grand." I was an audience of one for my friend's urgent need to vent his indignation, which suddenly would boil up to fever point as he related the indignity of his son's treatment as a soldier at the hands of hectoring sergeants in the filthy barracks where the boy was quartered. Reshad was particularly disgusted by the servility of many of his former friends who now cringed before Enver and Talaat, proclaimed a fanaticism which they did not feel, and a hatred of everything Western that was not even sincere. A deliberate attempt was with tragic humour being fostered from Berlin, to persuade the Turks to preach a Holy War. The excess of this fanatical zeal disgusted Reshad but amused the cultivated Persian Ambassador, Mahmoud Khan, who showed me some excellent rotogravures, made in Germany, that represented the Sheikh-ul-Islam inciting the Faithful to exterminate unbelievers while himself wearing a laundered dress shirt, which was rank heresy in orthodox Moslem eyes. The Holy War, then spectacularly announced at Constantinople, fell quite flat, in spite of the agitated efforts of a few hysterical Germans at Aleppo, who did their utmost to incite the Turks to massacre.

I can still see my friend Reshad swaying his enormous body to and fro, and looking at me pathetically as he foretold the ruin ahead for Turkey. He loathed the war, and he loathed the adventurers then at the helm, who were leading his country to destruction; he belonged to that earlier generation who still retained their English and French sympathies. There was nothing these men could do, for all knew that the Sultan was only a benevolent half-wit and that no appeal to him could be of use. The Grand Vizier, the Mongolian-featured Egyptian Prince Saīd Halim, was little more than a vain and pompous figurehead who understood nothing of what went on, but talked glibly about the conquests by which he proposed to extend the Turkish Empire. The Grand Vizier spoke English and French perfectly, and passed every afternoon playing billiards at the club. He had become of late fanatically anti-foreign, and in his private house he dressed in Oriental robes. He was the centre for a group of violently anti-British Egyptians at Constantinople, one of whom was fighting at the Dardanelles because of having been black-balled at a club in Cairo.

Military authority in Turkey was under Enver Pasha, who relied on his German advisers to make up for his own mediocrity. He was a man of great courage and of still greater confidence in his own star. The loss of an army that he had led to destruction in the snows of the Caucasus did not alter this pleasing belief, for he recalled that Napoleon had lost a much larger one in Russia. Like Napoleon, to whom he was not disinclined to compare himself, he had married a princess, and back of his mind lay the hope that with victory he would become heir to the throne after having set aside the unworthy princes of the House of Othman. Meanwhile he was buying up, for next to nothing, vast tracts of land in Anatolia, and using soldiers to build roads for his private estate on the Bosporus.

The civil authority in Turkey was entirely in the hands of the Committee of Union and Progress, and many believed that its leaders were wilfully encouraging Enver's abuses in order to hold him in their power. In postwar terms, the Committee would have been styled a fascist party. There was no single dictator, but a small body of men met, in secret, in order to rule an empire in which public opinion did not exist, and to enforce drastic measures on a submissive and long-suffering population. The most conspicuous member of this Committee was the masterful Minister of the Interior, Talaat Pasha. He was less omnipotent than many believed outside Turkey, for there were other members as influential, like Dr. Nazim, who worked in the dark. Talaat acted as the link between the Committee and the outer world. Unlike Enver, whose ambitions were far more personal, Talaat's loyalty went whole-heartedly to the Committee, and I doubt if he entertained any greater wish than to serve its interests. Unlike Enver, he was indifferent to money, lived modestly, and boasted that his entire fortune did not amount to a hundred pounds, a circumstance which never seemed to prevent his playing poker at the Club for very high stakes.

I found him, however, a different man from the one I had known six years before. He had become as obese as he then was slim, and his former pleasant expression had hardened to one of cruelty and callousness. I have never seen a greater facial alteration than had come over Talaat, nor a physical appearance which more befitted the deterioration of his character. Swift and authoritative in his decisions, his bloated and dissipated appearance made him look every inch the Oriental tyrant. With this, he kept a rough sense of humour, and when he drafted convicts from the prisons to despatch them to the front, he would jest about this, saying that if they killed the enemies of Turkey they benefited the country, and if they were killed they benefited humanity. Of his early gypsy origin he retained principally the adventurer's spirit. War suited his temperament, and its duration guaranteed the Committee's retention of power. Knowing that nothing could shake this so long as hostilities went on, he was cynically to admit the worst misdeeds, and I have seen him smile with keen amusement when a diplomat called him a devil to his face. There were few things he enjoyed more than to flout the foreign ambassadors whom in the depths of his heart he despised.

The relations between Turks and Germans had passed through several different phases before they became established by the events themselves. When war broke out in Europe, in spite of the German military mission at Constantinople and a secret pact signed early in August 1914 Turkey was less in Teutonic hands than was then supposed, principally because Berlin at that time felt little inclined for any closer intimacy. Former German military calculations regarding the value of the Ottoman army had gone so far astray during the Balkan War that in the summer and autumn of 1914 Berlin still regarded the Turks as a most uncertain factor and feared that their participation might be more of a liability to them than an asset. Paradoxical as it may seem, those Germans in Turkey who knew the country best felt no desire for a real alliance and little confidence in the value of the assistance which they could expect. They dreaded lest Turkish intervention should prove to be a dangerous boomerang by providing England with an easy victory and allowing the Allies to open communications with Russia. In this early stage, the German wish was only to have Turkey mobilize and then, by maintaining an attitude of armed expectancy, oblige the Entente to divert forces to watch her, without giving Great Britain an excuse to break through her defences.

Two events that happened unexpectedly were to put Turkey in Germany's power. The first was the intense indignation aroused against England for having seized the two Turkish battleships just completed in British yards and intended to bring about the recovery of the Greek islands. Notoriously the Turks had made the greatest sacrifices to obtain these ships; women had offered their wedding rings and the government had borrowed money at twenty per cent to pay for their construction. When war was on the point of breaking out, the last instalment was just due. The Turks, who enquired in London if there were any use in making this, were advised to do so, but immediately afterwards the vessels were seized and added to the British fleet. It would have been far better if the two battleships could have been despatched to Constantinople with British crews under the crescent flag, nominally to assist Turkey to preserve her neutrality, for if this had been done no secret pact might have been signed with Germany. Instead, the seizure of these ships was dramatically followed a few days later by the Kaiser offering as a free gift to Turkey the *Goeben* and the *Breslau,* which had just then miraculously escaped from the British fleet at Messina and had found refuge in the shelter of the Dardanelles. The two German vessels, as soon as they anchored in the Straits, had perquisitioned English ships and destroyed the wireless apparatus on a French boat. Yet the British fleet, which was only a few miles away, refrained from following and sinking them at anchor where they lay, for Great Britain, having just denounced the rape of Belgium, was not yet ready to commit an obvious breach of neutrality and did not foresee that the results of Turkish intervention would soon be measured in the defeats of Gallipoli and the humiliation of Kut. The Turks, however, contrasted the behaviour of England towards them with the gift received from Germany.

Strangely enough, the arrival of the *Goeben* did not make the Germans at Constantinople any more anxious to have the Sultan as an ally. Six months after Turkey entered the war, I had a curious talk with an old friend, Paul Weitz, the well-informed correspondent of the *Frankfurter Zeitung* and himself a man of moderate views, who had always been intimately associated with every German Ambassador. To my amazement he answered a remark I let drop that if Baron Marschall had been British Ambassador he would have found means to keep out of the war, by saying that this would have happened if Baron Marschall had been the German Ambassador. He hastened to add that by expressing this opinion he did not imply any criticism of the then Ambassador, Baron Wangenheim, but the latter possessed less personal influence at Berlin than did his predecessor and was obliged to carry out his instructions. After the defeat of the Marne, when things were not going well for Germany, insistent orders had come from Berlin to bring about Turkey's entrance on their side. The Germans used the obvious argument that if Russia was to be victorious, the fate of the Turks would be sealed. The latter now had a golden opportunity to ally themselves with a first-class military power whose armies were certain to triumph. No great effort was necessary to convince a small group of adventurers already more than half won over and who would have chafed if they had continued to remain in a secure neutrality. The British blockade of the Dardanelles in this way unexpectedly played into German hands, for it gave the Turks an excuse to mine the straits. Open intervention was then precipitated by the *Goeben's* bombardment of Sebastopol, after a plot which was known beforehand only to Enver, Talaat, and the Germans, but had been kept a secret even from the Grand Vizier.

The greatest fault that can be committed in dealing with an Oriental power is to display weakness, and British policy had been guilty of this toward Turkey. Next to weakness as a sin comes bluff, for bluff is a blunder almost as great. On March 9th, 1915, a British admiral sailed into Smyrna harbour, demanded the immediate unconditional surrender of its forts and batteries, under threat of the sternest reprisals, and announced that if this was complied with he would place a large sum of money for the poor at the Vali's disposal. The governor of Smyrna was then Rahmi Bey, an able official who was particularly friendly to the many English residents under his protection. Rahmi felt so embarrassed by the offer of this clumsy bribe that he published the Admiral's letter in the Turkish press, and when the British fleet sailed away without carrying out any of its threats, it took with it much of the prestige which is so necessary in the East. Later, when I mentioned my regret at this unfortunate affair to Sir Edward Grey, it was characteristic of that statesman that he had never heard of it.

The difficult liaison between Germans and Turks was managed by Captain Humann, the son of the distinguished archaeologist who had excavated ancient Greek cities in Asia Minor. Humann, brought up in Smyrna, spoke German with a Levantine accent, but was fluent in Turkish and Greek. He possessed few advantages of birth or rank, and would have remained an obscure naval officer if he had not become the intimate friend of Enver when the latter was military attaché at Berlin. This friendship made Humann's fortune, and after Enver became Minister of War the sailor was sent to Constantinople to be the indispensable link between the German Embassy and the most powerful man in Turkey.

I came in touch with this naval officer in an odd way. Some Greek ladies had asked my wife to intercede for a few tons of coke requisitioned from a charitable society and without which the laundry work that it carried out could not go on. Certain cousins of my wife had formerly been childhood friends of Humann, and on the strength of the connection she wrote to ask him if it would be possible to release this trifling amount of coke. He answered her with that fondness for didacticism which is so tiresome a German trait, and entered into a lengthy political argument to explain the many reasons why the Turkish government felt so unfriendly toward the Greeks. The reasons were excellent, but my wife had made a simple request which he was at liberty to comply with or to refuse, and neither of us saw any cause why he should find it necessary to give her a somewhat offensive political lesson. Together, we concocted a suitable reply. She wrote that her intention was solely humanitarian, and she finished her letter, which was in French, by expressing the hope that she might soon have "l'occasion de vous servir." Before sending it, we read the text to the Italian Ambassador who begged her not to transmit it, as the impertinent ambiguity of this particular phrase would certainly lead to an incident and a likely demand for my recall. I told her, however, to go ahead. Perhaps Humann did not understand the true meaning of the French idiom, for a few days later, much to our amazement, came the authorization for the coke.

The German Ambassador at Constantinople was Baron Wangenheim, a diplomat who had a mercurial and not unsympathetic personality, with an expression which was half satanic and half that of an artist. His tact may be judged by the visit which he paid at the American Embassy to announce the sinking of the *Lusitania.* Apart from politics, he was an agreeable colleague who loved his game of bridge every afternoon at the Club. A few Greeks with whom he played were flattered by the Ambassador's company at the bridge table and frightened enough to applaud his frequent violent outbursts against the Allies. On these occasions he would thump the card table, and shout that England wanted the war; and his bridge companions, more terrified by Wangenheim present than by John Bull absent, would repeat after him in chorus, "Yes, England wanted the war."

In the middle of July 1914, Wangenheim returned to Constantinople from a holiday in Germany and called at once on the Italian Ambassador Garroni to congratulate him on his birthday. He then related to him that the Kaiser, before sailing for Norway, had summoned the principal generals, bankers, and captains of industry for a conference and asked them if they were ready for war; and that all had assured him that they were fully prepared. This story, related to me by the Marquis Garroni with dramatic effect, was also repeated by Wangenheim to the American Ambassador, Henry Morgenthau, and is the origin for the legend of a Crown Council said to have been held at Potsdam early in July 1914, at which war was decided. Prince Lichnowski has related having heard something of this sort when he passed through Berlin in July 1914. German historians are morbidly sensitive regarding the question of war guilt and have made much of the fact that no real Crown Council took place at this time in Potsdam. But the account I heard, and which I have every reason to believe was true, might as well have presupposed a series of informal conferences of which no regular record need have been kept, rather than a formal Crown Council. Presented in this light the tale is as difficult to prove as it is to disprove, and I think that the importance attached to the story has been needlessly exaggerated. It would have been far more surprising if the Kaiser, who knew of the warlike intentions of the Austrian government, and had already assured the latter of his support, the proof of which is all on record, should not have taken every means in his power to ascertain the degree of his country's preparedness.

At Constantinople early in March 1915, a general feeling of pessimism had prevailed. The Dardanelles were still virtually defenceless against an attack from the land, and neither Turks nor Germans felt any confidence in the ability of the forts to prevent the passage of the ships. The government treasure and archives had been despatched into the interior, and at Haidar Pasha, on the Asiatic side opposite Constantinople, trains were kept under steam for instant departure. The German and Austrian ambassadors had both called to request the United States to take over the protection of their interests when they would be obliged to leave the capital and follow the Sultan's government to Eski Chehir. The Turkish authorities intended, however, to defend the city and frankly informed us about the preparations that they were making to establish a neutral zone in Constantinople for foreigners and noncombatants. Certain police officials were to remain and keep order in the difficult interval anticipated between the evacuation of the capital and its occupation by the Allies. That this occupation would happen was regarded as a foregone conclusion, and with tens of thousands of foreign subjects in the city, as well as several hundred thousand Greek and Armenian inhabitants and an unruly mob which might run amok, the problem was avowedly an anxious one.

The armed protection which the Embassy had at its disposal consisted of some fifty or sixty sailors from the American guardship *Scorpion*. Arrangements were made for this force to be divided between the protection of the Bible House at Stamboul, which was a natural rallying point for our missionaries, and the Embassy. In a Chancery cupboard were kept a dozen rifles. We might be able to defend ourselves for a short time against a mob, but it was impossible to hold out long in case of real trouble, and how serious this might be no one could say. I heard a remark made by Hassan, one of our *cavasses** who had served at the Embassy for many years, that we had nothing to fear in his opinion, for if the time ever came for a massacre he offered to despatch us himself in the most humane and painless fashion.

After Turkey entered the war, the protection of many thousand Allied subjects was at first divided between the American and the Italian embassies. The Italian Ambassador, the Marquis Garroni, was a former Prefect of Genoa and an intimate friend of Giolitti, who had appointed him to obtain orders to build some Turkish battleships in Italian yards. When Garroni left for his post, he tacked on to his name the title of Marquis, but it was difficult to detect anything aristocratic in a man who possessed the pedestrian and cautious commonsense, the kindly obligingness, and the wily cunning that is so frequently met with in the Italian middle class. I saw much of him, for I had to do with Italian interests, and his homely comments on military events invariably amused me. Thus, after the first British attack at Gallipoli had failed, he compared this to a man who attempts to break into a house and, unable to force the front door, proposes to try the window.

* A cavass was an armed guard and courier at consular offices and legations in Near Eastern countries.

And the protracted Roumanian agitation for intervention he described as being like the chorus of an Italian opera eternally singing "Partiamo, partiamo," but never leaving.

Garroni was not in sympathy with his government and hated to see the rapid shift toward intervention which was taking place at this time in Italy. The Ambassador frankly favoured neutrality, and in this way he managed till the end to keep on the best personal terms with both Austrians and Turks. The impression he gave of disapproving of his own government while at the same time conscientiously carrying out his instructions may have been lacking in dignity, but it was sincere, adroit, and intentional. It was also to the advantage of some twelve thousand Italians who remained in Turkey and after his departure were turned over to my special care. Shortly before the final break occurred and while relations were already highly strained, Garroni had been the victim of an incident which might have precipitated the rupture. The Marquis was trying to cross a street along which troops were marching when a Turkish officer, unaware of his identity, slashed him across the back with the flat surface of his sabre. The Italian Ambassador then acted intelligently and with great restraint. At all costs he wanted to avoid contributing by any personal grievance to inflame a situation which was already far too strained for his taste. He concealed all knowledge of the incident until after he had obtained the apology which he demanded from the Porte, not as an Ambassador but as an Italian. No one had any suspicion of the offence until an announcement was made simultaneously describing the incident and stating that it was already settled.

The American Ambassador to whom I had been attached as a Special Agent was then Henry Morgenthau. Constantinople was his first government post, and he brought to his duties a quick and pliable intelligence, a vivacious and imaginative mind, much initiative, and an untiring energy. All these were useful qualities to handle a situation which allowed little scope for the practice of the more ordinary diplomatic methods. There was no time to wait for answers to notes addressed to the Porte, or to employ the customary leisurely processes of polite diplomacy. A state of war breaks down the respect for peacetime precedents, and the Turkish government, which was fighting for its existence, cared little for any former traditions. Circumstances thus transformed the Embassy into what was substantially an enquiry office where business was always pressing and demanded immediate attention. An immense number of individuals belonging to countries at war with Turkey, who were imprisoned or molested, often for no cause, looked for their only protection to us. To help these unfortunates meant innumerable visits and telephone calls, usually to the police or at the Ministry of the Interior. Sometimes these were successful, although our arguments, unbacked by force, could never have appeared very persuasive to the practical Turkish mind. Quite as often, such representations led to infinite bickerings and refusals. Many petty police officials were then thoroughly enjoying their new opportunity to act high-handedly toward people who formerly had been shielded from the Turks by their embassies.

Every day would bring fresh cases of interference against enemy subjects who were under our protection. Sometimes the charges were farcical, as when the police arrested the manager of a large store in Pera. As they had found some French toy soldiers on his premises, they tried to compel him to sign a paper by which he admitted having enemy uniforms and flags in his possession. Sometimes the cases were more tragic. The police, at a moment's notice, expelled French nuns from their convent and took an inventory of a room in which a sister lay dying. At another French orphanage, the children were turned out homeless into the street just as they were about to sit down to lunch. The Mother Superior rushed to the Embassy in despair, and I went to intercede on her behalf with the Minister of Education, Chukry Bey. Chukry I knew to be an atheist and a fanatical nationalist, for in Turkey, as in other lands, the old order was reversed and while religion had become liberal, politics became fanatical. The Minister frankly wanted to drive every priest out of the country in order to get possession of the religious schools, which he called "palaces," and use these for Turkish institutions. To my astonishment, Chukry received me that day with unexpected politeness, commiserated with the misfortune of the poor people expelled, and threw all the fault on the military who, he said, were looking for convalescent homes. His explanation was so convincing, and his manner so affable, that I regretted not having any further business to take up on an occasion when I had found him, unexpectedly, in so conciliatory a temper. The affair was then brought to Enver's attention, who knew nothing about it. Bedri, the Chief of Police, was more outspoken in calling the Minister of Education a cur who lacked the courage to admit his own misdeeds. Soon afterwards I had again occasion to see Chukry on a similar matter, and this time he justified his expulsions by citing lynch law and telling me that anyhow Turks were regarded by us as barbarians. I answered that as a well-wisher of Turkey I found it hard to understand how, in an age of progress, they could make war on women and children and act in a way which Abdul Hamid's tyranny would never have attempted. The Minister merely shrugged his shoulders and remarked cynically, "Our faults are the same, and our former chivalry has gone."

The Embassy, among its other tasks, had to arrange for the distribution of relief to enemy subjects who could not be repatriated and would otherwise have starved without this assistance. After the rupture with Italy, the United States had inherited the care of Russian interests, and I was placed in charge of the Czar's subjects at Constantinople, nearly all of whom were Greeks, Jews, and Armenians. These unfortunates were also being systematically robbed by their own minor Consular officials who had been left behind to take care of Russian government property and administer the relief funds. The Embassy, for instance, issued certificates of protection to enemy subjects under its care. We gave such papers gratis, but they were sold to their unfortunate nationals by the Russian Consular officials, who pretended that the fees demanded for this service went to the Americans. As if this iniquity were not enough, they kept their accounts in gold and paid the relief in silver, which enabled the rascals to retain a regular percentage on all the funds which passed through their hands.

The situation of the Allied subjects in Turkey changed for the worse after the failure of the British and French fleet to force the Dardanelles, on March 18th, 1915. It has often been said that the Turks were running out of ammunition just as the attack was called off, but from accounts then given me by Captain Morton, the commander of the *Scorpion,* who visited the forts soon after the bombardment, and from Austrian friends, I do not believe that there was any truth in this opinion. English sailors, like Admiral Keyes, remain convinced that the Straits could have been forced, yet the failure to do so at that time may have been a blessing in disguise. The Allies had then no troops to support the ships, and if the fleet had arrived before Constantinople it would have been separated from its base by a difficult and dangerous communication, and unable without an army to occupy the capital. The ships would virtually have found themselves prisoners in the Marmora, and might in the end have been compelled to fight their way out. Hardly was the attack over before General Liman von Sanders went to inspect the Dardanelles. On his return he reported that in another ten days he would make the peninsula impregnable. Instead, the British gave him six weeks' time to complete his preparations.

One fact had impressed itself on the Turkish mind after the unsuccessful naval attack. The Committee of Union and Progress up to that time had dreaded the British fleet. Talaat was then to put the situation in a nutshell. "Hitherto we used to fear England and France. Now we know they can do nothing to us." As soon as the Turks felt confident that the Dardanelles could not be forced, they saw before them an unexpected opportunity to destroy the Armenians, who were the real victims of the naval failure. No other government except the Turkish, while at war against some of the most powerful nations in the world, would have dared to carry out the deliberate extermination of an important though almost helpless minority. The systematic method by which this revolting policy was put through appeared all the more incredible because, prior to the massacres, the two races had been living peacefully side by side, on friendly terms, and with little or no popular animosity or religious fanaticism. Turks and Armenians only a few years before had worked together at a time when both were revolutionaries, and certain members of the Committee were under the deepest personal obligations to individual Armenians, which they were now conveniently to forget.

To understand the devilry of what took place, one must put aside all preconceived ideas of racial hatred, or the more modern explanation of an alleged economic exploitation. To comprehend its cruelty, it is necessary to go back to those political beliefs which brought about the massacre of St. Bartholomew.* Probably few members of the Committee of Union and Progress, beginning with Talaat himself, felt any real hatred for the Armenians, and the latter was prepared to admit that his personal estimate of the loss to the country as a consequence of destroying this industrious community might run to five million pounds. Talaat explained the measures they were about to take by say-

* The killing of thousands of Huguenots, instigated by Catherine de Medici and King Charles IX of France in 1572.

ing that they feared the Armenians because the latter knew their secrets. This was however only a trivial excuse for a nationalistic racial policy of ruthless cunning and deliberate devilry carefully prepared and skilfully carried out with a minimum of publicity.

The real explanation for massacres in which nearly a million people perished and a great community was pitilessly destroyed lay in the conviction that an Armenian minority, culturally more advanced than the Turks and enjoying certain international connections, particularly with Russia, could not exist without encroaching on the rigid framework of a purely Turkish racial state, which the Committee of Union and Progress was then aiming to build. With half Europe kept at bay outside the Dardanelles, and the other half unwilling to restrain the Turks because they were allies, the latter knew that, for the first and probably the last time, their hands were free and that a unique opportunity, which might never occur again, lay before them to put through a policy which they had planned long before but which until then had not been practicable. It was no sudden crime they committed, but a scientifically prepared savagery, the perpetration of which seemed for political reasons as desirable to the Committee of Union and Progress as did the murder of the Huguenots to Catherine de Medici.

The excuse put forward in order to prepare domestic opinion for the impending massacres made much of the fact that when Turkey entered the war the Armenians in the Southern Caucasus had formed some bands of irregulars. Those who joined these bands were Russian subjects, and many of them had been refugees who escaped from former massacres and were filled with a fierce hatred against the Turks, which the memory of ravished wives and murdered relatives had burned deep into their hearts. These bands crossed the mountainous frontier in sufficient numbers to capture Van, with its governor, who was commonly known as "the blacksmith," because his favourite torture had been to rivet horeshoes on the live flesh of his victims. The Armenians also shod the torturer in the same way as he had done to many of their race, but it was unfair to find any connection between the excesses of a few irregulars and the immense majority of peaceful Armenian communities in Turkey. At the very time when, with unconscious humour, the Germans were circulating at Constantinople an official White Book containing reports of atrocities inflicted by barbarous Belgian civilians in gouging out the eyes of the Kaiser's inoffensive soldiers, I heard Turkish officials express a sincere indignation at the atrocities which Armenians had committed on inoffensive Moslems. A shred of conscience usually makes an assassin try to explain his crime with a lie. The Turkish government, which planned the murder of a defenceless minority, felt obliged to find an excuse, and in order to justify itself resorted to a loathsome vilification, knowing it was a lie.

The first warning about the impending massacres came to me from a Swiss engineer who had just come back from travelling in the interior. At different localities he had been shown some antiquated weapons which the police were then carefully collecting. These were to furnish the flimsy pretext of having discovered evidence for a supposed rising of the Armenians, which naturally had to be suppressed. The allegation was so preposterous that it was soon abandoned, but the authorities were then busily organizing the criminal elements of the population into a so-called constabulary whose pleasurable duty would be to murder their victims.

I recall once having seen a thriller at the Grand Guignol in Paris in which a man hears his wife scream through a distant telephone that she is being murdered. At Constantinople, in 1915, I understood what he must have felt. An Embassy is not unlike a telephone room in which the staff takes the place of operators who receive, connect, and disconnect messages, and usually can do little more than pass these on to a central exchange, which in our case was the State Department. Vicarious accounts of calamities, as a rule, leave us calm. One reads that a million Chinese have been drowned by a Yellow River flood, without being able to visualise the immensity of the disaster. Human sympathy is a strictly limited article that fails to grow in proportion with the numbers of the afflicted. At Constantinople, even without the physical spectacle of the horrors committed, one felt an inward rage at one's powerlessness.

Massacres did not take place in cities, and rarely before foreign witnesses, for appearances were kept up, and the Armenian community of Constantinople was hardly molested. The method of destruction then adopted was much more cunningly cruel. Orders of deportation would suddenly be issued for all the Armenians in a town to leave at an hour's notice. They were directed to take with them only such effects as they could carry, for a destination in the Mesopotamian desert which would later be announced. Men, women, and children were obliged to leave their homes and belongings so they would have to sell these instantly to Turkish buyers for a pittance. In this way, fresh consignments of rugs, which were really Armenian loot, reached the bazaars at Constantinople, where the more decent merchants regarded such articles with disgust. The wretched Armenians, after bundling the few effects they could carry on their person, would then be made to march off with their Turkish guards. These marches went on day after day, with the sick and infirm left to die on the roadside. Parents, in their despair, would beg strange Turks to take their children, and many of these regarded it as a charity to do so. More often than not the poor wretches would be murdered, usually at night, either by Kurds or by the bands of criminals who had been drafted for that purpose. Every day brought some fresh tales of incredible horrors which filtered through in spite of the strict censorship exercised. Not a few decent Turkish officials were revolted by this murderous policy, but those who refused to carry it out were summarily dismissed. I heard of an Arab officer who had been placed in charge of one of these human convoys. Day after day, he marched from one town of Anatolia to another, only to be told to march back again to his starting point. The orders given him were so senseless that at last he asked for an explanation. He was frankly informed that he was expected to get rid of the Armenians in any way he chose, but until this happened he would have to go on marching. The following morning the Arab took a dose of calomel, pleaded illness, and turned his wretched convoy over to another officer.

The position of the United States in Constantinople, at this time, was unique. After Italy entered the war, America was the only neutral great power left in Turkey, and the consuls and missionaries in the interior kept the Embassy fairly well informed about the massacres. Mr. Morgenthau repeatedly made representations on the subject to Talaat Pasha, who was himself their principal organizer, and the latter would listen and smile as if he enjoyed the joke when the Ambassador accused him of this crime. The Austrians also were revolted by a cruelty which they could do nothing to prevent. It is not possible, however, to absolve the German Embassy from a considerable share of responsibility, which was all the greater because many kindly German missionaries in the interior did their best to help. Certain German consuls would have desired to use their influence to protect the wretched

Armenians, but all had received the strictest orders not to interfere in Turkish internal affairs, and the German Embassy merely prepared a hypocritical paper record of protest to have ready for its later protection. The explanation for this callousness was simple. In the life and death struggle in which the Germans were engaged, many of them felt that nothing counted except victory and that they could not afford the risk of appearing to be censorious of any ally. Yet I have always thought that Berlin deserved the severest blame for taking this attitude, for they alone might have prevented these massacres. Nor do I think that Washington can be entirely absolved from criticism, although it is most unlikely that any steps which the Embassy could have taken at this time in Constantinople would have stopped the Turks from continuing their murderous policy. In a few individual instances, the American Ambassador was able to render an assistance which could not have been given in the event of a rupture. Yet I should personally have preferred to see our intercourse broken, and to have published the reason to the world, instead of carrying on friendly relations with a government of murderers, as soon as it became plain that we could do nothing to prevent their crime.

Perhaps we accomplished more by acting as we did. Certainly the missionaries did not wish a break, and President Wilson acted principally on their advice. Many of them had been through the previous massacres, when there were always survivors who needed assistance, and the missions had been able to collect relief funds in America. There was, however, another and more important reason that, unconsciously or otherwise, influenced their judgment. The missionaries feared for the fate of their institutions, and this apprehension had a great deal to do with determining their attitude and that of Washington. Undoubtedly the Turks would have welcomed an excuse to take possession of the missionary property. Moreover, the Turkish policy of extermination was directed against the Armenians of the National Gregorian Church, and applied with less cruelty to the smaller Catholic and Protestant minorities. If America had broken with Turkey, the feeble protection which the latter enjoyed would at once have been withdrawn, all our missionary institutions would have been seized, and the patient work of a century might have been uprooted in a month. There were certainly some excellent arguments to offer on the side of noninterference.

Probably no American threat of rupture would have caused the Turks to desist from these massacres once they had begun, for they foresaw that a world divided by war had no time or inclination to concern itself with their crimes, and rightly believed that after the peace nothing would be done. The violent deaths met later by Enver, Talaat, and the Grand Vizier, the two latter at the hands of Armenian avengers, were merciful by comparison with the sufferings which they had inflicted. It is a comforting opinion to believe that the just will be recompensed and the guilty suffer, but the religious doctrine which relegates questions of reward and punishment to the Day of Judgment unfortunately comes nearer to historical truth.

As soon as it became apparent that the Italians would declare war against Turkey, I tried to persuade Garroni to include these massacres as among the reasons for a break. Even from a selfish point of view, I argued that such a ground might be found useful in case Italian colonial ambitions were later advanced in Asia Minor. The Ambassador professed to agree with me, but his relations with Baron Sonnino, who was Minister for Foreign Affairs, were not friendly enough, he said, to encourage him to put forward any personal suggestion. The rupture between Italy and Turkey thus took place without any particular reason or hostility on either side. I do not know if pressure to bring this about was exercised by the Allies at Rome, but there was no ill feeling of any kind at Constantinople.

The night before the Italian departure, Garroni, after dining with Bedri, the Prefect of Police, and Pallavicini, the Austrian Ambassador, embraced them and they wept in each other's arms. When the Italian Embassy left next day, the scene at the railway station resembled a wedding more than it did a declaration of war. A company of Turkish soldiers was drawn up as a guard of honour, and everyone embraced, for Latins enjoy displaying an emotion which in English-speaking countries has ceased to be fashionable since Nelson gave his dying kiss. Colonel Mombelli, a good friend who was military attaché and afterwards commanded the Italian Army in Macedonia, somewhat to my embarrassment kissed me on both cheeks before he boarded the train.

My wife, who was worn out by the strain of Constantinople, needed a change, and Garroni kindly offered to take her to Italy. She left with the departing Embassy and hardly had she gone when she regretted her decision. In vain the Ambassador tried to convince her that she had been wise to leave and predicted imminent massacres and incendiarism in Constantinople, an argument which made her more than ever regret having left me. The Italians were obliged to wait a few days at the then Bulgarian port of Dedéagatch for the ship which was to fetch them. Instead of the luxurious vessel which they expected, their government had despatched an old freighter that had been used for the transport of prisoners in the Libyan War and which, with no cargo aboard, rode uncomfortably high above the water. My wife, still torn between the wish to go and the regret at having left, felt a little ashamed to return, but allowed herself to be coaxed on board by a Secretary who admitted that he was most anxious for her company, as the presence of an American would constitute a protection from German submarines. But when she stepped on the deck of the ship, she broke down and insisted on being put ashore at once. She returned to the convent at Dedéagatch where she had stayed and telegraphed me that if nothing stood in the way she would return to Constantinople. The difficulty was her French maid, for enemy subjects could only enter Turkey by special permission from the Minister of War. I tried my best to hasten the necessary arrangements and sent her three urgent wires not to start before these could be completed. But Enver was then absent from the capital, and no one else dared to assume the responsibility of allowing a French maid to imperil the safety of Turkey. So I wired her to exercise patience, not wishing to mention that, in the Ambassador's opinion, the arrangements would need at least a fortnight to complete.

At four o'clock on the morning of the third day, I was awakened by someone entering my bedroom door, and to my amazement saw my wife enter the room, not a little annoyed because no one had been sent to meet her at the station. She was just as astonished to find that I did not expect her as I was to see her, for neither of us had received each other's urgent telegrams. The method which she adopted to get round the stringent official regulations, of which she knew nothing, had been simple but effective. She had called on the Turkish Consul at Dedéagatch. His office hours began at nine in the evening and he was out when she arrived, but she found his children in his office and had played with them. When the Consul returned she complimented him on their remarkable beauty till he beamed with pleasure, and then related to him that she had been honoured by the Sultan with the order of the Shefekat. After some more talk of this nature, when they had made friends, she produced the passports, and he raised no difficulty in visaeing that of her French maid. Next morning at the Turkish frontier a woman inspector entered the railway carriage and asked to see her papers. My wife produced some medical prescriptions which anywhere else would have been regarded as highly suspicious, but which the woman could not read. The female inspector drew down the blinds and announced that she proposed to search her, whereupon my wife threatened to slap her face if she tried. The rest of the journey was uneventful, and at four in the morning, in defiance of every Turkish war regulation, she arrived at Constantinople with her French maid.

I hesitate to speak of one of the great dramas of the war which was then being acted at Gallipoli, little more than a hundred miles away. Of the drama itself, although so close, I had only indirect and belated knowledge. Civilians in wartime are like listeners to a radio description of a football match, except that, whereas the match is accurately described, military operations rarely are. Such experiences as I had during the wearisome months of depression I have already described in a diary which was published in 1917, when America entered the war,* after cutting out from its pages any references which might have compromised friends who were still in Turkey.

It was hard enough in wartime for a civilian to keep up his spirits in an atmosphere where everyone felt in sympathy, but in Constantinople I was made painfully aware that Turkey was an enemy country. The news of the April landing, with the prospect of the Allies breaking through, had momentarily lifted this depression. No one, least of all the Turks, believed their own war bulletins, and for this reason the early reports of the fighting at the Dardanelles seemed less depressing, for I was persuaded that the announcements of Turkish victories were only the customary subterfuges given out to conceal defeats. At that stage of the campaign, all those who were of Allied sympathy in Constantinople, and probably many Turks and Germans, were convinced that it was merely a question of time before the British would break through, and the apparent confidence displayed by the officials did not shake this belief. Turkish officers later told me that they felt somewhat apprehensive at the beginning, when they did not know the effect which the fire of big naval guns and the bombing from aeroplanes

* *Inside Constantinople* (London, Murray, 1917). *L.E.*

would produce on their men, who were still unaccustomed to these engines of war.

Much has been written about the opportunities neglected at Gallipoli, but in spite of reports to the contrary, only once during the fighting at Suvla did the Turks actually run out of ammunition for twenty-four hours. I profess no competence to discuss the strategy of this campaign, but still recall a suggestive plan which a Levantine outlined to me of how the original attack could have been made. His idea was that two thousand carpenters should first have been sent to Cyprus to put up barracks for two hundred thousand men, with the strictest orders that no one would be allowed to leave the island. Naturally the news would have leaked through to the Turks, and almost certainly have led to their distributing the greater portion of their army around the Gulf of Alexandretta, in the expectation that England was planning to cut off Syria. Once this military concentration had been effected, the attack on the Dardanelles would have come as a much more likely surprise.

As it was, no campaign was ever better advertised at the wrong moment and in the wrong way, and no defence was ever given more time to prepare. The effectives which the Turks could put in the field were estimated in England as being 150,000 men at Gallipoli, and as many more between the Straits and Constantinople. Could it reasonably be expected that a numerically inferior number of troops, however gallant, as soon as they had lost the element of initial surprise, would be able to drive out a superior enemy from a series of strongly defended positions in which they could easily be reinforced? When one considers the enormous casualties inflicted by a single, well-concealed platoon of Turks on the splendid men of the 29th Division at the time of their landing, one feels at a loss to know whether to be more amazed by the audacity of this desperate enterprise or its seemingly unnecessary nature. The argument used in its justification, that if it had been successful it would have shortened the war, is no truer than the reverse, that the dismal and costly failure of the Dardanelles, in spite of many heroic memories, unquestionably prolonged it.

Why it was ever made without the certainty of being able to dispose of a far greater number of trained effectives than the Allies could count on at that time, I have never understood, for the Turks were the only Central Power who, left to themselves, could not have been dangerous.

Always stubborn fighters in any defensive position, they were notoriously too weak for any offensive, whether against the Suez Canal, where the difficulties of transport were far too great for their resources, or in the snows of the Caucasus, where they already had lost an army and where, even if successful, they could have done little harm. Turkey was then cut off from Germany except by the most precarious communication. If half the effort expended at Gallipoli could have been despatched, in time, to Salonika, it would have kept Bulgaria from entering on the side of the Central Powers, secured her as an ally, and maintained the Serbian front intact with which to threaten Hungary, help Roumania, and connect with Russia.

The psychology of war develops a kind of fatalism among civilians who subscribe to its hardships, partly because they cannot do otherwise, and also because they feel ashamed of how small these are when compared with the dangers that are undergone in the trenches. A resigned fatalism fitted easily into the Turkish character and made up for the absence of the feverish patriotism which prevailed in all Western lands. Few Turks had their heart in the war, and I could discern little feeling among those I knew either of hatred for the Allies or of sympathy for the Germans. In spite of bulletins of official praise for their soldiers' heroism, I greatly doubt if any real enthusiasm existed. The wounded, whom occasionally I saw in the hospitals, seemed in their Oriental way resigned to suffer, without the satisfaction of having done their bit which one noticed in Western countries. My Turkish friends whose relatives were at the Dardanelles openly commiserated with their hard lot. Many Turks would have been delighted to see the British fleet enter the Golden Horn, and the entire Christian population would then have gone wild with joy. A reign of terror kept down any expression of Allied sympathy, and people were arrested and tried secretly before military courts, often in ignorance of their supposed offence. In spite of the announced victories, I saw no sign of any real exultation, and such demonstrations as took place were ordered by official command. One hardly knew even the names of the principal generals, and I for one never heard until considerably later of Mustapha Kemal. I would often watch reinforcements on their way to the front march silently through the streets of Constantinople without any of the gaiety of the British Tommy, or the set resolution of the French. There was no elation before a prospect of terror, and only a placid and submissive obedience. Once I saw a few thousand Arabs, freshly drafted from their villages, march through Pera at night, looking more like Biblical herdsmen than modern soldiers. They wore rags, for they had not yet received uniforms, and their general appearance was one of sheer misery.

The position of a neutral diplomat in a country at war is not a happy one when all his sympathies lie on the other side. He is an object of suspicion, and he is obliged to keep a bridle on his tongue and be careful whom he sees, in order not to endanger friends whose personal security may be less great than his own. Worst of all, he feels the smallness of his effort and the difficulty of accomplishing anything of real utility. I had been profoundly unhappy in Constantinople during all these tragic events. Also, the protection of Allied interests had gradually subsided into a routine which left one with not even the illusion of being any longer of use. There was no special reason for my remaining, and it was evident that Bulgaria would shortly enter the war. Sofia had become the new point of interest, and I hoped to be sent there when I left Constantinople in the middle of September 1915.

# 7. *Sofia during the War*

Bulgaria remained neutral and seemingly undecided during the first year of the war. In order to hide his real plans until the moment was ripe, Czar Ferdinand, who in August 1915 had signed an agreement with Germany, still appeared to many a month later to flirt with the idea of coming in on the side of the Entente. The supposed indecision of the Czar's tortuous policy had encouraged a kind of auction by both sides, in which the Allies acted more or less as unconscious dupes. Whenever French emissaries arrived at Sofia to visit Ferdinand, he would boast to them of his Bourbon blood and enjoy watching the satisfaction of his visitors when he made them believe that he was loyal to his French ancestors. The call of Henry of Navarre heard across three centuries would have made a touching story if Bulgaria had entered on the side of the Entente, but, as the contrary happened, this tribute was promptly forgotten.

The bidding for Bulgarian support was flattering to the vanity of certain Sofia politicians and not unremunerative to others. The Czar had at that time some two million pounds on deposit in London and made it a condition that, whatever happened, Germany had to guarantee this amount before he was willing to join the Central Powers. Also, England and France resorted to certain questionable financial tactics in order to create what was euphemistically described as a current of sympathy for the Entente. From Paris and London some million gold francs then flowed into the pockets of a considerable number of Bulgarian politicians who were requested to purchase wheat with the proceeds and asked to store the corn indefinitely wherever they liked. At Sofia, when the news of this leaked out, it was current gossip that many parliamentarians who suddenly became grain merchants might even, in that agrarian land, have found it difficult to distinguish a blade of wheat from a sheaf of barley. It was particularly unfortunate that the French financial delegate who took charge of this delicate operation neglected, even after the rupture of diplomatic relations, to take away with him the receipts for this expenditure, which he kept locked in his safe. Hardly had the Entente missions left Bulgaria when the Prime Minister, M. Radoslavoff, ordered the safe to be broken open and used its contents to bring out the turpitude of his opponents; political purists at Sofia considered it somewhat less sporting on the part of the Prime Minister to publish only the receipts of his political enemies and conceal the signatures of his friends. Certain of these latter soon afterwards conveniently left the country in Radoslavoff's company when he went on a visit to Berlin.

In the Balkans, the Great War meant primarily a knockout fight between Bulgaria and Serbia. A vindictive resentment left over from the Second Balkan War had created the belief that the peninsula was not large enough to contain two small Slav states and that one or the other would have to disappear. Two circumstances stood, however, in the way of giving too early an expression to this destructive conviction. The first was the British at the Dardanelles; the second was the Russians, who at that time were still holding the crests of the Carpathians. So long as the Russian Czar's armies threatened to descend on the Hungarian plain, the Bulgars would never have moved. Only after the English failure at Gallipoli became evident, and the Russians had been dislodged from the mountains, did Ferdinand's belief in the victory of German arms develop into a certainty. The Macedonian tail had often before wagged the Bulgarian dog, but Sofia as a first dividend intended to rake off a little to the southeast, for one effect of her intervention had been to guarantee Turkey's exposed flank from danger and allow Constantinople to look forward to an uninterrupted communication with Berlin. The Turks did their best to stave off compensation in return for such benefits, and made some lavish promises for the future, but the Bulgars insisted on getting their pound of flesh before they consented to move.

The difficult negotiations between two parties who had always been enemies, and who distrusted each other profoundly, were skilfully conducted by Baron von Neurath, the Counsellor at Constantinople, who later became German Minister for Foreign Affairs, to finish his career before the Nuremberg Court, and Colonel von Leipzig, a man of great personal charm, who was the German military attaché at Constantinople, and whose accidental death during these parleys, in a small Turkish railway station, led to some sinister conjectures. The price agreed on was the cession by the Turks of a strip of territory which ran to the sea along the right bank of the Maritza River. Negotiations between Balkan powers are rarely marked by any excessive confidence in each other's word, and those between Bulgaria and Turkey, although engineered and guaranteed by Germany, were no exception to this rule. It was, for instance, stipulated that as soon as the Bulgarian notice of mobilization had been publicly announced, the Turkish Minister was to report this fact by telegraph, after which a protocol between the two countries was immediately to be signed, and the steps preliminary to the cession of territory could then take place. The call to arms was in fact posted at midnight early in September on a kiosk of the boulevard at Sofia. As soon as this had been officially recorded by the Turkish Minister and telegraphed to the frontier, this notice was torn down, as the Bulgars needed a little more time in order to prepare their mobilization. All this was in strict accordance with the agreement, though certain Allied diplomats were even then not yet convinced. The pact to enter on the side of the Central Powers was kept a secret till the last possible moment, and the actual surrender of Turkish territory to Bulgaria only took place as arranged on the opening day of hostilities.

Later, at Sofia, I heard of a pathetic incident which occurred as a result of this negotiation. An Armenian family with several small children had miraculously been saved from the massacres in the interior and, disguised as Turks, after living for five months in continuous danger and having many hairbreadth escapes, had found means to reach Constantinople. They pretended to be Turkish emigrant settlers, and as such had taken the train for Adrianople. In order to reach this city, the railway track crossed the Maritza River and traversed a strip of land which as a consequence of the cession had become Bulgarian territory. The Armenian calculation was based on this circumstance, and as soon as the train stopped for a moment at the junction which had just become Bulgarian soil, they leaped out, feeling that at last they were safe from their long nightmare. To their horror, the Bulgarian authorities informed them that it was illegal for them to remain without proper papers and that they would have to be deported back to Turkey. This meant death for the Armenians, who carried poison with them and declared that they would first kill their children and then themselves sooner than return to the hell from which they had just escaped. After some discussion, the matter was referred to Sofia. An American traveller who had witnessed this pathetic scene described it to me as soon as he reached the capital. I went at once to the Foreign Office to intercede for the poor wretches. I never knew if this was necessary, but the Armenians were permitted to remain.

My own appointment to Bulgaria came as a surprise after leaving Constantinople. I had gone to Scotland, and was actually on the grouse moors at Yester when a man on horseback rode up to my butt with a cable from the Secretary of State, asking me to proceed at once to Sofia in order to open an office in that capital for the protection of the Entente interests. Washington had been requested to look after these, but the State Department began by showing some reluctance. When at last it was prepared to take them over, the protection of these interests had already been given to Holland and, not without some difficulty, Great Britain recalled hers from the Dutch on the plea of an old regulation providing that whenever England was at war the United States should be asked to look after British nationals.

I left Yester that same night and for the second time within a month I recrossed Europe. At Bucharest, I enjoyed a talk with the brilliant Take Jonēscu, the leader of the Roumanian Ententophiles, who gave me a cheery warning that, for every two words I should hear at Sofia, three would be lies. Next day I crossed the Danube at Roustchouk, and entered a country which already bore the marks of war. The windows of the railway carriages were painted white in order to prevent passengers from looking out. Travellers were not even permitted to leave the train to stretch their legs at the interminable stops. Late at night, when I arrived to open the mission at Sofia, I could not even find a porter to carry my luggage.

At Bucharest, I had called on the Bulgarian Minister, who for my benefit drew the picture of an imaginary Macedonian attempting to return to his home only to find the way barred by a Senegalese Negro who kept him out in the name of the principle of nationality. This image was much more striking than true, for the Senegalese who were sent to Salonika had arrived only in time for the retreat. As usual, the Allies came too late. The unfortunate Serbs, buoyed up by hopes never fulfilled, had pathetically erected triumphal arches at Nisch to welcome a support which was always reported as imminent, but had failed to come in time. The Serbs, surprised by an overwhelming offensive which was revealed only at the last moment, had to yield before the double flanking movement of Germans and Austrians, descending from the north, and two Bulgarian armies pressing on them from the east. To avoid being surrounded, they abandoned their country in a heroic but terrible starvation march across the Albanian mountains to the sea, where the tracks over which their army passed were littered by their dead. Meanwhile at Sofia I read every day the victorious Bulgarian war bulletins, which began by announcing the capture of innumerable bathtubs sent by the American Red Cross, and ended by announcing the capture of motor cars, without mentioning that these had been thrown into the bottom of a deep ravine when the Serb retreating army was about to enter the Albanian wilderness. On everyone's lips at Sofia one heard the words *Finis Serbiae.* It was generally supposed that that small kingdom would be carved up between Hungary, Montenegro, and Bulgaria. Even the Serbian Legation at Sofia was seized by the Bulgarians, on the ground that it had belonged to a country which existed no more.

To the credit of the Bulgarian people, the victory over their neighbour did not seem to fill them with any particular elation, and the nearest approach which I saw to public rejoicing was a police-organized manifestation held after the capture of Nisch. Later, when Monastir fell, a procession of school children, headed by a regimental band, marched by my hotel playing the song of hate, but it needed no practised eye to see that there was nothing spontaneous in this demonstration and that its real purpose was only to emphasize the Bulgarian claim to that city. Every day the official press repeated the hackneyed phrases about how their dead heroes would rise from their graves unless they retained these conquests, which meant only that the Bulgarian government proposed to grab everything they could. In spite of a succession of alleged victories which were principally rear-guard actions, I could detect no real feeling of rejoicing. Perhaps the population preserved too vivid a recollection of their tragic experiences in the Second Balkan War, but there was also a good deal of latent Slav sympathy for the Serbs.

The principal monument at Sofia is that of Alexander of Russia, the Czar Liberator, to whom the country owed its independence from the Turks, and many Bulgars hated the idea of finding themselves allies of the Sultan against the White Czar. I understood how deep was the discomfort of this feeling when a Bulgar told me, with every mark of approval, that some Russian prisoners who passed through Sofia had flatly refused to work, declaring that their fathers had shed their blood to free Bulgaria and that they would not slave for the sons of men whom they had liberated. General Fitcheff, the former Chief of Staff, resigned sooner than fight, and General Dimitrieff left Bulgaria to take service in the Russian army. The former Prime Minister, Mr. Guechoff, whom I saw frequently, made no secret to me of his Entente sympathies and threw the blame for his country's participation on the absence of statesmanship. He took pride in showing me a room in his house in which the Balkan Alliance had been signed. Bulgarian intervention had now destroyed Guechoff's work. More than once he repeated what was evidently a favourite phrase of his, "From us peasants of the Danube one cannot expect statesmanship, but there is also a dearth of this in England, France, and Russia." This was a polite way of intimating that if timely concessions had been made in Macedonia, Bulgaria would have kept out of the war.

Until I arrived, there had never been a permanent American Legation at Sofia, and my first duty was to find an office. This was extremely difficult, but I was able to rent two rooms at the Hotel de Bulgarie, which maintained a high Balkan standard of discomfort although it was the best hotel in the place. Such articles as boots placed outside my bedroom door at night would never be seen again, braces disappeared from my trousers, and I met with other flattering attentions to the choice of my wardrobe. A single bathroom was regarded as sufficient for the wants of the many guests, and usually six German soldiers slept in this, who were considerate enough to leave at the hour of my ablutions and allow me to approach the tub through an entanglement of spiked helmets and rifles. This hour was also convenient to the police agents, who usually selected it to inspect the contents of my desk.

The Ministry of War was across the street, and from my windows I could watch the sentries pace up and down in front of it. The sidewalk of this government building was strictly forbidden to passersby, lest they should feel inclined to throw bombs through the windows, a precaution which did not save the Minister of War from later being killed by one exploding during a service in the Cathedral. Four times every day I was obliged to give this pavement a wide berth on my way to the Club for meals. Even this short walk was not without some excitement. Once I saw two men lying dead in the street outside the Opera House, which was just beyond the Ministry. They had killed each other, for similar spectacles were not unusual in a capital where hatred was fierce and political passion ran to excess.

The Roumanian envoy, Derussi, who afterwards became Minister for Foreign Affairs, would often ask me, after dining at the Club, to walk back with him to his Legation, as he feared that an attempt would be made on his life. I suggested that in case of a mistaken identity the consequences might be awkward for me, but my company seemed to reassure him and Derussi was an excellent companion. Safe in his office, he would entertain me by playing Viennese waltzes and afterwards, as a return, I would help him to cipher messages to Bucharest. A declaration of war with Roumania did not seem far off, and at the Foreign Office Derussi would jokingly be warmed by the Under Secretary, Kosseff, that on the outbreak of hostilities they proposed to confine him in a small Balkan village for the duration of the war. This would lead to the retort that the Bulgarian Minister at Bucharest was to be interned at Sinaia* and properly debauched by his dissolute countrymen. After more exchanges of similar pleasantry, the Under Secretary suggested that it would be better to "manufacture" friendship between the two countries, and he promised, in that case, to close the little grocer's shop opposite the Roumanian Legation from which spies kept watch on every visitor. The tension between the two countries was already at fever pitch when news came that two Roumanians had been arrested, in suspicious circumstances, on the Bulgarian shore of the Danube. The strange explanation the prisoners offered was that they were trying to catch frogs for the table of Sir George Barclay, the British Minister at Bucharest; this seemed unconvincing, but happened to be true; even in wartime, George Barclay remained an epicure.

The Bulgarian Premier, Dr. Radoslavoff, was also Minister for Foreign Affairs, a circumstance which instead of facilitating diplomatic business rendered it more difficult, for that statesman was never to be found at the Ministry. The usual explanations given for his customary absences would have led one to believe that high dignitaries in Sofia spent most of their time in Turkish baths while their country was at

* A Roumanian town close to the Hungarian border at Predeal and a favorite resort for Bucharest's social elite in the late nineteenth century. A monastery at Sinaia was a residence of the Roumanian royal family.

war. The shadow of the crescent was very noticeable in dealing with Bulgarian officials, though in his personal appearance Dr. Radoslavoff resembled neither a Turk nor a Bulgar. His long, dark, silky beard made him look not unlike a Greek Orthodox priest in mufti, and his enormous head overweighed a rather small, corpulent body which rested on diminutive and carefully shod feet. The suspicious overrefinement of his manners approached the genteel and contrasted sharply with the more stolid peasant rusticity displayed by most of his countrymen. The Prime Minister seemed to spring from another stock and his ways, instead of being bucolically crude, were mellifluously suave. His language was surprisingly moderate, and like a Grand Vizier he employed the Turkish trick of professing to feel an inordinate personal distress at having to refuse any request. To his credit, I will say that after the Cabinet decided as a reprisal to retain all the English in Bulgaria, he allowed them to leave freely without exacting any conditions, but this consent was given me during the honeymoon of our relations. Until I later fell from favour, I had found him conciliatory, seemingly friendly, and amiably responsive to whatever I asked. In the Balkans, the idea of truth is somewhat at variance from the standard of Western lands, and only exceptionally was any credence ever given to Dr. Radoslavoff's polite assurances. As soon as I attempted to have these in writing, I discovered that my courteous and urgent notes, intended to remind him of our conversation, were not often honoured by a reply, and my perfectly innocent requests would afterwards be represented by him as the most preposterous and outrageous demands.

The Secretary General, Mr. Kosseff, who was acting head of the Bulgarian Foreign Office, had obtained his early training for diplomacy by selling corn behind a stand in the marketplace at Roustchouk. He was an elusive and argumentative official, with piercing black eyes which would cast on me a glance as little benign as any I have ever observed. One of our Red Cross commissioners was so struck by the unaltruistic nature of his expression that he wanted to obtain his photograph in order to take it back to America to offer as a specimen of what the Balkans could produce. Kosseff was Radoslavoff's right-hand man, for the Prime Minister knew that his Secretary General could be relied upon never to embarrass him by complying with even the simplest request. As soon as Kosseff's confidence in victory increased, his demeanour also became more arrogant. At one time he attempted to prevent my using the English language to correspond with other Americans in Bulgaria. This was probably owing to the difficulty in the Post Office of reading my letters. I protested that this was going beyond the limits of any restrictions attempted in Turkey. The mere suggestion that anything Bulgarian could be like anything Turkish infuriated him, for he hated the Turks even more than he did me, so that I had no need for any further argument on that score.

A number of our missionaries who had resided for many years in Bulgaria and felt only the most disinterested friendship for a country to which they had devoted their lives discovered, to their sorrow, the growth of a new feeling of official hostility toward everything American. The old sentimental ties of association with Robert College had suddenly snapped, and any traces of gratitude for the helpful sympathy of the United States given during the First Balkan War were conveniently forgotten. Bulgarian officialdom in 1915 and 1916 regarded us as enemies who did not have the manliness to come out into the open, and German influence helped actively to pin suspicion on everything American. The haphazard, half-Oriental administration at Sofia yielded submissively to any suggestion from Berlin, and as it felt unequal to its task owing to the strain imposed by war conditions, it was forced, even more than the Turkish had been, to accept the consequences of Teutonic superiority. Little by little, the Germans occupied the principal strategic points in the country. They dominated the Bulgarian police; they took over the management of the railways and increased immensely their transport capacity. Through a "Committee of Purchases," whose consent was required before a single car could be moved, they controlled the entire export trade. Banks and commerce, sanitary and hospital services fell under their direction. At Sofia, most of the Legation wires were handed to me on forms printed *Deutsches Reich.*

Czar Ferdinand delivered Bulgaria to the Germans, not out of any personal sympathy but because confidence in their victory and ambition caused him to make the second great mistake of his career. His people followed, not because they loved him or trusted his leadership but only because the lines of political cleavage were so evenly drawn in Bulgaria that the Crown became the arbiter when it came to the final decision.

I saw Ferdinand, at the opening of Parliament, walk, with an arrogant look, through the Agrarian Centre, which kept an icy silence as if to mark its disapproval. Its leader, Stambulitzky, who afterwards was tortured before he was murdered, was then locked up in prison. In his speech from the throne, the Czar dwelt on having been obliged to send his armies into Serbia in order to end the sufferings of their brethren and expel the French, and the British who, to the shame of civilization, had entered Macedonia. The packed government majority rose to cheer his words; only the Agrarians kept their seats in dead silence. The frigid attitude of these red-sashed peasant deputies was most impressive. When the Czar had finished, he kissed the ring of the Metropolitan, shook hands with Radoslavoff, and completely ignored the remainder of the Cabinet. After Ferdinand had left the Chamber, Orthodox priests in rich gold vestments pronounced the benediction and chanted deep-toned Slavic liturgies.

Czar Ferdinand, whose portrait in the robes of a canonized Byzantine emperor adorned Bulgarian postage stamps and, executed in mosaic, decorated the walls of the Sofia Cathedral, was less saintly in his feeling than in the taste of his attire. He hated England, it was commonly said in Bulgarian Court circles, because at a coronation he had been forced to sit in the same carriage with two Indian rajahs. He hated diplomats and particularly the Austrian Minister, Count Tarnowski, who had a charming wife and the only agreeable house in Sofia, probably because the Count was too clever for him. The Czar could be most engaging when he wished, and as he wanted to show his dislike to the Minister he would go out of his way to shower favours on his Counsellor, Baron Mittag. The latter was often invited to the Palace, and one day he found Ferdinand reclining on his divan, looking the picture of misery. The Counsellor politely enquired about the state of his health; the Czar replied that his suffering was not physical but due to his moral isolation. The Austrian suggested that His Majesty might find agreeable relaxation in frequenting the charming society of Sofia. The Czar curtly replied that his subjects were all uncouth boors, an opinion which he was fond of expressing, to the embarrassment of foreign guests to whom he would describe graphically how they would throw stalks of asparagus on the carpet at Court banquets. The Counsellor suggested that His Majesty might find pleasure in exchanging ideas with certain of the more cultivated diplomats. "Diplomats," retorted Ferdinand, "are either vile intriguers or half-wits," thus leaving the

Counsellor in some doubt as to his own classification. Sometimes the Czar got as good as he gave. Once he taunted an Italian Minister, as famous for his avarice as for his wit, on the antiquity of a particularly shabby fur coat which the latter was in the habit of wearing. "Yes, Sire," came the quick retort, "it is even older than your kingdom."

I knew that Ferdinand had refused to grant audiences to neutral diplomats at this time, and not wishing to meet with a rebuff he had administered to certain of my colleagues, I refrained from asking to be received. Naturally I made no effort to see Queen Eleanor. Shortly before the outbreak of the war, an American Minister to the Balkans, on his own initiative, had invited the Queen of Bulgaria to visit the United States. The Queen accepted, but as soon as Washington was apprized of this, the envoy had been directed to recall his invitation. I was therefore taken aback when an aide-de-camp called one morning to tell me that Her Majesty was surprised at my having neglected to solicit an audience, all the more so as she had heard that the Czar felt a great personal sympathy for me. The aide-de-camp suggested that I should call on the Grand Mistress of the Court to request an audience. I offered my apologies for this unintentional remissness on my part and hastened to pay the visit. Next day, in a letter addressed to me as "Dear Madame," the Russian Grand Mistress of the Court wrote to say that the Queen would be pleased to receive me.

Princess Eleanor of Reuss, a middle-aged spinster of plain appearance, had arrived at Sofia from her small German principality to marry the widowed Czar. She was full of admirable intentions, but misfortunes fell on Bulgaria soon after her arrival, and popular gossip attributed these to the ill luck which she brought. The Czar showed himself quite as indifferent to her virtues as to her looks, and seemed to take a special pleasure in thwarting her benevolent wishes. The devotion she would have loved to tender him as wife and queen went to waste, and she was left an unhappy and a lonely woman, with nothing beyond a royal crown and an ardent wish to do good. She did this inconspicuously and bravely. In the wild Balkans, a German queen, at no little risk to herself and out of her private purse, gave five thousand francs to relieve some of the wants of British prisoners.

Queen Eleanor's personal experiences as a nurse during the Russo-Japanese War were responsible for her taking a keen interest in hospital work. She intended to found a training school at Sofia, and had brought over for this purpose a highly capable American nurse named Helen Hay, who enjoyed her confidence and her friendship. After the Queen discovered that I had not been received by the Czar, she changed the place for my audience from the Palace to a house she had lent to Miss Hay, which was situated in a small street on the outskirts of Sofia. Only the principal thoroughfares of that capital were paved, and the wheels of my carriage slithered uneasily through deep ruts of Balkan mud which forced me to step out at every puddle to avoid being bespattered. The coachman, who had begun by nodding assent to my direction, did not know the address, and neither my knowledge of Bulgarian nor of Sofia topography was sufficient to enlighten him. At last I identified the house, which was of a type common to every American small town, by seeing a car with the royal arms standing before the door. I rang the bell, embarrassed at arriving late for the audience after having been remiss in asking for it. A plain and simply dressed middle-aged woman, wearing glasses and with a pleasant smile, opened it and by way of introduction said to me in English with a German accent, "I'm the Queen!" She invited me to follow her into Miss Hay's room, where my compatriot lay ill in bed suffering from a rheumatic attack. The Queen then produced a pat of butter, remarking that in wartime one brought butter, which was far rarer than roses, to an invalid. She sat down to make tea, and for an hour we chatted pleasantly about the lighter sides of war.

Queen Eleanor possessed the well-bred woman's gift of putting her guest at ease. She was a kindly soul with simple dignity, and many were the teachers and governesses who counted her as a friend and never appealed to her in vain. One of our missionaries, for instance, in order to evade the censorship, felt no hesitation to address a letter in the Queen's care for her to forward abroad. I doubt if his expedient was successful, for when I left Bulgaria the Queen asked me to post a letter for her in England, which was seized by an official at the German frontier and only returned to me, some weeks later, with an apology. At Easter, I received from her a small enamelled egg bearing her monogram with a crown. The year following I learned, with regret, that she had died alone and unlamented by her subjects, just as she had lived a lonely and unhappy existence in the land over which she was supposed to reign.

With the advance of the armies of the Central Powers, American doctors and nurses, driven from hospitals in the war zone, kept arriving at Sofia, usually with only Serbian money on their persons which no one would change except at a fraction of its value. All of them had adventures to relate. Thus a surgeon from Buffalo, named Dr. Boddy, with two American women nurses, had defended a hospital at Nisch from a drunken mob of stragglers during the anxious hours which had passed between the evacuation of that city by the Serbs and the entrance of the Bulgars. The surgeon had armed his nurses with broomsticks to guard the doors at either end of the hospital, while he acted as a strategic reserve. He told me this story humorously, but the risk that these three ran was real, for Balkan comedy is never far removed from tragedy. The doctor also related another experience which took place at Nisch and illuminated me on an aspect of Balkan racial hatreds. When the Bulgarian commander entered the town, he had sent for the American surgeon to ask him how many beds he could dispose of for his wounded. "Four hundred," the general was told. As I knew that there were many wounded Serbs at this hospital, I wondered how he had been able to provide for these, and with some misgiving I asked how many Serb wounded he had to look after.

"Four hundred."
"What happened to them?"

The doctor's solution was so brilliantly simple that I never would have guessed it. In the bed of every Serb he had placed a Bulgar, and these wounded enemies got on splendidly together.

Military occupation by the Central Powers put an end to the Allied and American medical missions in Serbia. An important one, headed by Lady Muriel Paget, arrived from Usküb, with an enormous staff of surgeons and nurses. In that typhus-infested district, her hospital had been so well managed that many Bulgars thought it would be a good idea to keep her as a prisoner for the duration of the war in order to run a hospital for them, and they gave as a reason that she had looked after many of their wounded with great devotion. The fact that certain of her orderlies were of military age provided an excuse for this plan. In difficult circumstances, Lady Muriel Paget showed much tact and refrained from pressing for rights which, if asserted too vehemently, would have certainly been denied. The decision hung in suspense for nearly a fortnight, and the authorization for her and her hospital to leave came only in the nick of time. Hardly were they out of the country and safe in Roumania before many of the Bulgars already regretted their generosity.

The excellent work performed by the American Red Cross in Serbia was stopped by the occupation, just when the need for relief was greatest, as many of the inhabitants were then literally starving. I went to enlist the help of Mr. Guechoff, who was President of the Bulgarian Red Cross, and suggested to him that Americans and Bulgars should undertake this jointly, an idea which appealed to him. On our side, the Red Cross asked only for a representative to remain at Nisch, in charge of their stores, who would pledge himself not to go outside the town, and allow the actual distribution to be carried out solely by Bulgars. Even this was impossible to obtain, and the military had the effrontery to suggest that all our Red Cross supplies should be turned over to them.

After the Serbian army had been driven into the Albanian mountains, a few bands of irregulars left in the hills managed to carry on a guerilla warfare. How they obtained provisions was a mystery explained in one instance when the Bulgars discovered that a Serbian peasant woman had been in the habit of crossing their lines at night, in order to bring food to her compatriots. To prevent a repetition of the offence, they cut off her leg. Years afterwards her exploit was related to Marshal Franchet d'Esperey, who commanded the victorious army which in 1918 brought about the Bulgar capitulation and who was then revisiting the scene of his triumph. The story of this simple peasant brought tears to the Marshal's eyes. He became enthusiastic on the importance of recording such deeds for future generations to admire, and urged that the woman should be proclaimed a national heroine, revered as a Serbian Joan of Arc. It was a little hard to have to inform the Marshal that this heroine had since been doing a flourishing business in her country district as the principal prostitute.

A party of American nurses and surgeons arrived at Sofia from Monastir, bringing with them a young Albanian girl educated at the American College for Women at Constantinople, whom they were eager to take to the United States in order to train as a nurse. This meant salvation for the girl, but as she was without papers of any kind, it was impossible for her to travel throughout wartime Europe. Her legal nationality was still uncertain, and to get to America she was ready to call herself anything. Her status was a typical Balkan puzzle. She had been born an Ottoman subject at Monastir, at a time when that town was still under the Sultan's rule, but my Turkish colleague whom I approached on her behalf insisted on having proof of birth before he would issue her a passport, and this could only be obtained at Constantinople, if at all, after a long delay. The Bulgarian Foreign Office also refused to issue her papers, as the future status of Monastir, which had belonged to three different countries in as many years, was still in doubt. No Albanian government as yet existed in spite of a gentleman who had lately called on me to request my intercession at the White House for the recognition of a republic which he hoped to establish on a mixed basis of scientific experts and tribal chieftains. In the last resort, there was the Ministry of the Interior at Sofia. They may have regarded my request as indicating an American recognition of their sovereignty; perhaps they wished merely to be obliging. At all events, the Minister of the Interior issued the girl a passport which everyone else had denied.

This solved only half the difficulty. It was easy to get an Albanian girl into neutral Switzerland, but beyond lay France where her Bulgarian passport would make her an enemy who would be interned as soon as she crossed the frontier. So I called on my Greek colleague, who was all the more friendly to me because of a recent success I had in resisting the Bulgars. After explaining the facts to him, I remarked that Monastir was only a few miles from the Hellenic border, on the other side of which lay the Grecian town of Florina. The girl, it is true, had been born at Monastir, but she might just as easily have seen the light at Florina. The Minister assented to this. Why not suppose that she had been born at Florina, in which case she would be entitled to a Hellenic passport? The Greek was intelligent, well disposed, and above everything he hated the Bulgars. He put only one question to me—was she a nice girl? It was unnecessary to enquire what particular value he attached to niceness, or if his interest was based on aesthetic or on moral grounds. I assured him that she was nice. He asked no further questions and merely remarked that it would be a pity to see a nice girl left as a Bulgarian—far better make of her a Greek. Perhaps he saw in her a new triumph for Hellenism; perhaps he wanted only to oblige me; but he immediately made out a Greek passport in her name, which was despatched by diplomatic bag to Berne, where she found it later. To Switzerland, the girl journeyed as a Bulgar; then, as a Greek, she crossed France and entered America. I have heard that she has since become the first native trained nurse in Albania.

The Allies, from the time that they landed at Salonika, had been worried by the consuls of the Central Powers reporting on all their military movements. At last they took a natural, though illegal, course —for Greece was then a neutral—of arresting and embarking them aboard a man-of-war for an unknown destination. Of the four Central Powers, the only ones to make reprisals were the Bulgars. A French Consul and an English Vice-Consul named Hurst had remained behind at Sofia to look after the property of their respective legations. On January 1st, 1916, when the news came about the Salonika incident, orders were issued by the Bulgarian government to arrest both these officials. The Frenchman was promptly incarcerated, but before I knew anything of a proposed arrest I had already sent for Hurst, who owed his escape to this circumstance. At the very moment that the news came of what had happened, the English Vice-Consul walked into my rooms at the hotel. As he had heard nothing, I told him to wait. I walked over to the Bulgarian Foreign Office and asked to see the Secretary General, Kosseff. This was our conversation:

*I.* "There's a rumour about that Hurst is to be arrested. I hope it isn't true."

*K.* (*dourly*) "He has been arrested."

*I.* "Any charges against him? Is he guilty of anything?"

*K.* "There is nothing against him personally; he is a charming fellow."

*I.* "Has the Bulgarian official who was left in London in the same capacity as Hurst been arrested?"

*K.* "Not that I know of."

*I.* "Only a few weeks ago, acting on instructions telegraphed me from Washington, I asked you to recognise Hurst as a member of the American Legation, and I mentioned that this was the practise at Constantinople in the case of enemy officials in similar positions. You replied that to do this was unnecessary at Sofia, as Bulgars were not Turks, and moreover that you would personally guarantee me his safety."

*K.* "When I gave you this guarantee, conditions were entirely different. Today, every Bulgarian is revolted by the brutality of British methods and their flagrant disregard of international law. This arrest was necessary in order to satisfy public opinion and has been made in his own interest in order to shield him from the violence of the mob."

*I.* "Not long ago I was greatly impressed by a remark made to me by Dr. Radoslavoff that the day was over when the street could rule the government. I do not believe myself that there is any danger from a mob and am quite prepared to keep Hurst at my own risk. If you now arrest him I must warn you that this will mean a violation of the American Legation."

*K.* (*taken aback, for until then the Secretary General had been convinced that Hurst was already under arrest, angrily*) "You have arranged this thing together between you. It will be for the Cabinet to decide if you are allowed to keep him."

*I.* "You can only arrest him by violating the Legation."

*K.* "Meanwhile he is your prisoner."

*I.* (*smiling*) "No, he is my guest."

In similar circumstances, a French official might have been quite as angry as Kosseff, but would have been icily polite. A British official would have hidden his real feelings and assumed a detached attitude. In the Balkans, men are more primitive. The Secretary General made no secret of the fierce hatred he suddenly felt for me, but the only means he had of showing this was to be as unpleasant as possible. At the very moment I was leaving, he snorted that he was obliged to impart something disagreeable. He professed to have just learned that the Bulgarian Minister at Washington was not permitted to use the cipher for his cables except on condition of depositing his code at the State Department. We had both known this for months, and knew also that the reason did not depend on the United States, but on the Allied governments. As a punishment, I was now to be prevented from making ordinary communications to Washington unless I was prepared to deposit my cipher at the Foreign Office. "You can protest if you like," Kosseff hissed as a parting shaft.

Through no wish of my own, I found myself unexpectedly in the position of having to flout the Bulgarian government in wartime without knowing how they would view this, or if Washington would back me up. Yet I could not act otherwise, for the only alternative was to allow a man who was under the Legation's immediate protection to be taken into custody and for me to consent to his indefinite confinement, if not worse, as a hostage in a Bulgarian prison. Meanwhile Hurst, who had been brought up in a tradition of rigid Palmerstonian deportment, kept up a brave front before his uncertain fate. It was easy for me to put up a bed in the small room which hitherto had served for the Chancery, and for the next month this was to be Hurst's sanctuary.

I telegraphed Washington to relate the incident, but purposely refrained from asking for any instructions, and dipped hurriedly into a few books of international law I had brought with me and looked up precedents regarding the right of asylum. Modern jurists were disposed to question the validity of the principle, and the most convincing illustration I found for this practise in Europe had taken place a half-century before, when a Danish Minister in Madrid gave shelter to some revolutionary leaders who afterwards, when they had established their government, showed their gratitude by conferring on the Danish diplomat the title of Baron Asilo. Lord Asylum sounded much funnier in English. The question of law was, of course, the weak point in this case, but fortunately this was not put to a test during the five weeks in which Hurst found sanctuary at the Legation. The Bulgarian government showed considerable ingenuity in resorting to other devices, but the Ministry of Foreign Affairs never attempted to overwhelm me with legal arguments, where my position was less easy to defend.

Most of the difficulties which now took place arose from the fact of my living at a hotel. The wretched quarters, which I pompously had to style the American Legation, consisted of two fair-sized rooms, one of which was the office and the other my bedroom. A third, smaller one, used as a Chancery and now occupied by Hurst, was just across the way from my office, separated by a narrow corridor which led to the hotel dining-room. The morning after the spar with Kosseff, I saw a number of plainclothes policemen loitering outside the door, and on returning from my bath I noticed that my private papers had been rummaged. The intention was evident, to arrest Hurst as soon as he set foot in the passage. I therefore wrote to the Prime Minister to say that his underlings were doing their best to stir up trouble in the face of the Legation's wish to avoid any incidents. For his information, I drew a plan of the quarters that I occupied and enclosed this in my note, mentioning that although the hotel corridor led to the public dining-room, it also formed an essential part of the Legation, and when it was used for such purposes it was extraterritorial. This led to my developing an argument based on a kind of diplomatic theology and maintaining the dual nature of a hallway, which was at the same time an ordinary passage and American soil. I ended with a declaration that an arrest made in the corridor would be tantamount to a violation of the Legation, and in the interest of good relations between our countries I begged Dr. Radoslavoff to call off his sleuth hounds. After this vindication of the inviolate nature of American soil in a Sofia hotel, the plainclothesmen disappeared from sight, and there were many Bulgars who were not displeased to enjoy a laugh at their government's ineffective attempt to make an arrest.

A few days after this had occurred, an unexpected bombshell was exploded in the following telegram which was sent me by the Secretary of State, Mr. Lansing. It read, "You may make strong representations in favor of Hurst but if the Bulgarian Government insists upon arresting him you will not continue to give him shelter in the American Legation." To make matters worse, in spite of having previously indicated to the State Department a safe route by which he could communicate with me in cipher, the Secretary had seen fit to despatch this illuminating instruction in the open, and the Bulgarian government had, of course, read the text before I had seen it.

Few diplomats have not at some period in their career been infuriated by their government. My own opinion of my superiors at that time did not bear repetition. The instruction received from Washington gave me, however, just enough leeway to answer the Secretary of State that I felt as if my representations had as yet not been strong enough, nor the insistence of the Bulgarian government sufficiently pressing to warrant such a disgraceful surrender. If I was forced to submit, I asked that my resignation be accepted at once, as it would be impossible for me to render any further service to American interests. This despatch I knew would take a few weeks to reach the State Department, and meanwhile the delay provided a breathing spell.

The Bulgars were now aware of my shaky position and at once resumed their previous tactics in a stronger form. The plainclothesmen reappeared next day in the corridor to carry out the old plan, which was to arrest Hurst whenever any necessity compelled him to leave his room. On these occasions I was always notified, so that I could head my own bodyguard, which consisted of a Legation staff composed of an Armenian clerk and a Macedonian messenger who had once been a rabbinical student. The three of us would solemnly stand outside the door of the toilet until the Vice-Consul was able to return under our joint protection to the sanctuary of the bedroom. What would have happened if this protection had been challenged, I do not know, but the international controversy of the extraterritoriality of the hotel corridor was fast becoming a joke.

The third act of the opera bouffe began when the hotel manager cut off Hurst's food, but it was easy to counter this move by sending out the Legation messenger to forage for provisions in town. Next came a letter from the German hotel keeper, who professed to have learned with horror that I was actually harbouring an enemy subject and stated that his guests were so indignant at my action that they all threatened to leave his hotel. He notified me that in order not to suffer this heavy material damage he had let my rooms, and he gave me three days' grace in which to find some other accommodation. His letter remained unanswered.

After the three days were up, a Bulgarian lieutenant in uniform asked to see me. He was followed by a picket of eight men with bayonets on their rifles. The lieutenant clicked his heels and saluted me. He explained that he came by order of the General Commandant of Sofia, who had certain questions which he wished to put to Hurst. The General was prepared to assure me on his word of honour as an officer that no harm would befall the British Vice-Consul, a statement which was repeated to me at least three times. In turn, I assured the lieutenant of my absolute confidence in the Commandant's word, but as a formality I asked for a simple statement in writing that, after the General had put his questions, Hurst would be permitted to return to me in the same condition as he had gone. The lieutenant's orders evidently did not cover this interesting point, for he seemed embarrassed. Meanwhile, the German hotel keeper, made bold by the bayonets of the soldiers, piped up to say, "Excuse me, Excellency, but you have not yet left your room, although the three days are over." I answered tersely, "Go to hell." The hotel keeper fled, and a moment later the lieutenant clicked his heels, saluted, and left. Next day the Sofia newspapers related that I had spoken very coarsely, but that my vulgar language had been of no avail. The press implied that in spite of my rude words, which offended their sense of delicacy, Hurst had been removed, and the news of his arrest was published next day by the official Bulgarian agency at Bucharest. In reality, after this had happened I was left in peace, for the incident had become a joke. Even the German press, sick of war bulletins, took it up humorously and asserted that I had gone on every day claiming more and more of Sofia as American soil. Personally, I was enjoying the humour of the situation far more than poor Hurst who, terribly mortified at the trouble of which he had been the innocent cause, called himself my Old Man of the Sea.

Not until five weeks after the affair began, and the Bulgarian Consul at Salonika had been allowed to cross the Swiss frontier, was the Englishman safe. I accompanied Hurst on foot back to the British Legation. The hotel bellboys had a broad grin when they saw the English Vice-Consul emerge from his sanctuary. In the streets of Sofia, where only a few days before he would have been arrested at sight, we walked unnoticed. Three months after the affair was safely over and half forgotten, most unexpectedly an instruction arrived from Washington that my action, which incidentally had brought up several new points of international law, had been officially approved.*

Until the Hurst affair took place, it seemed incredible that in the midst of a world war a diplomat's life in the capital of a belligerent state could be as monotonous as mine. Only after the arrival of the prisoners did matters begin to change. Late in November, when the weather had suddenly turned bitterly cold, came the news that four hundred British had been captured on the Doiran front. I wrote to Radoslavoff to express my hope that Bulgaria would seek to win the same honour for her humanity as for her arms. I asked for the prisoners' names in order to transmit these to England, and requested permission to relieve their more pressing wants. No reply came, but a week later I discovered that the British and French prisoners had arrived at Sofia. By accident, I was allowed to see part of the camp in which they were to be confined and talked there with some Serbs who looked wretched and had only dirty straw on which to sleep. One of their number, who was a lawyer, complained bitterly about the food and the lack of proper medical care, and contrasted this with the freedom which his countrymen had accorded to Austrian prisoners at Nisch.

* Most of the despatches regarding this incident have been published in the 1916 Supplement to *Papers Relating to the Foreign Relations of the United States,* (Washington, Government Printing Office, 1929), pp. 825 ff. *L.E.*

Although I was not permitted to see the Tommies, I found seven English officers from Kitchener's new army, who belonged to a division which had been on the way to India when fresh orders despatched it to Salonika. They were quartered, none too badly, in a well-heated room. Only later I talked with many of the prisoners. I did this by going daily the rounds of the hospitals at Sofia. Except for a sprinkling of old enlisted soldiers, the others were principally Lancashire mill hands and Irish, mostly of poor physique. Their division had been sent to the Doiran front just as the Balkan winter set in, when the mercury dropped to forty degrees below zero. Two companies were sacrificed to protect a retreat, and had been compelled to surrender. On the road to Sofia the prisoners were made to march, in icy weather, twenty-five miles a day, at times with only a crust of bread and a bit of cheese to eat, carrying the wounded with them as best they could. The Bulgarian officers had been kind to the British officers and shared their meals with them, but the soldiers had fared worse, and none of the prisoners possessed anything except the clothing on their backs.

Permission to see the men in the camp had to be given by the Chief of the Prisoners' Bureau at the War Office who, in civil life, was a professor of geology. With Melvill, the sympathetic Dutch Minister, whom Kosseff described as my Siamese twin because we protested together, for he was in charge of French interests, I sent in my card to this authority on stones. The Chief of the Prisoners' Bureau replied that he was too busy to receive us. The real reason for his refusal was that, being without any power, he had been appointed only for ornamental purposes because Western states had prisoners' bureaux. The professor in fact found it prudent not to talk to any foreign diplomats. But we were angry and asked to see the Minister of War, General Naidenoff. The General was small, trim, and looked physically a Tartar, although Radoslavoff had assured me that, unlike certain other generals, he was not really a bad man. He was perfectly polite, but as soon as we asked for permission to visit the prisoners, he refused this, giving no reason except to say that it was impossible. I pointed out that in every other country of Europe the visits of friendly neutrals to prison camps were solicited. The General answered that Bulgaria was unlike any other country and that he personally commiserated with the prisoners' distress, for he had been in Europe and knew how much higher was its standard of comfort. Evidently he did not regard Bulgaria as being a European country. When we pressed our point, he affirmed that he had no personal objection to our seeing the prisoners but that the authorization was contrary to military regulations, and would have to come from the Prime Minister.

This explanation seemed plausible, and the next move was to get in touch with Radoslavoff, whose secretaries showed immense resourcefulness in inventing alibis for their elusive chief. A friendly Bulgarian had brought me news that the prisoners were in a deplorable condition. The men were in rags, many had no coats, and all suffered from the extreme cold. They were covered with vermin, and the huts in which they were housed were intended only for summer use, made out of the thinnest boards and put up in a frozen quagmire. Their most urgent need was for the great sheepskin coats which are worn in the Balkans. It was out of the question to buy many of these at one time, for the military authorities would at once have requisitioned them but, little by little, a sufficient number were obtained. The wool of the sheepskin offered a perfect nesting place for vermin, and it was impossible to disinfect the poor wretches for whom they were intended. But their immediate wants were so pressing that this risk had to be taken. The coats were paid for by me out of the British Legation safe, where a small portion of the grain corruption fund still remained. The money had never been employed so usefully. London, informed of this, approved at once of what I did, and the gold intended to warm the feeling of Bulgarian politicians for the Entente served instead to warm British Tommies from the fierce cold of the Bulgarian winter.

When at last the Prime Minister consented to receive me, it was to say that permission to visit the English could only be given by the still more inaccessible General Headquarters. Diplomacy regarding the prisoners had become a game of hide and seek, which would have been comic without the suffering captives. At a loss to know what to do, I left a note with Dobrovitch, the King's secretary, which I asked him to lay before His Majesty. I referred in this to the Czar's well-known feeling of humanity and expressed the belief that the King of Bulgaria could not wish prisoners of war in his power to suffer unnecessarily. The secretary promised to submit this to Ferdinand, but that chivalrous monarch remarked that the English and French prisoners had "only got what they deserved." At last, word came through

Prince Boris, who took a more sympathetic interest in their hardships, that the fate of the prisoners depended solely on the Minister of War.

With Melvill we called once more at the War Office to ask to be allowed to send the men a few extras to add to their Christmas fare. This well-meant offer produced a contrary effect. Radoslavoff declared that I demanded two beefsteaks a day for every English soldier, and that it was impossible to permit foreign ministers to offer a banquet to their prisoners. The immediate result of our request was that all the captives were packed off, at two hours' notice, to Tatar Bazardjik, a small town in the interior where they would be well out of our reach and news would be almost impossible to obtain.

Except for the warm-hearted Queen, no Bulgarian official seemed to care a straw what happened to the prisoners, but they resented any criticisms. Among the better elements of the population, many felt a latent sympathy for England which they found it wise, at this time, to repress. Formerly the British had been looked up to in the Balkans like superior mortals, and it was in order to counteract this feeling that the official press was deliberately preaching hate. The English were accused of using dumdum bullets, and the wire cutters that were found on them were described as being instruments to make these. The harsh treatment of prisoners was in fact a typically Eastern method of dispelling the former legend of British superiority. Yet it was not entirely deliberate, for there was also much Balkan negligence mixed with this. Bulgarian noncommissioned officers and soldiers were generally decent and often kindly disposed peasants, but they were Oriental in their native disorder and the evil effects of practises and regulations which, in a country like Germany would be restrained by a stricter discipline, were accentuated in Bulgaria, less through intention than by sheer carelessness.

In the hospitals of Sofia, where the prisoners were well treated, there were some distressing cases, like that of a blind Tommy I had found in a ward where no one could speak a word of English. The poor fellow had been told that he was at Gladstone, which was the name of the institution, and at first thought this meant that he was back in England. There were also numerous instances of kindness, and whoever was attended to by Dr. Kara Michaeloff, a splendid Bulgarian surgeon who had an English wife, owed him a debt of gratitude. One day the doctor called to ask me to speak to an Irishman in his hospital who was slowly dying of gangrene. The only means to save him was to cut off his leg, but the prisoner stubbornly refused permission. I went to the sick man's bedside, and talked sentimental Ireland to the poor fellow. It was St. Patrick's Day, and I asked what he would have done if he had been in Ireland. He answered, "Sure I'll not tell you a lie, I'd have got drunk." "Don't you want to get drunk again?" He nodded approval. Next day the leg was amputated.

The best-appointed hospital was that of the Knights of Malta. It was under Austrian direction, and Count Mensdorf, admittedly homesick for Mayfair, had come to Sofia to inaugurate this. I found there a young English lad of nineteen with both his feet cut off. His story was simple, and he related it as if it were any ordinary occurrence. He had been sent to a labour camp under a Turkish overseer who maltreated the prisoners. Whenever one of these fell ill, the sick man would be accused of shirking, and on the plea that he did not work, would be left intentionally without food. For three days the poor fellow had lain helpless in an open shed in icy weather. Both his feet became frostbitten by the exposure and the boy had to be sent to the nearest town, where they were amputated.

A few days later, there was more cause for my indignation. A hundred and fifty French and English prisoners were being temporarily detained at the railway station at Sofia, on their way to a labour camp. Dr. Plotz, an American bacteriologist, who was investigating typhus, had been given a military car driven by a soldier chauffeur. Owing to this circumstance, it was possible to talk to the men and hear some harrowing details of the conditions in which they had been confined at Tatar Bazardjik. The prisoners were covered with vermin which they had never been able to get rid of, and half of them ought then and there to have been in hospital. Although in no shape to work, they were on their way to Radomir, where a violent typhus epidemic was raging. Dr. Plotz felt certain that in the weak condition these men were in they would fall an easy prey to any epidemic.

It was natural to go at once to the Minister of War and not overpolite on my part to accuse him of sending these prisoners to their death. General Naidenoff answered me sharply that he was prepared to assume this responsibility. He intended to use the English to do some necessary work on the railway, and as there was a large military and civilian population in that district, he saw no reason why enemy prisoners should be treated with any greater leniency than the inhabitants. Nor would he admit that it was a different thing to send men covered with vermin and weakened by exposure into a typhus epidemic, which meant certain death for them. The General then reminded me that if there were any further remarks to make to him, the proper procedure was to address these to the Foreign Office. We were both standing on our feet as he said this, for our talk had been excited, and I expected any minute to be shown the door. Technically, he was of course right and he had put me in the wrong, but as a last resort I declared that my warning was that of a friend, and that future complaints would now be made through the channels he suggested. To my amazement, just as I was about to leave, the General suddenly began to climb down and whimpered that because Bulgaria was a small country was no reason to speak to him in the way I had done. He pleaded that there were things which could not be granted, but in case a doctor should assure him that the men were unfit to work, they would not be sent to Radomir, and he added, "Now that you have your own physician for the prisoners, if he reports that their state is really as you have represented, they will not be sent."

It was easy to answer him that Dr. Plotz, who was a specialist of typhus, would draw up a medical report. After this our talk became much friendlier. The Minister of War promised that the prisoners would be moved at once to Philippopolis, where they could live in more favourable conditions. The tension between us was unexpectedly over, and from that time we chatted together amicably. When I left him he held out his hand and said, "Now we are once more friends," and the same evening came a personal note from the General, confirming his conversation and authorizing me to see the prisoners. He tried, I think, to keep his word, and a serious effort was made soon afterwards to improve their treatment.

With the Dutch Minister Melvill, and accompanied by several Bulgarian officials, we left by the night train for Philippopolis. It was mid-March, and the air in Eastern Roumelia is much balmier than at Sofia and was springlike when we arrived next morning. Flanked by an official escort, who had received strict orders not to leave us out of their sight, we walked to a large prison camp, dating from the Balkan Wars. It was located a mile away on the outskirts of the town and seemed healthy and suitable, but we found it almost empty except for some Serbian crippled soldiers and officers. The latter kept up a remarkably smart appearance in spite of their captivity, and wore on their *képis* the enamelled royal monogram of King Peter. A British officer offered to get me one of these as a souvenir, but he soon discovered his mistake. Prisoners though they were, they declared that they were ready to sell their souls but not their King's emblem.

The British officers, with their tempers somewhat frayed by the strain of captivity, had been quartered in a small but not too uncomfortable house. They were full of plans for escape, regarding which they naïvely asked my advice in the presence of an English-speaking Bulgarian. The Tommies, however, had all been whisked away that morning to different labour camps, and the purpose of allowing our visit at once became plain. We were expected to report favourably on the camp and on the condition of the officers, while the men themselves were kept out of our sight. The Commandant was a youthful lieutenant who waxed eloquent on the subject of his own superior virtues, which would have put an archangel to shame, but offered no enlightenment regarding the condition of the common prisoners. Melvill and I were furious at what seemed to us a trick, and by way of protest my Dutch colleague returned that afternoon to Sofia. I stayed on and asked to visit General Kovatcheff, a veteran of the Balkan Wars who then commanded at Philippopolis. He showed himself sympathetic and amenable, and offered to bring back the British prisoners at once.

Late that afternoon, a few hundred miserable creatures in rags, with Balkan sandals instead of shoes, straggled back to the prison camp. I recall once having seen Beerbohm Tree act "The Man Who Was," Kipling's story of the British officer captured by the Russians who was reduced by suffering to a miserable creature who had lost all self-respect and even the recollection of his own identity. Beerbohm Tree played the part admirably, and was made up to resemble a cringing native who whined in terror before any officer. In this prison camp I experienced something of the same impression of horror and pity which the play had left on me. The men were drawn up in line, like a legion of the damned on parade. When questioned how many were sick, nearly half stepped from the ranks, yet they had not reported illness because the care which was given in the hospital at Bazardjik had been so bad that they preferred not to go there. Here were prisoners who only a few weeks before had been able-bodied, fresh-looking English boys, now reduced by ill treatment to human wrecks whose spirit was crushed. And yet much of this suffering was not intentionally inflicted, but came as the result of Balkan mismanagement and callousness. Thus, the Commandant related that the prisoners took three days to march from Tatar Bazardjik to the camp, but had been given rations for only one day. Admittedly this was a mistake, but the official in charge had no authority to obtain more. Certain complaints made were less distressing. The English did not relish their food, which was prepared in the camp by some of the French prisoners. I asked to taste the soup and found it quite palatable, but the Tommies complained that the meat which lay at the bottom was kept by the French for themselves, who then doled out to the English only the clear liquid.

On my return to Sofia, I addressed a note to the Prime Minister worded without any rhetoric, for I allowed the facts to speak for themselves, but with enough evidence of bad treatment to form a terrible indictment. This was all the more unexpected as the Bulgarian officials hoped for compliments about their prison camp. Radoslavoff was furious when he read it and denounced me to several of my colleagues as an "enemy of Bulgaria," going so far as to advise the Roumanian Minister not to frequent me. The Chief of Police sent for the only American resident in the capital and warned him also to keep away from the Legation. Even the poor Queen found it necessary to silence Miss Hay when innocently she mentioned my name while talking to her on the 'phone. In the dreary monotony of a neutral's life at Sofia, the only pleasure left me was the self-complacent one of having become an untouchable whom no Bulgarian dared any longer to approach. But the result of my note was beneficial to the prisoners.

My wife's illness brought to an end a situation which could hardly have been strained much further. She was at that time in London, suffering from a serious nervous breakdown that came after her stay in Constantinople and was caused by the anxieties of the war. I was summoned by wire to the nursing home in which she lay.

Just at this time, Lord Newton, who was in charge of the prisoners of war, saw fit to quote me in the House of Lords as his authority for the bad treatment of the British in Bulgaria. His knowledge on this subject was derived from my confidential reports to Washington, of which I had sent copies to Mr. Page, our Ambassador in London. The British government had already asked my permission through the State Department that these despatches from Sofia should be published in a Blue Book, and I had refused consent, for it was one thing to blame Bulgar officials to their face and another to allow my accounts of their misdeeds to be used as propaganda in a country with which they were at war. When I saw Lord Newton a few days later, I told him that he had made my return to Sofia impossible. His ingenuous reply was, "Why should you want to?" Actually, I was not overanxious, nor could I blame the Bulgarian government for asking that I should not be sent back.

# 8. *Prague Memories*

In mid-December 1921 the night train from Vienna brought me to the Masaryk Station at Prague, perhaps intentionally so that travellers from Austria would have to associate their first glimpse of the Czech capital with the name of the President of the new Republic. The other much finer station formerly called after the Emperor Francis Joseph had now become Wilson, although the Czech porters still faithful to the Habsburg tradition merely linked an American president's name to that of a deceased emperor.

Prague was already under snow, the Vultava was frozen over, and on the hill, half veiled in mist, rose the famous Hradcany, which under its white mantle looked an appropriate castle for the unfortunate Winter Queen of Bohemia. We crossed the medieval fortified bridge where baroque statues of saints stood like graceful sentinels, between the Gothic towers, to enter the Mala Strana.

The architecture of every city tells a good deal of its story. New York explains itself by a jumble of styles which have emerged from the brownstone age to create new babels by an infinite repetition of small units piled skyward. Prague offers a sample board that extends over seven centuries. Yet the Mala Strana quarter in which most of the diplomats lived was unique in Europe. Modernity had not been permitted to intrude in its deserted streets nor deface the ancient palaces with their hidden gardens behind.

In no other capital were diplomats lodged with a greater architectural splendour. There was a reason for this. In the early days of the Republic the old aristocracy to whom the palaces belonged were terrified lest all their possessions should be seized, and they were glad to rent them for a pittance, and afterwards to sell them to foreign governments who benefited from this fear. The Yugoslavs leased, and lost an extraordinary opportunity to buy, the Palace of the Knights of Malta which was filled with beautiful Beauvais tapestries, which in themselves were worth more than the purchase price of the building. The

British had acquired the Thun Palace, which was a grim fortress-like structure from outside, but contained some agreeable surprises, not the least being a wonderful garden terrace entered after climbing up three flights of stairs.

My predecessor, Richard Crane, had purchased the Schönborn Palace, which is one of the largest and finest of the ancient buildings in Prague. It was in a somewhat dilapidated condition, and, like most of its kind, was badly in need of modernizing, but it contained a hundred rooms and three courtyards. At the end of the great central court rose a double flight of steps which led up to the garden and to another entrance of the palace on the floor above. There was a legend that these stairs had been built by the first owner, Count Colloredo Mansfeld, who having lost a leg in the Thirty Years' War, used to ride his horse up these steps into the palace. At a fancy dress dance which we gave later, Count Kinsky entered the ballroom in this way, riding a stallion covered with the splendid trappings which two centuries before had served his ancestor at an emperor's coronation.

Only a few of the old aristocracy had then rallied to the new Republic. One of these was Prince Max Lobkovicz, whose castle of Raudnice, which was greater than many a royal palace, contained a notable gallery of pictures, a famous library which was still kept up, and the musical instruments of a private orchestra which had been maintained by his great-grandfather, who was Beethoven's friend. Raudnice is not very far from Dux, where Count Waldstein had provided Casanova with a roof for his old age by employing him as his librarian.

Once, visiting a friend in Bohemia, I heard an authentic story about this great adventurer. After the Venetian, already advanced in years, entered the Count's service, his neighbours would call of an evening and send for the old man to hear him relate the picturesque gallantries of his youth. But they showed a little too plainly that they did not understand Casanova's real worth as a man and cared only to be amused by the story of his less estimable side. Casanova's pride was hurt, but the adventurer did not dare to offend his patron's friends and so risk the loss of his livelihood. Intentionally, therefore, he would repeat the same tale to the visitors night after night till they believed that the old man was in his dotage and then left him undisturbed to enjoy the peace of his library. The Venetian, who was once known in every capital of Europe, now rests in a nameless and unidentified grave in a small churchyard at Dux.

The Austrian aristocrats who, after the Roman example were called the "Blacks," were a caste who had survived from the wreckage of the Habsburg Empire. Most of them still lived in a self-centered world of their own which was restricted, but less altered by outside events than might have been supposed. Many resided in their castles, a very few keeping up feudal practises with pensioned retainers in private uniforms. Some preserved the old courtly manners and one of these, Prince Thun, in his castle at Teschen, looked as if he might have stepped out of a Van Dyck. Their invariable preoccupations were their estates, their shooting, and the endless chronicle of birth and death and marriage, in a society where all were closely related. They came to Prague principally during the carnival season, when a few wealthier ones like Prince Schwarzenberg* gave balls to which no Czech of the new régime would be asked. One saw them also at certain legation entertainments. As a political body they were leaderless and unreconciled save for a few like Count Eugene Ledebur, a charming man of the world, who had become a German Christian Socialist senator, and adopted toward the Republic a reasonable attitude of constructive criticism until he was led astray by Hitler.

Many of the younger branches of great families who possessed no places of their own resided at Prague. One of these, who had been the aide-de-camp of the last emperor, was Prince Zdenko Lobkowicz, a retired general, who lived with great dignity in a small apartment which he graced by his courtly manners, while his daughters found work of a clerical kind. We had many friends among the "Blacks," and at small gatherings at the Legation it was easy to avoid asking them at the same time as Czech officials, although when they met unexpectedly the situation became icy. More than once I have seen a young woman who belonged to the old order and was employed as a typist in an office run out of the Legation in order to avoid encountering Dr. Beneš, who had come to play tennis with me. Towards the end of our stay at Prague, an improvement was already beginning to take place in this

* The Schwartzenberg family possessed one thirty-first of the Bohemian lands at the outset of the Czech Republic's existence.

respect, and not a few of the Blacks accepted invitations to attend the presidential receptions.

The cause for much of the bitterness was the Land Reform Act which had broken up the great estates. Passed immediately after the war when it seemed as if Central Europe would go Red, Czech politicians claimed that it had saved the country from Bolshevism, as the new class of independent landowners which had been created would no longer listen to Communist ideas. Before the war, the surplus population had been obliged to emigrate, and the division of the land made room for increased numbers of small farmers. Fair-minded landowners admitted that some reform was necessary, for the ownership of a good deal of the soil had been on a kind of feudal basis, with too much of it held in too few hands. Prince Schwarzenberg, for instance, owned fifty-seven estates that extended over half a million acres, and other great nobles also possessed enormous tracts of land. After the Republic was established, the new law limited private ownership to a few hundred acres according to the quality of the soil, but compensation was provided on a basis of former average value. As meanwhile the currency had depreciated, this meant that the government gave about one seventh of its actual worth, although by amicable arrangement as much as a third of the real value would be paid. Other legislation had, however, been enacted of a semi-confiscatory kind, like the capital levy, so that the state virtually could pay the former owner what it liked. Spoliation in a revolution is usually a quick act of violence committed in the heat of disorder. With a slow and methodical people like the Czechs, something resembling it went on for years during a period of perfect tranquility as a deliberate legalized process. Inevitably the seizure of so much land from which came their wealth and prestige was bitterly resented by the former owners, and naturally, but most unwisely, the aristocrats who were the victims of this act denounced it as Bolshevistic robbery.

The Western world had been slow to understand that in Central Europe the social consequences of the 1914–18 war had been quite as significant as the political. One of the unavowed purposes of the Land Act was to break the power of the great territorial aristocracy. Some of these were still faithful to the Habsburgs, or else were feudal magnates. Others had been won over to Pan-German ideas, but almost to a man all were avowed enemies of the Republic, and they openly displayed their hostility at a time when less intransigence might have secured for them better terms. In fact, President Masaryk offered to select anyone they liked to administer this Act. The unfriendly attitude which they adopted was partly explained by the fact that at first they did not believe that the new state would last, and it was too late when they understood their mistake. It would have been hard, in any case, for a semi-feudal caste, singularly lacking in political wisdom, but firmly imbued with the feeling of their superiority, and which for generations had been artificially separated from the people among whom they lived, to have acted differently.

The expropriation which had been carried out in the French Revolution left the aristocracy who fled from the country still Frenchmen. In Bohemia, the situation was otherwise. Many of the nobles did not speak Czech, and to some extent they were strangers in the land, for many descended from the soldiers of fortune who had been given the confiscated estates of the expelled Czech nobels after the Thirty Years' War. The remembrance of the Habsburg Empire was still so near that it was natural for them to have everything in common with the members of their caste in neighbouring states, and nothing in common with the Czechs, who looked on them as an inimical and alien element. Only a few aristocrats regarded themselves as Czech patriots because their grandfathers had encouraged a Czech movement among their then feudalized peasantry. Nearly all would have found it difficult suddenly to display a convincing sympathy for the particular brand of lower-middle-class nationalism which lay at the foundation of the Republic. So they became the victims of their natural prejudice, for the new government was not altogether displeased to assert its authority over a class which held it in contempt.

Landed property, great and small, was therefore ruthlessly parcelled out, partly as a social measure carried out ostensibly in the interest of the peasants, but also for political beneficiaries. As any perfect division was impossible, the Land Act recognized reasonably enough that there were certain portions of every estate which could not be equitably divided. Former owners, however, were not allowed to buy these back. But in practice this clause of the Act was somewhat scandalously made use of for partisan purposes and the so-called *"Restgüter,"* or undistributed parts, were usually sold, on highly favourable terms, to friends of the Agrarian Party.

The division of the forests which afterwards took place was in principle much less justifiable than that of the soil. Bohemian forestry, like its agriculture, was of a high order, and vast tracts of land cleared of undergrowth and planted with conifers in a monotonous regularity covered a ground which was generally unsuitable for other crops. The trees were felled in a rotation of from eighty to a hundred years, and only exceptionally, when threatened by the ravages of a disease like the nunworm, did the state grant permission to allow any earlier cutting. Immense woods which covered tens of thousands of acres and teemed with deer had been the special pride of the great landowners. Count Kolowrat's great forest of Dianaberg near the Bavarian border was large enough for a railroad merely to cart the timber, and a favourite sport there was to jack deer at night by the flash of a lantern from an open truck attached to an engine.

For me a far greater pleasure of the woods was stalking capercailzie.* This bird is about the size of a turkey, and the learned Czech foresters, who knew everything, would explain its names to me in Latin and Greek. To hunt capercailzie, I slept in a lodge in the forest, to rise an hour before dawn, in order to follow the gamekeeper through the woods, in a darkness so great that repeatedly I stumbled over invisible tree trunks. The blackness of the night turned this experience into an adventure. In spite of the cold April air and the balsam of northern pines I understood what the Emperor Jones must have felt when he was lost in the tropical forest. I had no idea how long it took to reach the spot where the stalk began, but a faint glimmer of light was already beginning to outline the shapes of the trees. Far away I suddenly heard two or three bars of liquid notes calling at first faintly, then louder. The forester whispered in my ear to be careful not to make a noise, clutched my hand firmly, and in that half-darkness, we sprang forward a few yards. Only when the bird, drunk with his love chant, pours out the fulness of his heart in the silence of the forest, is it possible to approach him. His liquid notes are short, and as soon as the caper stopped singing the forester would halt me abruptly. Then the bird burst into song again, and we would rush the short distance that it was possible to cover during the few seconds that his love call for his mate had lasted. The passionate melody of the lovelorn capercailzie,

* The largest variety of European grouse.

dancing on the top of the woods, was as enthralling as it was indescribable. Then for an unknown reason the bird ceased to sing and the forester imitated the raucous squeak of the female; for by an irony of nature this hideous screech evoked in response the exquisite notes of the cock. A series of short rushes brought us, at last, full in sight of our quarry perched on the highest branch of tall fir, and not suspecting that we stood underneath. I did not care to shoot, and daylight ended his song. He flew away just as the silver dawn of early morning was transforming the forest glade into an abode of magic. The Emperor Jones had changed into Young Siegfried who listened to birds piping in the day, while all around fleeting deer rustled through the thickets.

Another wood near Prague belonged to Count Silva Tarouca, who had made it the finest arboretum in Europe. Every year the Count planted himself many thousands of trees with specimens of every variety that could be grown in a northern climate. The war, and other misfortunes, had deprived him of his former immense wealth and left him nothing except this park which, once his pastime, had then become his only remaining property. Even this estate came under the Land Act. The arboretum fortunately was recognised as an institution of national utility, and the Count was beyond any doubt the forester best able to look after it. The state therefore appointed him to be curator of his former property and moved him into a small house opposite his castle, which was then taken over as a summer residence for the Minister of Agriculture.

Every autumn diplomats would be invited by this Minister to shoot at the great archducal properties confiscated to the state by the peace treaties to demonstrate that the world had been made safe for democracy. One of these was the Archduke Frederick's estate at Ziedlochowice in Moravia. This was a favourite place for sport, and although situated in a densely populated district, more than thirty thousand head of game were shot there in the course of a year. Diplomats were asked there for the partridges in August, when incredible hordes of beaters would march between the guns in sight of the Column of Austerlitz, which crowned a neighbouring hill. This cumbersome manoeuvre, carried out under a torrid sun, invariably flushed enormous coveys at a great distance, without ever breaking these up, which helped me to understand why Napoleon always beat the Austrians. Seemingly the elusive partridge had learned his tactics. In the late autumn, the Minister's invitations would be repeated for a gigantic slaughter of pheasants. These shoots lasted for three days, during which we lived in the Archduke's castle, an agreeable but far from luxurious residence decorated in the fashion of Central Europe, with gigantic antlers, each pair inscribed with full particulars, as well as the name of the exalted personage to whose gun the stag had fallen.

The Archduke was the richest of the Habsburgs and the decoration of his country house was not without interest. The states carved out of the Habsburg inheritance still preserve earlier designations. In Republican France styles are still labelled with the serial numbers of former kings, whereas monarchical England gives to its furniture the names of plebeian cabinetmakers. The greatest of Austrian empresses attached her name to a style followed by that of the obscure Biedermeyer. The Archduke's castle was gorged with exuberant Maria Theresa and slimmer Biedermeyer furniture. Neither possessed any particular merit. There was in fact little luxury, yet a moderate comfort which was much greater than the Archduke Charles, the future Emperor, enjoyed when he inhabited the castle of Brandis near Prague, which possessed neither bathrooms nor plumbing of any kind. Like most Austrian country places Ziedlochowice was built close to a public road on the outskirts of a village. It possessed no avenue of trees such as leads up to the most modest English country house. Nor did it have any garden worthy of the name, but only a few small flower beds. Instead, a large beet sugar factory built on the estate very near the residence gave it a utilitarian aspect.

The planting of the archducal coverts had been most carefully designed, and in several stands the pheasants flew high and were not merely the low birds of Central Europe, which are as easy to shoot as they are distasteful to slaughter. In winter, when the mercury was close to zero, and the ground lay covered with hard snow, a difficulty which never prevented a hot lunch from being served in the woods, a couple of thousand birds and hares could be killed there in a few hours. These shoots were most carefully prepared, and between beaters, keepers, and stops, three hundred men would be called out in order to provide a day's sport for eight or nine guns. A few of us who were friends, like the English and Dutch ministers and myself, would enjoy there a house party without a host, for the officials from the Ministry of Agriculture tactfully kept to themselves. Our participation, however, was not without some value to them, for many Czech politicians also enjoyed this sport, and when some socialist asked an inconvenient question in Parliament as to why the archducal shooting should be kept up in a republic, he would be informed that this was only done as a courtesy for the entertainment of diplomats.

Another great shooting estate was the forest of Topolcanky in Slovakia, which formerly belonged to the Archduke Joseph and was used as a summer residence of the President. Before the war, this Hungarian member of the Imperial family had bought up entire villages in the foothills of the Tatra Mountains and destroyed these in order to create a vast game preserve. I was shown his carefully worked out statistical estimate of the stags, wild boar, and moufflon, which he expected to shoot in increasing numbers every year.

The most famous of the different Habsburg estates taken over by the Republic was, however, Konopisht, not far from Prague, which had belonged to the murdered Franz Ferdinand. Popular Czech gossip related that the World War was hatched there during the German Emperor's stay in June 1914, just before the Archduke had set out for his fatal journey to Serajevo. This legend was currently repeated in Bohemia, without there being a word of truth in it, for after the Kaiser had left, the Archduke sent for his gamekeeper and ordered him to prepare another great shoot for the autumn when he was expecting to receive the visit of the King of England. These Imperial shoots required immense preparations, for the gamekeepers had to trap the stags and fallow deer that were to be slaughtered and then confine them within a stockade. The size of the bag on these great occasions depended solely on the number previously trapped and not infrequently ran into hundreds. The day of the shoot the animals would be let out, one by one, in such a way that they would have to cross rides cut out of the forest where the guns lay in wait.

The Archduke's gamekeeper described to me how Franz Ferdinand used to sit in the forest reading his Vienna newspaper. When the game appeared, the keeper would shout, "Imperial Heir to the Throne, there is a stag on your left." The Archduke fired and then resumed his newspaper until the next call: "Imperial Heir to the Throne, fallow deer on your right." Unlike the kindly Emperor Charles, the Archduke, although an excellent husband and father, was brutal to his inferiors. I was told that once when a loader had handed him an empty gun he knocked the man down. But he was a magnificent shot who could kill a hare with a rifle, and the walls of his castle were lined with innumerable trophies of the chase. It is typical of the man that Franz Ferdinand kept a detailed record of a million head of game which had fallen to his gun.

Along with a few of my colleagues, I had several times refused invitations to shoot at Konopisht. The Habsburg properties taken over by the Republic seemed to me to be legitimate war spoils, but Konopisht was in a different class. The Archduke at the time of his morganatic marriage had taken an oath that his children should never be in line of succession to the Crown. Yet his sons had been denied their father's property on the specious ground that, as the Republic did not recognize morganatic marriages, it recognized these children as being Habsburgs and therefore subject to the disqualifying provisions against that family. The Ministry of Agriculture must have suspected my reason for invariably refusing their invitations, and this made them the more desirous to have me shoot there. One year I had returned late in December from a holiday in the United States, and was hardly back before the Under Secretary rang me up to say that, in spite of great pressure, they had delayed the diplomatic shoot at Konopisht on my account, and that my British and Italian colleagues would both be there. Not wishing to appear more royalist than the representatives of two monarchies I therefore accepted, and next day the official Gazette came out with a photograph of all the diplomats who had attended the shoot.

The Republic was not averse to an almost lavish scale of entertaining and regarded this as propaganda. The setting of its festivities was usually the great castle of the Hradschin, in which there is said to be the largest ballroom in the world and perhaps the longest banquet hall. It also has splendid gardens in which tulips were first introduced in Europe and which was famous in the sixteenth century when Prague was an Imperial residence. The King of Egypt was to be the first sovereign to honour the new state with his visit. In his honour there was the inevitable official banquet, which was preceded by a levee at which Czech democrats were delighted to make their bow before an Eastern potentate. King Fuad looked little amused by the array of captains of Bohemian industry who had been brought before him, and the royal boredom was later taken out on his unfortunate chamberlains. His Majesty displayed some further ill humour after he had been compelled to sit through the performance of a dancer whose exemplary virtue as wife and mother was warmly praised by Madame Beneš to the less enthusiastic Sultan. Not till the next day did Fuad recover his good humour.

King Fuad, in the grand manner of the East, had commanded the purchase of a legation at Prague solely in order to return the hospitality received by offering an entertainment of his own. Forty of his domestics and five of his cooks had therefore arrived from Cairo for this purpose, and after a two-day visit the Sultan left the castle to stay in his own Legation. That evening the happy monarch gave a party, with the most sumptuous buffet I have ever seen, composed of every delicacy that East and West could offer and served by a host of Nubian domestics attired in scarlet and gold. The King was once more in a jovial mood and related stories to his guests which caused respectable Czech ministers' wives to blush. The dancing lady he had engaged for the evening's entertainment may have possessed less virtue than the one whose performance we had so lately watched at the castle, and certainly she had on much less attire. The President sat inarticulate through the spectacle but the Papal Nuncio found it desirable to bury his face in his programme and keep it there somewhat conspicuously. Ecclesiastics can be embarrassed for different reasons than appear, and the same high dignitary of the Church complained to me, on another similar occasion, that although the dancer's absence of costume was indifferent to him, he did not relish being stared at to see if he was looking.

A Nuncio's position at Prague was far from easy, and I watched an incredible controversy develop between the government and the Holy See about a man who died more than five hundred years ago. Early in the fifteenth century, John Huss, condemned by the Council of Constance as a heretic, was burned at the stake, but his name still means so much to the Czechs that when a Lord Mayor of London once visited Prague he was frantically applauded because he spoke of "us" which his audience mistook as being a homage to their national hero. Not a little of this martyr's popularity came, however, from the pleasure it gave anticlericals to bait the Catholic Church which, before the war, had been closely identified with the Habsburgs. The Vatican is very tolerant toward Protestant and even non-Christian powers, but finds it hard to swallow heresy no matter how ancient is its date. After the Huss anniversary had been made an official holiday, the black flag of the Hussites flew from the President's window in full sight of the Archbishop's palace across the square. The Papal Nuncio lived there in an apartment hung with splendid Gobelins that represented the animals of the jungle, but no tropical heat in which these animals had thrived could equal that of the controversy which then suddenly developed. When the Nuncio saw the black flag flying from the President's window, he at once broke off relations between Prague and the Holy See, and left by the next train for Rome.

My French colleague, Mr. Couget, facetiously suggested that as the Church had burned Joan of Arc and later canonized her, the only way out of the difficulty would be to make John Huss a saint. But after more than a year had passed, and both sides had enough, Dr. Beneš found an easier solution and explained that Huss had been honoured, not as a heretic, but as a Czech patriot.

The fertile soil of Bohemia was endemic with ancient rows, and before the war politics had meant wrangling fights which always went on between Germans and Czechs and in which both sides displayed a spirit of incredible pettiness. They refused to frequent each other's houses, or go to each other's cafés, or attend each other's plays. If a Czech went to a German theatre, his name next day would be pilloried in the Czech newspapers, or vice versa, and anyone bold enough to transgress the rules of this boycott became a marked man. Occasionally feeling would be stirred till it led to a riot, and German and Czech students would then break each other's heads and windows. Many traces of this animosity still remained at Prague, although fewer than those that existed in the German-speaking regions, where the inhabitants were bitterly resentful of Czech domination. A friend of mine, who was a German politician, told me that he owned several houses in a manufacturing town of northern Bohemia, which he would have liked to sell. He had been obliged to refuse some advantageous offers for these as the prospective buyers were all Czechs. Although he had little prejudice of his own, he was forced to do this not to lose influence among his constituents.

The Germans were still convinced that they were a far superior race, and whenever I had the chance it gave me a puckish pleasure to remark that, except for language, I could detect few differences in the characteristics between German Bohemians and Czechs. Many of the former bore Czech names and vice versa, and the two so-called races looked alike and lived in the same way, with, so far as I could see, similar virtues and similar faults. A good deal of intermarriage had taken place between them in the past, and many Slav leaders have been of mixed blood. And it was a little disconcerting to discover that in the same family one member might call himself a Czech and the other a German. The linguistic frontier between the two languages began about forty miles west of Prague, after which the signs were nearly all in German, but except for the language the villages were quite alike in appearance, whereas between a German-Bohemian village and a neighbouring one in Bavaria, or in Saxony, a marked visible difference existed.

During a thousand years of turbulent history, the inhabitants of Bohemia have taken part in many wars, though virtually none of a racial kind. It needed the educational pedantry of the nineteenth century, exploited by politicians in the name of patriotism, to manufacture a largely fictitious racial pedigree to justify their own petty bickerings. After they had lived together peacefully for centuries, one result of popular education was to produce a political agitation of flamboyant nationalism among Czechs and Germans, till both regarded each other as strangers and hereditary enemies. And this feeling developed at the same time as the real differences which formerly had existed between the two were in process of disappearing.

In all the countries of the Danube Valley, German influence then percolated through every form of social organization, and often those most anti-German in their ideas had German mothers or had been trained by German methods. Certainly the Czechs had learned how to resist Teutonic encroachments by organizing themselves along similar lines, and during the last century before any political expression was allowed in the Habsburg Empire, they had revived Czech nationality on a basis of language, music, and gymnastics, at the same time maintaining an increasingly resentful attitude towards Vienna. Even after obtaining their independence, the Czechs seemed a little inclined to forget that they were no longer a subject race, for they still continued to impart to every artistic expression an incredible amount of patriotic significance. Even the Czech wife of a distinguished French general complained bitterly to the French minister that the alliance with his country had been of very little use because the Paris opera had not yet produced Smetana's *Bartered Bride.*

In a land where five different "races" dwell together, this overexuberant nationalism was fostered by politicians who found its expression considerably to their advantage even when it became a nuisance. President Masaryk wisely opposed every form of chauvinism, and his moderating reasonableness caused many of the worst excesses to be avoided. Another effort to break down the former barriers was also made through sport. The fashion for games had originated so recently that there was no ancient precedent against Czechs and Germans playing tennis and football together. Yet hatred is a hardy annual in Central Europe, and ancient grievances have been carefully nursed for generations without there being enough memories to share in common, or enough sense of national pride shared by minorities, which in Western lands brings citizens of different origin together.

A Czech journalist at Prague once asked me for an interview and wanted to know my opinion about the faults of his countrymen. The Czechs, like all young nations, are abnormally sensitive, so wishing to avoid facile generalizations which mean little and refraining from empty compliments, I answered that if they had faults these came largely from their not eating enough vegetables and not laughing enough. This remark was repeated to the Prime Minister, Mr. Švehla, who sent me word that I understood his people. This was as near as I ever came to seeing that leader. He was the most influential politician in his country and repeatedly Prime Minister, but he was always unwilling to meet foreign diplomats. Like many Czech politicians, Švehla called himself a peasant, but he was a well-educated man, and this leader of a Slav state, with his own roots lying deep in the soil of Bohemia, looked the typical John Bull. His shyness came partly from a distaste for all ceremonial occasions and also because the only medium of intercourse he had with foreigners was German; in the early days of the Republic, it was not politically prudent to converse in that tongue. Later, much of this feeling tended to wear off, and many politicians began to take up French. The study of that language, along with learning how to ride, were the certain signs by which anyone could detect those politicians who nurtured presidential ambitions.

Apart from a few outstanding personalities, social Prague contained some incongruous elements. There was a Czech and a German society, constructed along similar but not very friendly lines, and composed principally of bankers and sugar barons, whose pattern of life was shaped after that of the aristocrats. Many of them owned castles and lived like the "Blacks," and nearly all liked to extend a generous hospitality. Certain of the politicians were people who had not shaken off their small beginnings and felt little at home in the social world. We used to sprinkle these at our parties, and I think that they came to them out of curiosity, for they did not seem to enjoy themselves and conversation often became a mutual ordeal. Certain of them neglected the more conventional social observances. Thus my French colleague related to me that he had asked a Cabinet minister to dinner on a certain Tuesday. Ten minutes before eight, the latter sent word that he could not come, and every Tuesday through the season he kept repeating his refusal always at the same hour.

The diplomats were really the only solvent among different castes who had never before mixed. Until we came to Prague, there had been no social intercourse of any kind even between the different parties of the left, and I recall the astonishment of a friend of mine, who was a socialist professor, when he found himself at the Legation in the company of guests of other political creeds. Diplomats acquired, in this way, an unexpected importance, and especially in the early days of the Republic we formed a happy family, thrown together, as at Peking, in an intimacy which was all the greater because there were so few other resources. In fine weather our tennis court brought everyone to the American Legation, which we called the Country Club, and where we made it a rule that ordinary formalities were to be dropped.

In the beginning of my stay at Prague, I was fortunate to find some exceptionally pleasant colleagues. The British Minister was then Sir George Clerk, afterwards Ambassador in Paris. On my arrival, looking through the confidential notes kept in the Chancery, I found him described as "austere but attractive." I was never struck by any special austerity on his part, but the second part of the description fitted him better. Few men are completely true to type but George Clerk's appearance of an old-world diplomat was so perfect that even Metternich would have been impressed. Yet behind this antique perfection lay hidden a keen and very up-to-date humour, a talent for enjoying the best of life, and a real gift for friendship. The Italian Minister was at first Antonio Bordonaro, whose untimely death a few years later, when Ambassador in London, will always be regretted by those who loved him for his warm heart. The Dutch lived in the magnificent Nostitz Palace, and no one was more popular than their able envoy, Edgar Michiels, who possessed an incomparable *joie de vivre*. Later, I was pleased to find as French Minister an old friend from prewar Constantinople, François Charles-Roux. Since those days he had married a charming wife whose vivacity animated everything around her, and he had further developed his talents as a distinguished historian, which did not prevent him from taking the warmest interest in the affairs of Central Europe.

I found friends also in my staff. I discovered a hard-working secretary in Howell Williamson, and a most popular one in Alan Winslow, who had lost an arm flying with the Lafayette Squadron and whose good looks endeared him all around. Every envoy had always a succession of Secretaries. One of these, Jack White, was the son of my former chief at Algesiras, and I found him both highly competent and industrious. I had a fine commercial attaché in Jim Hodgson, who was indefatigable in smoothing out the many difficulties over the importation of American cars, and an excellent military attaché in Colonel Warner McCabe, a unique Virginian and the best companion in the world. The Colonel's great delight was to make humourous remarks to rude Czech officials, for he knew they would not understand his wit, which was fortunate, as otherwise international complications might have ensued.

One day, when he was returning from an excursion over the Saxon border, the frontier guards tried to examine his luggage. The discussion which followed gave McCabe an opportunity to bring out the superiority of Virginians at an epoch when he pictured the ancestors of these customs officials swinging by their tails from the primeval trees of the Bohemian forest. Fortunately these remarks were made in English. The customs autocrats explained that they were acting no differently than they would to President Masaryk himself. The Colonel's reply was magnificent. The President's family had always been struck by the remarkable resemblance which he bore to him, "but I guess he'll have to shave off those whiskers."

Ministers at Prague were rather sharply divided between those who had been lucky enough to find palaces and less fortunate envoys who did not play tennis or bridge and were condemned to live in hotels and look for other distractions. So it happened that one of these who had left his family in a distant land found solace in the company of a pretty typist. The echoes of this friendship were loud enough for the wife to hear them from afar, and she arrived in order to investigate her husband's unofficial activities. The Minister feared some inconvenient disclosures and sent for his Secretary, who was unmarried and for whom he supposed that matters of this kind could make little difference. He persuaded the bachelor in case of discovery to explain that any gossip was due to a misunderstanding, and that his chief was innocent and he alone was guilty. When the time came, the loyal Secretary insisted that the wife's discoveries referred only to his own misconduct. The irate lady therefore denounced him as a creature of Satan and declared that she could not be in the same room with so sinful a man as the Secretary, and she forbade him the use of the Legation. All this took place in the presence of the husband, who was obliged to acquiesce in his wife's stern virtue, for she insisted on his joining in censuring the bachelor for his reprehensible conduct. Perhaps she suspected the truth and used the Secretary as a whipping boy, but the rumours of the scandal reached the Secretary's father who, ambitious for his son's future, feared that, with a moral character so smirched, his marriageable prospects would be irretrievably injured, so that he demanded a retraction.

At Prague, we lived in a magnificent palace that was also a slum. Housing conditions after the war were very bad, as they were everywhere in Central Europe, and, apart from diplomats, no one was allowed to occupy more than a limited number of rooms. The others were allotted to poor tenants who paid little or no rent, but could not be evicted even by a Legation. Under one of our principal living rooms, there dwelt an entire family, consisting, as my social secretary explained, of a mother with her daughter, the daughter's "fiancé" and baby, and her son with his "fiancée" and baby, all together. The south wind blew garlic-scented smoke from their fire into our drawing-room and often rendered this uninhabitable, but in spite of persistent efforts to find them other accommodation it took me five years, after the acquisition of the property by the American government, to be rid of these tenants.

In spite of its inconveniences, the palace possessed some immense advantages. One stepped from the drawing-room into a splendid garden, known in Central European phraseology as a "Voluptuar." This extended over seven acres of open space that ran up a hill situated in the heart of the city. Like several other gardens at Prague, this one had formerly been laid out in the Italian style, but all recollection of this early design was lost, and for many years the place was left sadly neglected. Gardeners are labouriously excellent in Bohemia, and one of my first cares was to revive something of the ancient glory of the place by planting an enormous number of bulbs and rose bushes, with the help of a gardener who did the work of four men and understood everything about flowers except where to grow them. An orchard on the hill bore a wealth of fruit blossoms which were a delight in the early spring, and from the top one had a famous view over Prague. The Czechs are rightly proud of the beauty of their capital, and it was always a duty and sometimes a pleasure to accompany every visitor to this Belvedere and admire the panorama, which embraced many great landmarks of Bohemian history.

Once I had occasion to show the Legation garden to a Cabinet officer fresh from Washington. Our conversation follows:

*He.* "Lots of good building land wasted here."

*I* (*fearing that he might recommend the sale of the garden*). "The ground is a bit too steep for building."

*He.* "In Pittsburgh they run streets up much steeper hills than this."

A moment later we reach the top, climb the steps of the Belvedere, and look out on the famous panorama. I wait in vain, expecting some sign of admiration.

*He.* "Lots of old buildings at the foot of the hill. Why don't they tear them down?"

*I.* "Many of them are historic."

*He.* "I never believe in letting history stand in the way of progress. Why, in Washington, where we have lots of historic buildings, whenever one becomes an obstacle to some improvement, they just tear it down and put up a tablet to record the name of the Cabinet officer who lived there."

My First Secretary at that time was Jack White, who inherited from his father Henry White an ambassadorial solemnity under which he concealed a keen sense of humour. The Cabinet officer handed him a telegram to forward, together with a banknote. White returned with the change, to receive from him a friendly pat, and was told to keep the money to "Buy yourself a cigar."

Later I took the same distinguished visitor to lunch with President Masaryk. On our return we had the following talk:

*He.* "The President has no sense of humour."
*I.* "Why do you say that?"
*He.* "I told the President, 'Mr. President, I like your country and I would be in favour of seeing the United States annex it.' The President answered, 'That wouldn't do!' "

This statesman was accompanied by a congressman from Louisana, and to meet these distinguished guests I asked Dr. Beneš to tea. The latter, just back from Geneva, came straight from the station to plunge at once into a lecture on Central Europe. He had not gone far when he became aware that his argument was somewhat above the heads of his audience. Dr. Beneš continued in a more elementary language which impressed the congressman, who turned around to ask me, "Who's the fellow talking?"

"Dr. Beneš."
"Smart fellow. Who is he?"
"The Minister of Foreign Affairs."
"How do you spell his name," He took out his notebook and carefully wrote it down.

I felt some misgiving lest a palace might seem undemocratic as a residence, so I made much of the fact that the Legation property had been cheaper and far more desirable than any modern building which we could have bought at Prague. One influential congressman found the site good but thought it would be necessary to tear down the "lousy old palace" and build something more modern. Another congressman, who served on the Committee of Appropriations, asked to be shown every nook and cranny of the building. His inspection was remarkably thorough, and I foresaw that it would allow him to speak from personal knowledge when the estimates came up before his committee. But his only purpose, as he told me later, was to see how a "real count" had lived.

In 1925, on behalf of the United States government, I was able to purchase the palace from its late owner at about the price it cost him, although he could have obtained much more. The Prague Municipality courteously waived certain restrictions which had previously encumbered it. When I left Prague in 1930, it was a satisfaction to find that the valuation given to the Legation property had increased enormously since its acquisition and was then from seven to eight times the amount paid for it. America owned the most ancient of its diplomatic residences in the youngest capital of Europe.

The interest that Prague offered me was not in the twenty-eight political parties wrangling in Parliament, nor in my preoccupations over debt settlements, nor in trying to overcome the ingenious hurdles set up against the importation of American cars. In much the same way as there was a unique view over the city from the top of the Legation garden, Prague offered a unique view over Central Europe. A German writer during the war had prophesied that the Bohemian capital might become the capital of Mittel-Europa. It became instead its principal observatory, and Czechoslovakia was the meeting ground of East and West, of Slav and Teuton, of an industrial and an agrarian community, of socialist and reactionary. From its ancient towers one saw the roads which lead south to the Danube, north to the Reich, and easterly across Poland to the Russian steppes. But there was also a road which took one to Western Europe, and this Masaryk and Beneš were doing their best to travel along. Before the war, Prague was only a smoky provincial town. It was to become the capital of a state with a more ancient foundation than the Habsburg Empire. And through the mist which hangs over the city like a November fog pierced lights underneath to show that this new state could also be an outpost of Western democracy.

One often hears it said that the Allies made their greatest mistake in destroying the Habsburg Empire. To those who share this view, a bit of still unpublished history can be given which I relate as I heard it from a former Austrian diplomat who, in 1914, had occupied an important post at the Ballplatz.* He told me that, after the Archduke's murder, the pressure of the generals deliberately forced the war. Count Berchtold, the nominal culprit, was only a figurehead. The military believed that Serajevo gave Austria its last chance. Notoriously, the

* The building in Vienna that housed the Austrian Ministry of Foreign Affairs.

Empire had long been honeycombed by sedition from the Slavs within. But the assassination had momentarily brought the sympathy of the world to Austria's side. They were convinced that if they allowed this occasion to pass, and waited until the Russian strategic railroads were completed, the Habsburg Empire would in a few years' time be carved up without even a fight. The ultimatum to Serbia was intentionally couched to provoke a war, but my friend thought that the Ballplatz had badly bungled matters. The long delay which took place between the Archduke's murder and the ultimatum had given time for the opinion of the world to change. Much the same thing was related to me more pithily by another former Austrian diplomat at whose country house I was staying. He put the matter bluntly. Neither England, France, Germany, nor Russia, he averred, wanted war. The only country to want war was Austria, and her only mistake was not to win it, for nothing except a victorious war could then have saved the Empire from disaster.

The peace treaties only confirmed an existing situation, and did not create this, as has often been said. The succession states had in fact established orderly governments eleven months before the Treaty of St. Germain, and twenty before that of Trianon, were signed. How then could the old Austria-Hungary have been restored when it existed no more? The new states would never have obeyed an injunction by the great powers to give up their freshly won independence and return to the Habsburgs, even if France, England, and the United States had suddenly broken the Wilson pledges and reversed a policy which had contributed to their victory. To enforce so surprising a decision the great powers would have had to resort to fresh hostilities against Czechs, Poles, Yugoslavs, and Roumanians, undertaken at a moment when their own rapidly demobilizing armies would have been most unwilling to fight a new war against former allies on behalf of a fallen enemy dynasty. Still less would public opinion in any Western land have tolerated an adventure of this kind. For better or for worse, Central Europe was divided by treaty only when Austria-Hungary had already been dissolved into the different national states and the restoration of the Habsburg Empire had become impossible.

A few days after my arrival at Prague in 1921 I met the builder of the new Czechoslovak Republic, one of the few statesmen whose reputation was enhanced since the war. I was asked to present my credentials at President Masaryk's country residence of Lany, which is at an hour's distance from Prague. To make conversation with the master of ceremonies who accompanied me I alluded to Masaryk's career as a professor. He said that he also was a professor. I asked what his subject was and he said it was social philosophy, for he taught the young men of Prague how they were to behave themselves in society.

The castle of Lany was an eighteenth-century building that had been comfortably modernised for the President's use. It lay on the fringe of a great forest that formerly had belonged to Prince Fürstenberg, but was taken over by the Republic in part payment for his capital levy. The situation was ideal for a Chief of State, who could live near enough to the capital to keep in touch with the government, and yet sufficiently far away to relieve him from the burden of receiving idle visitors. Etiquette in a new Republic can neither be so formal as to suggest the imitation of royalty nor so informal as to pass unnoticed. At Prague, in 1921, it was still in the moulding, the President's staff inclining to elaborate ceremonial practises and Masaryk himself preferring an American standard of simplicity. The informality of the White House is one more of manner than of substance, but in Czechoslavakia the recollection of Imperial etiquette was still near enough to preserve certain trappings around the head of the state, at a time when it was highly desirable to build up the prestige of the Republic. This resulted in a striking contrast between the pomp of the presidency and the personal simplicity of the President. Masaryk, for instance, would have preferred to continue to dwell in the small apartment which he occupied as a professor, and had to be persuaded to take up his residence in the great Imperial castle of the Hradcany.

Later, after Masaryk's severe illness, Lany was acquired for his convalescence, and in order to show himself in different parts of the Republic, he spent a certain time every year in former archducal residences located in Moravia and Slovakia, which had been taken over by the new state. The President's household was administered by a chancellor, and he had a military guard always on duty, whose protection in the early days of the Republic was thought necessary to shield the head of the State from a possible *coup de main*. This display, which far exceeded anything at the White House, surrounded a man who genuinely loved simplicity for its own sake and who not infrequently would walk to the Legation to have a quiet chat with me—a man who detested every kind of pomp, and whose personal character was no more affected by his sudden elevation to the highest dignity than it had been cast down during a long life in which he had encountered much adversity, unpopularity, and slander.

Everyone knows that Masaryk was the son of a Slovak coachman and was first apprenticed as a blacksmith. The smithy may be a good school for statesmen to learn how to hammer iron on an anvil, for Mussolini's and Hoover's fathers were both blacksmiths, but the President's origin had little connection with his subsequent career. He has been described as the "Philosopher-Statesman," but except that he was a thinker, such description seemed beside the mark. Certain specialists have told me that his philosophical writings possess little original value. This opinion may or may not be true, but his intellectual speculations appear to me as irrelevant as is the quality of some politicians' French, and he could be neither more nor less highly regarded as a statesman because of them. The greatest democrat becomes a dictator in the classroom, and an academic career gave Masaryk the assurance which so often accompanies the teaching profession. The positiveness of the opinions he expressed seemed to me to come more from his training as an educator than from his position as Chief of State. So far as I could judge, his literary style was steeped with the jargon of the German university. Earlier writings, like his book on Russia, which he gave me, are full of those long and ugly half-philosophical, half-mystical words which learned Germans delight to parade and the ponderous vagueness of which contributes so often to their reputation for depth.

As President Masaryk gained in political wisdom he gradually discarded much of this Teutonic vocabulary and shook off some of his earlier academic inheritance. His attitude also became more tolerant towards everyone except perhaps professors. University appointments in Czechoslovakia were made by the President, and he complained to me about the intrigues which invariably surrounded them. To my query how men of learning could so demean themselves, the President caustically replied that professors and learning were far from being identical. At a time when many professors in German universities were veering toward a truculent nationalism, Masaryk kept his tolerant views. I believe that his greatest merit was to preserve the liberal spirit undimmed and stamp this on the new state during the black reaction which left democracy tottering in Central Europe.

Unlike most of his countrymen, Masaryk did not begin as an enemy of the Habsburgs. For many years he favoured a federal solution for the Dual Monarchy. Only toward the end did he see that this was impossible. When he attempted to compose the differences between Vienna and the southern Slavs he met with repeated snubs from Count Berchtold. His intimates say that he reached the conclusion with extreme reluctance that Czech grievances could never be satisfied within the framework of the Austro-Hungarian Empire. When I sat down to chat with the President in his study at Lany, it was hard to imagine the wild adventures which this kind-looking, quiet old man had gone through in creating a new state. The principal impression he made on me was one of natural dignity. He seemed to have none of that compelling force which made anyone who fell under the spell of Theodore Roosevelt ready to follow him as a leader, right or wrong. I could discern in him little of the intellectual vitality of Charles Evans Hughes, which was so practical that it bordered on opportunism and so authoritative that it left his listeners without an argument.

Masaryk's strength seemed to me to lie rather in a quiet reserve of moral force, a shyness with authority, and an inherent goodness which was simple without being gullible. His verbal expression was even a little elementary. He repeated truisms, and his outlook seemed to me neither original nor striking, although occasionally his insight cut deep below the surface. He neither strove for effect nor did he seem to care if he created any impression on his listener. He was more human and less of a superman than I had anticipated. There was no trace of affectation or vanity in his speech, which was that of man to man. Underneath this homely benevolence ran a strain of what for want of a better name can be called idealistic opportunism. I suspect that his most important decisions were taken in the silence of his thought by moral instinct more than by reason. To me he observed that there was something in the Czech character which courts martyrdom, and in saying this he may have had himself in mind, for there was a touch of John Huss in his soul, and if he had failed in his task or had fallen into the hands of his enemies, instead of escaping from their clutches in the nick of time I am convinced that he would have walked to the scaffold with the same fortitude.

Probably it is a mistake to expect the more shallow signs of human greatness to strike the eye. Certain statesmen who possess a theatrical side take delight in flashing epithets and strive to create an impression by exhibiting their less commendable talents. There was nothing histrionic about Masaryk, not even glibness, nor any trace of the politician's tricks. His handshake was not hearty, and it was impossible to imagine him striving for popularity by any cheap devices. But his outspokenness was engaging, and I admired the profound sincerity of a man who had enough moral courage to refuse to flatter the natural pride of his people and appeared far more inclined to criticize than to praise them. This was nothing new, for on two occasions before the war he had made himself the most hated man in Bohemia by taking up unpopular causes. Before questions of moral principle he was adamant.

Neither arrogance nor vanity are faults peculiar to any station of life, but those of lowly origin who rise to exalted positions often become the worst offenders. Masaryk was without trace of either weakness. His great achievement in a land long divided by bitter racial, religious, political, and social hatreds was to offer an example of moderation, and malice to none. As a Czech leader, he held out the olive branch to the Germans, who recognised his worth even when they disliked his ideas. He showed neither hatred nor vindictiveness in his character, or if he ever had any its expression was kept well concealed. A Slovak friend, who later counted himself among the President's warmest admirers, related to me that his father, for political reasons, had felt so bitter toward President Masaryk that, as a boy, he was never permitted to play with the latter's children. Afterwards in Siberia, the Czech Legionaries had elected the Slovak as an army delegate just when Masaryk was trying to win their support. My friend, who was still under the impression of his early memories, offered to resign to avoid any embarrassment, but the future President would not hear of this.

At the time when the recognition of the new state was sought for in Washington and in Paris, the grating sound of a then unfamiliar name like Czechoslovakia had first to be made acceptable. This in itself was a *tour de force,* for, strictly speaking, no such country, name, or race had ever existed. Czechs and Slovaks initially possessed a kindred origin, but during a thousand years of history the two peoples had passed through very different experiences. Masaryk would personally have preferred a return to the historic name of Bohemia, but this did not sufficiently assert Czech supremacy, left out the Slovaks, and contained too many Teutonic connotations at a time when it was desirable to bring out the Slav foundations of the new state. Already the number of Germans included in its future boundaries was sufficiently alarming to make the Czech leaders anxious, and at the Peace Conference they would gladly have relinquished to the Reich the aggressively Pan-German district of Eger although this had belonged to the Bohemian Crown ever since in the Middle Ages it had been pledged to a king of Bohemia as security for a loan. Dr. Beneš went so far as to propose a plan by which the million Germans in that region were to be exchanged for a few hundred thousand Lusatian Serbs, who are a peasant community living across the border in Saxony. This proposal was submitted to Lloyd George, but that statesman was reported to have dismissed it with the words, "On the one hand they want to give up, on the other to take. Let them stay as they are."

President Masaryk had also declared repeatedly that he would favour returning to Hungary those districts along the Danube in which the Magyars formed a majority. Unfortunately, this cession would not have gone far to satisfy Hungarian irredentism. The Slovak question is as much social as it is political, and Western students may discover to their surprise that the same terms convey very different meanings in Central Europe. Slovakia was a kind of Czech Ireland, and its inhabitants are separated by temperament and tradition from the Czechs. But in spite of much friction between the two, there was no reason to suppose that the Slovak peasantry, who had benefited greatly from the agricultural policy of the new state, felt any wish to return to their former Magyar masters.

President Masaryk's name is invariably associated with that of Dr. Beneš, for the two men had worked together during so many years. At the beginning of his administration, when the President fell gravely ill and believed he would die, he called the political leaders to his bedside and asked them to give their solemn pledge to elect Beneš as his successor. His opinion never changed in this respect. Yet intellectually the two men were very different, and temperamentally I suspect Masaryk to have been the younger, for under his calm appearance lay hidden a still youthful fire. Beneš, on the other hand, possessed a mental outlook which refused to be affected by any emotion or impulse.

Once Beneš was having tea with me, and a young diplomat who had dropped in asked him why the Czechs were so wanting in the graces of manner. I winced before an exhibition of tactlessness which it was impossible for me to stop, but Dr. Beneš appeared not in the least sensitive as many a lesser man would have shown himself. He frankly admitted this deficiency and explained it by describing the social history of his people. There was no Czech whose father or whose grandfather, he stated, had not been either a peasant or a workman. Yet after two generations they had been able to create a professional and an industrial class and to build up the solid structure of their state. Manners and graces would all come in due time. The doctor was certainly not aware of what John Adams had written when he expressed the hope that, until the third generation, Americans also would refrain from pursuing the graces of life.

With all his hard matter-of-factness, Dr. Beneš was perhaps, although unconsciously, the truest romantic I have known. Once I mentioned this to him, and the remark must have pleased, for a few days later I heard him so describe himself. His romance came from the fact that as a poor peasant boy he had worked barefoot in the fields to gather potatoes for his parents' supper. Since the age of twelve, he had been thrown on his own resources. But always he had dreamed of the fate of the great Austrian Empire which, more than anyone, he helped to destroy. At eighteen, he had left for Paris to round out his education, with two hundred francs in his pocket. He discovered as a student what hunger meant, yet he learned foreign languages by memorizing the Bible, which for him had no other spiritual meaning. Even then he wrote a French thesis for his doctorate on the necessity of preserving Austria-Hungary, but insisted that it could be preserved only by granting autonomy to the subject races.

He met his wife when the two were young students, and they had married on nothing. During these early years when he was a teacher of sociology at the Commercial Academy at Prague, Madame Beneš managed to save something out of the pittance of his salary. She then had a small inheritance from an aunt, but as soon as the war broke out this little fortune went to the Czech cause. Beneš then escaped to Switzerland to avoid arrest, and for four years he was not able to see her again. But instead of teaching sociology to Czech students at Prague, he taught the intricacies of the Czech problem to Allied leaders in Paris. Madame Beneš meanwhile was thrown into the common prison in

Vienna. I did not learn this from her, for although I used to see her continually, never once did I hear her allude to past sufferings which she had bravely undergone. On one occasion she had to act as hostess at a great banquet given at the castle in honour of Dr. Schober, then Austrian Chancellor, who had been the head of the police at Vienna at the time when Madame Beneš lay in prison. What thoughts ran through Dr. Schober's mind I cannot say, for he must have been aware of this circumstance, but no gesture or word on the part of his hostess reminded her guest of that not very remote past.

Dr. Beneš possessed two seemingly contradictory talents; one of these he would call objectivity, and the other was propaganda. He was a born propagandist and quite unable to meet anyone, however insignificant, without trying at once to win him over to his point of view. At times he employed for this purpose the nebulous philosophical jargon with which, to the horror of Anglo-Saxon minds, German training has poulticed Central European thought. But this practice was a blind, for Beneš was never unintentionally vague. His mind was always precise, and no one could be more practical. When he adapted his argument to his audience, no detail was too elementary to be remembered.

Once he was my guest in Florence, and we met a young Italian nationalist. Beneš had no idea who the man was, nor did my friend realize at the time to whom he was talking. The Italian expounded broad views of statecraft with the superb confidence which comes from reading the popular press; Beneš listened to all his solemn nonsense as attentively as if he were hearing some eminent politician at Geneva, and then argued back so effectively that my friend was reduced to silence.

If Beneš had remained at the university he would have made his mark, for he possessed an uncanny talent for analysis, a lucid power of expression with the ability to draw a historical parallel, and in spite of his fondness for propaganda he was able to take, when he chose, as detached a view of current events as if they had happened under the Pharaohs. As soon as he began an argument, he marshalled his facts like a German university professor, enumerating point after point, and labelling these *primo, secundo, tertio*. He possessed the equipment of an intellectual machine, a card-indexed brain, a marvellous memory, an enormous capacity for work, and a mind fertile in resources. The facts of every controversy were at his fingers' ends. In

Geneva he was seen at his best, always able to offer a concrete plan which was usually so persuasive that less laborious delegates from other states discovered that Dr. Beneš had admirably expressed their own convictions.

In the early years after the First World War, Beneš was flitting busily between Paris and London, trying to effect a compromise between Poincaré and Curzon and to preserve the mask of a united front. Czech views regarding Germany were nearer to those held in London, but Beneš remained closer to Paris, frankly giving as a reason that in case of trouble the French would help him but he could expect nothing from England. These were the days when Secretary Hughes was not unsuccessfully striving to rescue a shipwrecked continent with a diplomacy which turned politics into economics and tried to give Europe the respite of a few years' prosperity. The Dawes Plan* was largely Hughes' achievement, and I felt proud to serve under a chief who never hesitated to provide a clear direction and would always breathe his commanding personality into the conduct of our foreign policy.

Beneš' prestige at that time stood higher at Geneva than it did in his own country, and it was said of him in jest that he was like the Czechoslovak Crown, whose domestic purchasing power at one time did not correspond to its external value. Foreign esteem for his ability was less advantageous to him at Prague. His people had not yet given him his deserts, and the immense services he had rendered them were deliberately largely ignored. Long ago the ancient Greeks observed that democracies are jealous, and the Foreign Minister's ambitious activities abroad were little understood and often resented at home. This was also because Beneš' personal baggage contained few of those lighter foibles which make for popularity. President Masaryk's dignified aloofness was accepted as appropriate for an elderly Chief of State, but not so the attitude of a minister whose giant strides had made him pass over the heads of political leaders well known when he was still an obscure youth.

* The plan for revising the schedule of reparations payments presented to the Allied governments by a committee headed by Charles G. Dawes. The plan called for the evacuation of the Ruhr Valley by Allied occupation troops and for the scaling downward of reparations payments. Even on this reduced basis, Germany was not able to meet its obligations for long, and the Young Plan of 1929 replaced the Dawes Plan as the basis for reparations payments.

When the Kellogg Pact* was originally broached, I doubt if Dr. Beneš entertained many illusions about its efficacy, but it happened to fit his policy and he took a hardly suspected part in its adoption. Secretary Kellogg had, at first, not been greatly concerned about Czechoslovakia, but when the Pact unaccountably hung fire for months in Paris, I notified Washington that certain of the reasons had to be looked for in Dr. Beneš' fear that it was incompatible with the terms of the French alliance. When Beneš returned from Geneva, he showed me a telegram from Paris asking him to state the conditions on which he would be prepared to give his consent. I cabled these to Washington, and a few days later Secretary Kellogg added the treaty of the Little Entente to the generous list of other exceptions that might justify war which his Pact had already recognised. The Secretary of State telegraphed his effusive thanks to Beneš, and the treaty was signed.

Dr. Beneš' policy aimed to place the protection of his country, so far as possible, in international agreements, and for this purpose he had always utilized Geneva diplomacy to its fullest limits. No one knew better than he the dangers of a state situated in the centre of Europe, surrounded on three sides by potential enemies, and with unassimilated, and partly hostile, minorities living within its frontiers. The Republic was confronted not with one, but with a dozen problems which touched at some point every combination of European politics and made it certain that the country could not escape from being dragged into any future conflagration. Although future forecasts are idle, one recalls the impressive prophecy of the great Czech historian Palacky, during a period of harsh repression, that the Czechs had existed before the Habsburgs and would continue to exist after they had gone.

Later I was to see much of Dr. Beneš when in 1938 he arrived in London as a refugee after the Munich surrender. The deep furrows that lined his face bore witness to the strain and suffering he had gone through in that crisis. He then lived very secluded in a small house in Putney. Although embittered, he was able to speak of Munich with a

* Also known as the Kellogg-Briand Pact for the Renunciation of War, it was concluded at Paris on August 27, 1928. The signatory states, including France and the United States, declared that they condemned "recourse to war for the solution of international controversies, and renounce it as an instrument of national policy in their relations with one another."

greater detachment than might have been expected. I asked him if he felt that he could have counted on Russian support had the Czechs resisted. He was certain of this, but it would have meant identifying his people before the world as Bolsheviks.

When the Second World War broke out, Dr. Beneš' position in London improved, although it took some time before the British government was publicly prepared to repudiate the Munich agreement. Dr. Beneš, however, was no longer described as a "sinister figure" nor vilified by many who thought that by blackening him sufficiently they would add respectability to the Munich capitulation. He ceased to be the ghost of a murdered state and became again the President of Czechoslovakia. With the progress of the war he soon regained his early confidence.

I had frequent talks with him regarding the future of Europe, and he made no secret of the fact that, although his own preference lay in attaching his country to the West, he realized that in the event of future trouble England would not send an army into Central Europe whereas Russia would. And because of that, he felt the compulsion to ally himself with Moscow. I asked him more than once if he did not fear Soviet interference in Czech internal affairs, but he would not at that time admit any such apprehension and mentioned matters that brought out the Bolshevik respect for Czech sovereignty, even in questionable instances where the reverse might have been expected. After he returned from Moscow, he told me that the Czech Communists had never even seen Stalin until he himself had introduced them. Nor was any attempt made at the Kremlin to censor his speech at the official banquet, although the Foreign Office would have required this before he could speak publicly in London. Dr. Beneš liked to repeat the old argument about the Czechs forming a natural bridge between Russia and the West, owing to their being Slavs by origin and Westerners by culture.

In spite of his seeming confidence, I cannot help thinking that there were already some glimmers of apprehension on his part, although he would have denied the charge. I was attached at that time to our Embassy in London, and early in 1942 I had been working on a plan that called for an American, British, and Russian committee that should study the various problems which were certain to arise in Central Europe after the conclusion of the war and try to reach an early agreement on as many points as possible. I showed this plan to Dr. Beneš, who expressed himself as being in hearty sympathy with my proposal but added that there was no time to lose, as the Russians were getting cockier and would become more and more difficult. I had already observed signs of this in the Soviet opposition to a Central European union that was then under discussion among the four exiled governments in London. Yet I do not believe that until much later Dr. Beneš foresaw the extent of the threat to Czech independence, and only on his return to Prague did he understand how grave was the peril and how worthless were the assurances that he had been given at Moscow. It was then already too late, and Dr. Beneš, enfeebled by a stroke, was no longer able to fight the danger to his country.

I must add a word about Jan Masaryk, although during the eight years that I passed at Prague he had as yet given few signs of his real worth. In part this was due to the eminence of his father, which inevitably placed the son under his shadow. And Jan, although worshipping his father, was himself the antithesis of whatever was academic. There also were other elements in the son's character which were not easily discerned by a superficial observer. Jan always did his best to conceal his deep melancholy under the surface of an apparent gaiety which often made him act the playboy. His outward jocoseness was usually a blind that even harmed him in the esteem of his compatriots before the war, for they were more accustomed to the pompous gravity of many of their public men.

Jan was at heart deeply patriotic, but his character contained very little of the Czech. Perhaps his American mother had something to do with this; perhaps it was the effect of early years spent in the United States. Certainly his personality was differently shaped from that of most of his compatriots. His merriment was much less a characteristic of his nature than it was a cover for much real sadness, which often was expressed when least expected. There is a famous restaurant in a cellar at Prague where there was then a remarkably fine violinist named Wolff. Sometimes late at night when the other guests had left and only a few friends lingered on, Jan would sit at the piano to play Slovak melodies with Wolff. And no one who heard him on these occasions can ever forget the deep pathos of his sensitive rendering. In his nature there was also a great kindness and great generosity. No one ever appealed to Jan in vain, and no man ever tried harder to be of service to the many who went to him in their need. Perhaps he derived an inward satisfaction in assisting the aristocrats who would once have looked down on him but then came in numbers to him for help in their troubles with the government.

He was almost painfully aware of the fact that the Czechs were somewhat wanting in social graces. He knew that they had risen too freshly from the soil, that their learning was still too new to have acquired the easy graces and amenities of life that were more current in nations which had preserved the vestiges of an aristocratic structure. He often took pains to point out and to emphasize these deficiencies, yet he suffered acutely when others alluded to them. But his natural kindness restrained him from displaying any ill will towards those diplomats who were tactless enough to express themselves on that thorny subject. Once at a dinner, a young Secretary had been particularly offensive, not knowing whom he was talking to, for the conversation had been carried on in English. But Jan never held this against him, though he could have asked for the offender's recall.

Particularly at the beginning of his diplomatic career, an uneasy humility and self-depreciation gnawed Jan. He was nervous when first appointed Minister to London, and he said to me in his inimitable way that he feared he was not yet sufficiently "housebroken." A few months later, while dining with me in a Piccadilly hotel served by a Czech waiter, he remarked that if it had not been for his father he might have been the waiter instead of an envoy. But the success he soon achieved went far to overcome this early diffidence. It was not long before no diplomat in London became more popular, and he had the rare distinction for a foreign envoy of being generally called by his Christian name.

This is not the place to speak of his distinguished service during the war or of the talent that his broadcasts displayed. Once he said jocosely to me that his real interest did not lie in Czechoslovakia, but that he was working for a Europe in which his nephews could sit of an evening in a beer garden listening to the music and be able to say openly, "To hell with the government."

He was, I think, already apprehensive about the Soviets, and once when mentioning a Czech diplomat he described him to me as being a "Moscow man." The last time I saw Jan was on the eve of his departure for Prague to become Foreign Minister. He made no secret to me that he went back with little pleasure. I think that even then he entertained deep forebodings. When I wished him luck, he said, "I shall stand it as long as I can but no longer."

# 9. *A Diplomat Bows Out*

In 1930, after more than eight years passed at Prague, I was somewhat tired of the monotony of diplomatic life. Such glamour as it ever possessed for me had long ago worn off, and though I liked the work, when work there was, I was bored by diplomatic entertainment and the continuous obligation of attending tedious banquets and talking to tedious people. I had then virtually made up my mind to resign unless I was able to obtain a more important post. But before I could do this, President Hoover relieved me of any doubts I had on the subject by accepting my untendered resignation. There were more courteous ways of dismissing an old public servant of some experience than the one that he adopted, although his method was by no means unusual in the conduct of our government. Mr. Hoover liked to be known as the great Engineer, but his zeal in advocating the preservation of natural resources did not extend to the human ones that were at his disposal. The ease with which he dropped many career men was not calculated to flatter their self-esteem, though doubtless it provided some lessons in humility. The presidential purpose was only one of utilising diplomatic posts as a hidden subsidy for administration politics. My successor at Prague obtained his training for world affairs by running a taxi company.

My own case was of slight importance, but the careless discard of trained human material offers a striking contrast to the success of American industry in the elimination of waste and helps to throw some light on the disparity between the efficiency of our private enterprise and the frequent inefficiency displayed by different branches of our government.

My old friend Justice Holmes, with his old-world standard of courtesy, wrote to me on that occasion (February 1, 1930):

> Many years ago I realized that we are brutal in our way of dealing with public officials and that men who in other countries would not

be allowed to end a long and faithful service without some mark of recognition here are simply dropped. Your case is not peculiar—it is I think what always happens—I am always shocked when I hear of it.

A few weeks later (April 15, 1930) Justice Holmes, who was then nearly 90, wrote me again and, perhaps vaingloriously, I quote a passage from his letter.

> This is merely a line interpolated between duties—to tell you that talking with Hughes C[hief] J[ustice] today he said that you were not only one of the most accomplished but one of the most efficient and useful as well as popular of our foreign representatives and lamented the loss to the service. There was no qualification but solid high appreciation that gave me great pleasure.

This praise was all the more gratifying because of the admiration that I had felt for Hughes when he was my Chief. Of all the Secretaries of State under whom I served, he seemed to me the ablest. It was a magnificent treat to listen to his crystal-clear exposition of a question when he would develop its different aspects and then draw a conclusion so convincing that it admitted of no further argument. With Hughes, action followed naturally as the servant of his thought. He possessed the rare gift of being authoritative without appearing to be dictatorial and yet preserving with this a keen sense of humour. I have been told that his character contained elements of deep emotion, but he concealed his feelings under an Olympian serenity that gave him, quite unjustifiably, a reputation for iciness. I had an inkling of this depth of feeling when on one occasion I asked him if he thought that we could have entered the war after the *Lusitania* had been sunk. "Certainly," was his reply. I expressed regret that he had not been President during the war years. I still can hear his answer: "If I had been, I would not be alive today."

Hughes was no exception to the American political axiom that only rarely do our ablest men reach the White House. He had come within an ace of election in 1916, when the *New York Times* conceded his victory. If he had then been elected President instead of Wilson, the fate of the world might have been different. It is idle to speculate about this, but when I mentioned the matter to him Hughes' complete detachment became apparent. He observed that his defeat was fortunate, for whereas the Republicans had supported the Democratic Administration in the war, it was more doubtful if the reverse would have happened. It has often been said that Wilson's greatest mistake lay in not sending men like Root and Lodge to Paris. Hughes gave me a novel explanation of why he regarded this as such a gigantic blunder. He said that whoever had gone to Paris would inevitably have been destroyed at the conference, and after that Wilson could have stepped forward successfully.

Hughes thought that 1908 had been the proper time for his candidacy, but Theodore Roosevelt was opposed to him, not desiring to see another prominent figure arise in New York. Hughes' failure to reach the White House in 1916 was due entirely to a petty factional fight in California which did not interest him in any way. He related the details of this incident, which had been largely distorted in the public mind. Next day I wrote down what he said to me.

Hughes had left the Supreme Court where, in his own words, he had grown "woolly," in order to enter the presidential campaign. He had a very meagre knowledge of politics, so he told me, and still less understanding of what partisan bitterness could mean. He was then the nominee of both the Republican and the Progressive Party, which after the disastrous split in 1912 had once more come together in their choice of a common candidate. In the course of his campaign Hughes planned to visit every state in the Union. The early reports that he had received from California did not indicate that anything was wrong there. When he left for the Pacific Coast, he asked to be met at the state line by representatives of both parties. This was done, but almost immediately afterwards the Progressive representative was summoned away, owing to the sudden illness of his wife. Hughes asked at once for another Progressive to replace him but no one came. He spent Sunday at Pasadena, going to church in the morning, which he remarked to me was an appropriate thing for a candidate to do. It was later suggested to him to take a drive down the coast. He stopped for some refreshment and then returned to Pasadena, where his manager told him that Governor Hiram Johnson had been staying at the Long Beach Hotel at the time of his visit there. Hughes asked why he had not been informed of this, as he would have liked to have called on the Governor. His manager answered that he did not know it himself and had only just heard it from a newspaperman. Hughes' personal relations with the Governor had hitherto been very friendly, and he had entertained him on several occasions when the latter went to New York. He sent word to Johnson that he would appreciate a message of welcome to California, to which he would reply in suitable terms, and suggested that they should agree on the texts of the letters exchanged before they were given to the press. Hiram Johnson answered that he would have nothing to do with Hughes so long as he was accompanied by a Republican but, as Hughes observed to me, he could not ask the latter to leave as he was also the candidate of the Republican Party.

This episode was outrageously distorted and made to appear as if it had been a wilful insult to Hiram Johnson. It resulted in Hughes losing the vital state of California by a few hundred votes which stood between him and the presidency. Hughes was not of the opinion that Johnson had deliberately set out to knife him, but that the latter believed at the time in his own great career and that he had planned to run far ahead of the rest of the ticket. He overshot the mark, and in so doing brought on Hughes' defeat.

Hughes related this incident to me at Prague in 1928, twelve years after it had taken place. He spoke of it with complete detachment and without any trace of rancour. In spite of the keen zest for life which made his personality so stimulating, Hughes had lost all political ambition. I remarked that I had regretted the statement he had made shortly before that he was too old to be President.

> What I meant [he said] was, not that I was decrepit, but I should have been 71 at the end of my first term and that is too old in America to start a second term. Consequently I should hardly be in office before Congress would begin planning as to who would be my successor and I would be deprived of the proper authority. I could not be the kind of President I would wish. Moreover the office holds no attraction for me, although the American people would never believe that. I know it inside out and it is a small office. I'd far sooner be the leader of a party in a Parliament for six months than President for four years. With the Senate as it is today what kind of support could I hope for? Whom could one depend on to defend the Administration? Nor was there any real demand for my candidacy nor any great issues to be decided. As, however, it is a common adage

that no one has ever refused the presidency, I had to be categorical. Hoover was very anxious for it and it wasn't fair to allow any uncertainty over my position.

Since that talk, the Depression and the war and its aftermath have immensely enlarged the dimensions of the White House. Whether the multiplication of government offices and government interference which has gone on steadily ever since is conducive to a loftier presidential authority or the reverse provides a moot point. Jefferson and Lincoln accomplished much without having large staffs. Today the creeping extension of legislative measures renders a huge personnel indispensable, although even so probably on a much lesser scale than what now exists. In my own small sphere, I recollect when I was a young Secretary at the Embassy in Paris in 1903, and again in London in 1905, that the entire mission from ambassador to messenger numbered only nine instead of the present figure, which is closer to nine hundred. Today nearly 23,000 officials are said to be on the payroll of the State Department.

Sometimes it has occurred to me that an international tourist agency like Thomas Cook could, with great convenience to the general public and considerable economy in personnel, rent, and time, carry out most of the routine work of diplomacy jointly for many nations. Such questions as visas and registrations and attestations could all be handled by a single bureau of this kind acting for different countries in different capitals. Routine business transacted through an international agency could lead to immense economies by reducing the present giant staffs, with correspondingly smaller rents, pensions, and other items of expenditure. Yet I fear that the mere suggestion of such a proposal would lead to so much general indignation that there is little hope for its adoption until a debt-laden world will be more ready than it is today to recover from its present drunken spree.

At the beginning of the third decade of this century, nations still seemed peacefully inclined. The world appeared better disposed to enjoy an era of calm, with nothing startling likely to occur in any early visible future. Germany was then behaving itself reasonably, and Hitler had only been heard of as an ignorant rabble-rouser whose star was believed to be already on the wane. Mussolini was thought to have sobered down, and many then saw in him a pillar of peace. Even Russia seemed uninterested by events outside its borders, and the opinion was frequently heard that Communism was gradually being modified into something different and more respectable. The prospects for a settled world in fact appeared to be extremely good.

In view of my retirement I had taken a house in London, which for family reasons seemed at that time to be a more convenient place than Washington. My house is now a gaping space, which is all that remains of its Georgian structure after the Nazi bombers passed over it. I then intended to divide my time between England and the United States. The American who lives outside his country is regarded with some unflattering oversimplification as being an expatriate. Yet it seems to me that expatriatism can be of the mind or of the body or both, and the one test to be applied of whether or not it is reprehensible depends on inner feelings and on outward performance far more than on the mere physical circumstances of residence.

I wanted to write, and in London I first completed a life of Theodore Roosevelt, already begun at Prague.* This was a labour of love, for apart from the fact that Roosevelt had originally appointed me to the Diplomatic Service, he had shown himself friendly on more than one occasion, expressing himself with that heavy emphasis which he was prone to give to all that he said and did. Two years before the First World War, I wrote an article to prophesy its imminence, and I argued that a defeat of the British Empire would also mean a defeat for the United States, to guard against which we ought to arm, and that we might have to intervene to preserve the balance of power. Such views were unheard of at that time and no American periodical would print them, so I sent the article to the *National Review* in London, where it appeared.† Roosevelt then told me that he agreed with what I said, but he was not surprised at the country's deaf ear to any warning. He had lately delivered an important address before the Rhode Island Historical Society that had passed unnoticed, for he stood then at the ebb of his political reputation and had not yet been forgiven for having split the Republican Party. I still recall an uncle of mine, who was the owner of a New York daily, coupling his name with that of Benedict Arnold.

* *Roosevelt: His Mind in Action* (Boston and New York, Houghton Mifflin, 1930).

† The United States and Anglo-Germany Rivalry," *National Review* (January 1913), pp. 736–50.

After we entered the war, the Columbia University Press reprinted my *National Review* articles with an introduction by Theodore Roosevelt.* He was then already fast recovering his former stature. He expected to be re-elected President and would have been but for his untimely death. He had sent me word that he wanted me with him. I felt a personal loyalty towards him as well as admiration for one who so closely resembled the great worthies of the sixteenth century. He too shared their ambition for a well-rounded life of thought and action. He too had their thirst for the varied experiences offered by learning and adventure, and he felt their wish for fame. It is easy to point out his mistakes. His real genius never was one of intellectual power but lay in the quality of a leadership that made him unforgettable and caused his admirers to be ready to follow him whether right or wrong.

Roosevelt's fame is today temporarily dimmed. He had foreseen popular fickleness, and when a wild enthusiasm greeted his return from Africa he remarked to a friend: "It is a kind of hysteria. They will soon be throwing rotten eggs at me." After another ovation he prophesied jestingly that before long many people would compare his character unfavourably to that of Caligula. What Roosevelt did not foresee was the indifference of oblivion which falls equally to the lot of statesmen, poets, and painters after they are dead. Yet this temporary apathy is not injurious to their permanent place in history, for it allows the cheaper trappings of tinsel glory to be forgotten and their real contribution to remain.

After finishing my life of Roosevelt I began a study of the Americans who were in England during the War of Independence, which was published under the title *Divided Loyalties*.† Moral values in history have always fascinated me more than facts, and what men have done is often of lesser consequence than the reasons why they have done it. The preparation for this book meant many visits to the British Museum and the Record Office, till I swore that never again would I embark on a similar labour of research. Searching through obscure records brings one into contact with some little-known men whose activities are often of greater interest than many more familiar characters. One lives with them in a past that seems alive and that makes the pres-

* *A Prophecy of the War* (New York, Columbia University Press, 1918).

† *Divided Loyalties: Americans in England During the War of Independence* (Boston and New York, Houghton Mifflin, 1933).

ent recede in its importance. The historian's sense of values and of perspective in this way can be changed by the illusion of time, until the personages of another age become alive to him and may even appear nearer than many of the people around him.

I took the keenest interest, for instance, in Dr. Edward Bancroft, who was a traitorous villain of the deepest dye but also a man of real accomplishments, a chemist, an inventor, a physician, even a novelist and a member of the Royal Society. He lived in the intimacy of Benjamin Franklin, whom he betrayed, and yet was never suspected by that wisest of men. Although professing to be an American patriot Bancroft, who was in Paris during our Revolution, reported regularly to Lord Stormont, the British Ambassador. He would place his communications in the hollow of a box tree on the south terrace of the Tuileries Gardens, where an English Embassy messenger would call for them. Bancroft boasted that he gave notice in London within forty-two hours of the secret negotiations at Versailles that led to the American alliance with France. He offered some excellent advice without realizing that the always stubborn George III refused to listen to him because the royal spies had discovered that Bancroft was "a meddler in stocks" who speculated, and the King regarded these warnings of the impending French alliance as "moves to depress the funds." George III wrote to Lord North to tell him that as Bancroft "was a stockjobber as well as a double spy no other faith can be placed in his intelligence but that it suited his private views to make us expect the French Court means war."

Historical research is like looking for gold. One digs where the soil seems promising, always hoping to find treasure, but usually the metal is of low grade and one must be prepared to meet with much disappointment. I had gone to the Royal Society to see if I could discover any traces of Bancroft and found there a photograph of his portrait which had been sent many years before by his grand-niece, a Mrs. Bancroft Vidal, who gave her address as Turnham Green. I wrote to her hardly expecting an answer, when to my astonishment I received a note by return of post to say that although she was a very old lady yet she would like to see me and would be glad to show me all the letters in her possession.

Then there came up for me a question of conscience. Did she know what I knew—that her great uncle had been a traitor, a spy, and a villain? Could I decently ask her to show me a correspondence which I intended to make use of to prove this? My curiosity was, however, too whetted to reach an immediate decision, and I made up my mind to delay this until after I had seen these letters. Next day I found a very old lady, who had all her wits about her and something more besides, for she both astonished and put me at my ease by asking almost immediately if her great-uncle had been a spy, as she herself could never make out. I tried to be evasive until she remarked that she did not care a rap. In fact, for a reason that will appear, she preferred to think he was one. The correspondence she showed me was of no particular interest, but she explained why so few letters were left. She had seen her uncle, who had been a general in the British Army, burning stacks of Bancroft's letters, saying as he stood before the fire that he was "a damned spy." For a special reason, Mrs. Bancroft Vidal entertained an amused interest in her great-uncle's guilt. She had a sister who lived in Philadelphia and wanted Congress to give him some adequate recognition as a great American patriot. Mrs. Vidal derived an unholy satisfaction at the prospect of her sister's discomfiture when she learned the truth.

Secretary Cordell Hull was the principal American delegate at the Economic Conference which met in London in 1933. No public man could make a deeper impression of sincerity or had a greater simplicity of manner. I enjoyed several talks with him, and when he left to return to Washington he asked me to write to him. I did so regularly until the beginning of the war, and repeatedly he was kind enough to inform me that he had circulated my letters among his associates.

Lately, after reading copies of this correspondence, I was surprised to find how accurately it had been possible to foretell the march of events that led to war. I claim no credit for this, as there were many others who in writing or by word of mouth vainly foretold the impending conflict. Mr. Hull was under no illusion of the dangers ahead and only entertained a hope that the democracies by arming might be in time to restrain the aggressor. It is tragic to think that the measures required to avert war were too unpalatable for peace-loving nations to adopt.

Among the many letters that I wrote to the Secretary of State I shall refer only to one dated May 8, 1936. It concerns a talk with French military men who spoke of their terror at the prospect of waking up one morning and finding that German motorized armies were halfway across Belgium and of their fear that the war might be decided against them during the first critical month. I mentioned that prominent French generals had expressed themselves in favour of cutting their commitments in Central Europe and abandoning Austria and Czechoslovakia to their fate.

I wrote about the opposition to Hitler in Germany and of the General Staff being against war, and of Dr. Karl Goerdeler who came to London in 1937 to advise against lending any support to the Nazi regime, which he predicted could only end in ruin. He had spoken with amazing frankness in spite of the risk that he ran—indeed he was later executed for heading the plot against Hitler. The former Chancellor Bruening also visited London secretly and counselled adequate armaments as the only way by which England could prevent war. But in influential quarters in the City and elsewhere, the belief still existed that Hitler could be "bought off" and that a prosperous Germany offered the best guarantee for peace. Neville Chamberlain was too cautious to listen to the only kind of advice which might have averted the conflict.

When I went to Washington, Secretary Hull suggested and arranged for me to see the President, with whom I spent a pleasant hour during which he did all the talking. I had brought him a memorandum on the future of Austria, but he surprised me by remarking that he read all the despatches from Vienna. I also handed him a plan to define aggression before the crisis occurred in order to forestall likely partisan bickering. To this he stated that he accepted Litvinoff's definition of aggression. Then, as I was leaving, he alluded to his difficulties in handling career men who had principally their wealth to recommend them for missions. I said the wrong thing by remarking that I was a career man, for I felt that he would have preferred another answer.

The impression Franklin Roosevelt made on me that afternoon over a glass of iced tea was one of charm and shrewd intelligence, but it was difficult to get an inkling of his character or to measure his real stature. Greatness, whether it is expressed in thought or in action, is a kind of intermittent spasm. Perhaps its test is one of power when confronted by difficulties yet achieving its aim. It is impossible to think of anyone as being great for twenty-four hours of the day, but even after the briefest acquaintance one associates some people more readily than others with its attributes. It was easy to detect certain visible elements of greatness in Theodore Roosevelt, in Charles Evans Hughes or in Justice Holmes, but in Franklin Roosevelt these were less superficially apparent to the outsider. The office of President can be compared, however, to a cathedral. Its foundations are sunk deep in the ground, so that something earthy clings to them and they are never quite clean. Its tall spires point toward heaven and are outlined in a clearer atmosphere, yet both form part of the same great edifice.

I wrote a number of articles on the international situation that appeared in boring American and British reviews which provide a suitable literary cemetery where the dead are at once forgotten. In accordance with a good old English custom, I wrote some letters to *The Times*. I lectured on Central European problems at Princeton, Johns Hopkins, and Vassar. Audiences were kindly, but all along I felt like a monkey nibbling at a nut without ever getting at the kernel. Diplomacy as a career had lately seemed vapid enough. Writing or lecturing about it seemed equally sterile. Plainly, great events were brewing on the Continent, but no cries of wolf seemed able to accomplish anything. After the flutter provoked by Hitler's rise to power, this was everywhere being calmly accepted as inevitable and even offering certain good sides. The seething German cauldron boiled over, but the British soup still remained tepid.

Certainly whoever listened to the siren song of life in London found its melody entrancing and could forget other preoccupations. England was a pleasant country in which to live and offered many easy satisfactions for every taste before the official regulations had begun to disturb the fabric of daily life. Weekend parties, which once were a great feature of that life, provided many opportunities for politicians and divorce lawyers. They have now virtually disappeared, killed by the axes of three executioners—high taxation, low rations, and scanty domestics. For similar reasons, even the dinner party as a form of entertainment has largely been replaced by the cocktail party, and many sympathetic aspects of the former British hospitality have shrunk sadly under the astringent effects of government measures. Even the excellent roast beef, which did so much to compensate for bad English cooking, is now a thing of the past. Lately I asked a debutante if she had ever eaten a dish of it and she said she had once—in Paris! There is no longer the same good nature that was prevalent before. At the

Athenaeum, after an innocuous remark on my part about the weather to a man seated beside me, his answer was "I don't think that we have been introduced."

During the 'thirties one could still play about pleasantly in England even if Europe was already in a ferment of unrest. Former friendships left me in touch with many diplomats, for diplomacy is a profession that keeps its hold on those who like myself were no longer in office. The rootlessness that is its bane finds some compensation in the easy friendship of its members who have known each other from former posts. The Belgian Ambassador Cartier de Marchienne had been a good friend ever since Peking days, for to be an "old China hand" is a link that is never forgotten. He asked me to join a little shooting syndicate of which the other members were Regis de Oliveira, the Brazilian Ambassador, who was a man of great personal charm and Dean of the Diplomatic Corps; Count Edward Raczinsky, the Polish Ambassador, whose fine dignity during his country's tragedy I later found occasion to admire; and another Belgian diplomat, Prince Eugene de Ligne. We would meet at Loseley Park near Guildford, an old Elizabethan manor where John Donne had once been tutor and where he had fallen in love with the heiress and been imprisoned for his audacity in marrying her. At Loseley we shot pheasants and discussed food at picnic lunches to which each of us contributed a dish. Gastronomy is a favourite subject with ambassadors, who wisely regard it as a meritorious and safe topic of conversation. In the midst of other anxieties Cartier and Regis, who were typical of old-world diplomacy, still found time to enjoy the amenities of life.

Diplomats in London had then acquired a fresh importance. This was partly because so little entertaining went on at Court, but more so owing to the diminishing number of great houses that had formerly been open during the Season. Some of these had been torn down in order to make way for office buildings, clubs, and flats. Grinding taxation was already more and more exercising its levelling influence, and the reign of the great hostesses was well-nigh over. Only a very few of these still remained. I recall one who belonged to another age and preserved a fine sense of authority that reminded me of Good Queen Bess giving orders. In spite of a somewhat ostentatious parsimony which she deliberately cultivated until it became a stock jest, she did much charitable work at the docks, where her racehorses helped to make her very popular.

Lady Oxford was another personality who provided many people with an endless subject of gossip. It was easy to make fun of "Margot," for she lent herself to criticism and remained perfectly indifferent to what was said about her. Such faults as she had were never hidden, and the frankness with which she expressed her opinions was often disconcerting to her friends. She was no hypocrite and unblushingly fearless in speaking out her mind. Thus she expressed to Ribbentrop her very unflattering opinion of Hitler. But she was quite as capable of saying at the dinner table either that she hated Americans or that she loved them. Neither remark, nor both, meant anything, and for those who knew and cared for her they had no significance. Curiously enough, although she had lived in a political atmosphere since she was a girl and her husband had been Prime Minister in critical times,* she herself knew astonishingly little about politics. To her, public life represented only certain men who had occupied important positions and many of whom had been her personal friends. In her opinion, the affairs of England and indeed of the universe were matters that could always be settled at the dinner table or in intimate talks at house parties. She would often quote remarks allegedly made by the great, but her voice in such instances became, according to Sir Edward Grey, that of a ventriloquist.

Except for an underlying liberal instinct which was real, it never occurred to her that politics might include principles and traditions. She was curiously ignorant of history and geography, knew little enough of England and nothing outside the British Isles. Yet in spite of many obvious weaknesses, she possessed a very remarkable personality which she impressed on every word she spoke and on every line she wrote, for she was gifted with a natural style. As a woman she was unforgettable. In her character there was something immaterial together with a vitality that made her personality unique. At the Wharf, her house on the Thames, I caught a glimpse of her once in the twilight looking more like a ghost than a living woman.

Let others chronicle the mundane pleasures of this period. If I have

* Herbert Henry Asquith, British Liberal Party leader who served as Prime Minister, 1908–16.

briefly alluded to the subject it is only in order to bring out the fact that most people refused to see the writing that was already written in great letters on the wall. A few believed even then that the British ruling classes were committing political suicide. J. A. Spender, the old Liberal publicist, observed to me sadly that a Cabinet of twenty men added up to one donkey. And a minor official wittily remarked in Chamberlain's time that England was governed by two men, but they had not been able to find out who the other feller was.

The contrast between Hitler's gigantic armaments and British unpreparedness hardly disturbed anyone's slumbers. In the light of events, it is today unbelievable that so much blindness should have prevailed in high places. Those who like Winston Churchill saw the danger ahead preached in the wilderness and were regarded with extreme suspicion as self-seeking alarmists. Yet during the Munich crisis the nation's feeling was considerably healthier in the pubs than in the clubs, where below the surface there was a certain stratum of defeatism.

Chamberlain's comforting assurances before and after Munich provided a dangerous temporary relief that equally misled many British and many Germans—the former because they hoped that his policy meant peace, and the latter because it was difficult for Hitler to understand that behind many weak and foolish words and gestures there still lived in Great Britain the clear spirit of a great tradition of pride and courage.

# 10. *A Spectator Gazes at the War*

It would be difficult to find anyone of any age or occupation who in some way has not been affected by the Second World War. In this sense, war has been thoroughly democratized and is likely to become still more so in the future. Yet the day when a world war was declared, London could not have been more peaceful. The weather was warm and sunny, of a kind all too rare in the British Isles. I took a walk through Green Park, where I noticed people lying on deckchairs reading and seemingly unperturbed by the news. It was impossible to imagine a more tranquil scene. Suddenly a siren sounded the alarm—no one knew why—but after a few minutes came the "All Clear." No war could have begun more peacefully.

The impending conflict had long been plain. At the beginning of the year, I learned at the French Embassy that their General Staff expected hostilities to break out in the autumn, but its imminence required no secret knowledge nor any gifts of prophecy. Nonetheless the atmosphere at the time of the Munich crisis the year before had seemed far more alarming than what took place in September 1939. One had then seen trenches hurriedly dug in the parks, which some people gloomily suggested were intended to bury the dead. The distribution of gas masks to everyone appeared half an ominous foreboding, half a joke. It was a preparation for the only danger that was never encountered. People were told to go out with these, but many soon discarded this bit of official advice. The war began, in fact, by providing its own anticlimax. Except in Poland, which was far away, few incidents occurred that even faintly resembled the wholesale horrors that everyone had at first expected. True, an Atlantic liner was torpedoed by mistake, with serious loss of life, and the French, as in the nursery rhyme, marched a few miles up some German hill and then marched back again. No wonder the war was soon called phoney.

This general inaction in Western Europe at first seemed to confirm the wisdom of Neville Chamberlain. His dry and sober speeches, even in their self-complacency, had something reassuring about them. The Prime Minister's restrained manner was the antithesis of all that Hitler stood for. It inspired confidence, and he seemed to represent the British people in their calm and silent determination. I find written in my diary in February 1940 that I felt no doubt about the underlying tough obstinacy of his character but was much more concerned as to his imaginative vision. Chamberlain's war preparations were seemingly planned to develop step by step in a careful and methodical manner that was characteristic of the man. Every two or three months a new batch of two hundred thousand men was to be called up. The Prime Minister kept reassuring the country at frequent intervals regarding the greatly increased production of boots and of yards of cloth. All this was good enough, but something else was also needed. I quote from an entry that I made on February 1st 1940:

> What will happen if some sudden stress or strain occurs, some unforeseen reverse or disaster which calls for the instant mobilization of every resource human and material. Wars cannot be carried on by a fixed pattern and there is too much of this pattern present in Mr. Chamberlain's rigid mind.

Doubtless many others then entertained similar thoughts, but they were not enough to exercise an effective pressure on a well-drilled Cabinet whose head had no intention to allow his government to be rushed into anything.

Two days later I wrote in anticipation of a German attack: "If the Allies can hold out till 1941 they are certain to win but I shall feel quieter once the Summer is over."

Then, instead of a German came a Russian attack on the Finns that diverted attention from the tranquil Western front to arouse a far greater indignation than that brought on by the Nazi attack on Poland. Many suggestions were made of how to help Finland, and one well-known serious journalist advanced the astonishing proposal that it would be easier to win a war against Germany if England should also fight Russia at the same time. A favourite idea was that it would only be necessary to bomb Batum or Baku, although few people could say which of the two should be the principal target. Volunteers were called for who knew how to ski, with hearts sound enough to resist intense cold. A friend of mine who had been a captain enlisted as a private for this purpose, and two battalions disguised as Scots Guards went to camp expecting to be sent to Chamonix in order to complete their training in deep snow along with the French *Chasseurs Alpins*. These leisurely and skimpy measures were adopted partly in order to say that something was being done. Perhaps they might be useful later in case of a Scandinavian campaign, but they did no good to the Finns, for it was impossible to aid them effectively without passing through Sweden, and that the Swedes would never allow.

It has always seemed to me that at this juncture Hitler lost his greatest opportunity to win the war. If he had announced that his quarrel was not with the West but with Communism, if he had then offered magnanimous terms to the Poles which he would later have repudiated, if he had invited the Swedes to let the Allies pass through their territory and announced his intention to join them in attacking the unprepared Russians, his appeal would have been very difficult to resist, particularly in France where there was the strongest reluctance to fight the Germans and where helping the Finns seemed like a decent excuse for not having helped the Poles. In England at this time the country had as yet not been touched by war. The small people, with their instinctive discipline, realized the necessity of going through with the fight at any cost, but many in Mayfair did not see how Germany could be beaten and looked with dismay at the misery and sacrifices that a long struggle would inflict. A little more subtlety on the part of Hitler might then have secured for him a bloodless victory in the West. If he had seriously tried to become an ally of France, it is far from unlikely that his blandishments would have been rejected, and within a very few years Great Britain might have seen the Germans threatening their existence from the occupied Channel ports.

When war broke out, I had offered my services at the Embassy, only to find them declined. A year later, after a very agreeable talk with the Ambassador, Mr. Winant, they were accepted. Winant then made a most favourable impression on me. His manner was sympathetic and his appearance was not unlike that of a handsome Abraham Lincoln who had passed through a beauty parlour. His conversation was simple and friendly, so that I looked forward with keen anticipation to working under him. "We will have fun together" were his words when I left. I assured him that I was eager to be of help in any way I could. Like the First Lord of the Admiralty in *Pinafore* I was even prepared to polish the door handles.

Under a very sympathetic appearance, Winant's character was not easy to fathom. His nature was kindly, and he wanted to do the right thing. He gave a fine example of courage during the blitz. Along with a considerable ambition, which he kept well hidden in the background, I suspect he suffered from an inner doubt that grew from his own sense of frustration at not finding himself qualified to attain the high goal to which he aspired. He was a poor administrator and lacked any sense of time, so that broken appointments and indefinite delays meant little to him. On the occasions when I wanted to see him, the hour fixed would be rarely observed, and this procedure of continuous postponements would then go on indefinitely. Not being asked by him to do any real work, I took it on myself to write memoranda on current events, more particularly on questions related to Central Europe.

In the winter of 1941–42, the Polish, Czech, Yugoslav, and Greek governments, which were all living in exile in London, were planning to confederate after the war. Quite unexpectedly I learned from Dr. Beneš that, in spite of the desperate straits in which they found themselves, the Russians opposed this plan although still willing to acquiesce in a Czech-Polish union and in one between Greece and Yugoslavia. Central European problems had already brought on two world wars, and it seemed clear that this might happen for a third time unless a proper settlement could be made. Eight countries with one hundred and ten million people stretching from the Baltic to the Aegean were too weak to stand on their own legs against powerful neighbours and too jealous of each other, if left to themselves, not to become a prey to dissensions brought on by the great powers. Even if one could not hope to settle all the questions that divided them, it was highly desirable to try to settle as many of these as possible instead of waiting to see them hurriedly considered as bargaining points at some future peace conference.

Mr. Winant, to whom I outlined my plan, observed that President Roosevelt did not wish any questions of frontier to be discussed, but there were plenty of others to try to agree on, as for instance minorities, communications, and economic problems, that required attention. In particular the future of the Danube Valley called for a study along fresh lines. Some agreement might be feasible if one could establish an international conservancy similar to the Tennessee Valley Authority which would make for co-operation and be of advantage to all the Danubian states. Dr. Beneš, with whom I discussed this idea, was heartily in favour and shrewdly observed that if only one country appointed a member to such a board the others would immediately follow suit. There was, however, no time to lose, for already, he remarked, the Russians, flushed by recent successes, were growing cockier and would be increasingly difficult to handle. My plan contemplated having an informal American, British, and Russian committee to meet inconspicuously in London to discuss these questions and to agree on as many of them as possible. Winant at first seemed mildly interested but remained uncommunicative and evasive. He spoke vaguely about mentioning it to Eden. I never knew how far his enquiries went toward ascertaining whether the plan was feasible. I still think that it would have been useful to have tried for an agreement over Central Europe with the Russians before their great victories had been won. Even if no agreement had been possible, the Western Allies would then have been in a better position to know what they had to expect later on.

My suggestion, like many another, was buried in silence. One has to be prepared to meet such disappointments, for war is as wasteful of ideas as it is of life. I kept on writing more diplomatic memoranda that in the absence of any fresh information were mainly evolved out of past experience and my inner consciousness. Sometimes I would meet Winant by accident, and he would stop for a second to say that a point that I had raised was new to him and he had mentioned the matter to Eden. Nothing further. More often I had the feeling that the dozens of memoranda which I addressed to him were read and then consigned to the Dead Letter Box. After more than six months of this, as I was not able to see Winant in person I wrote to ask him if he was still of the opinion that I could render any service to the Embassy. There was no answer to this, so I wrote again to say that if I did not receive a reply by a certain date I would assume that I was of no use, and in that case I could be of greater service feeding pigs in Scotland than sitting idle at an Embassy desk. There was again no answer, so I left for Yester, which was my son-in-law's place near Edinburgh, where I worked in the piggery and hoed potatoes.

In a future war I strongly recommend feeding pigs as a useful occupation. They are reasonably intelligent, easy to handle, and providing they are properly fed make no further demands.

No more tranquil locality can be imagined than Yester. It lies in a splendid park at the foot of the Lammermoors, five miles from the nearest town. Yet in the beginning of the war, I had seen there the first German plane brought down in the British Isles. The fight took place at a low level and at one moment was directly over the house. Three Spitfires, coming from the Forth, attacked and then brought down on the moor a large Heinkel observation bomber. While this went on, innumerable starlings, woodpigeons, and gulls flew about excited and terrified by the sharp rattle of the machine guns. Only a few minutes later, when the Heinkel lay dead on the moor, I heard a nearby grouse clucking as though nothing had happened.

That day was a proud one for our local constable, who arrested the only uninjured German in the plane and at first refused to surrender his prisoner to the military. The villagers spoke almost with affection of the Heinkel, which they called "our plane," as if they also had a share in bringing it down. They were indignant when the newspapers printed that it had fallen near another village. Next day many people thronged to see the first enemy trophy. A boy with a Red Cross collecting box was sent to the moor, and that evening I helped to count its contents, which exceeded £13 mostly in threepenny bits. Scottish parsimony is an eighteenth-century legend hard to die, for no one could be more open-handed than those villagers.

Soon after, I admired another example of this generosity at an agricultural Red Cross sale that took place in the cattle market at Haddington and was attended by two or three hundred neighbouring farmers. The auctioneer talked broad Lowland Scotch that would have made his fortune on the vaudeville stage and which he enlivened with quips of his own. He created a contagiously humorous atmosphere which helped the bidding. A black-faced Highland ewe at first auctioned for £6, which already was twice its value, was then given back to be bid up again and reached £208. A diminutive Irish donkey caused so much hilarity that it was finally auctioned off for £190. I went away with a different impression of Scottish economy.

In the early days of the war, the great preoccupation in the village had been the evacuated children who came out of the slums of Edinburgh. Few of these knew what a breakfast was, for their mothers had been accustomed to give them a penny every morning with which to buy fish and chips. The children were distributed among the villagers and nourished in the village hall with excellent hot meals, which by a triumph of local organization, helped by a few gifts of rabbits and vegetables, cost only twopence a head. The filthy habits of many of these slum inmates came as a sad revelation. Hardly any of them had any idea of the most elementary sanitary behaviour, and their mode of life would have disgraced an African tribe. It took a war to focus attention on the terrible conditions in which these people had lived in the capital of Scotland.

In the village, men who were too old to join the forces or who were in reserved occupations like farmers now became special constables and helped patrol roads at night to see that the blackout was observed and to arrest suspicious characters. So far as I am aware, none was ever discovered. There were some denunciations of alleged fifth columnists at Haddington, attributed to private spite, and some gossip about signalling from lighted windows during air raids, but these were only indications of vigilance.

I saw how easily suspicion could be aroused by something that happened at Yester. The house stood in the midst of woods, a mile from the village, and the greatest care had always been taken with the blackout. One evening a message telephoned from the aerodrome at Drem, ten miles away, said that an intermittent light like a flash signal had been observed at Yester. A round of the house showed complete darkness, but then a second message came to repeat the first. The explanation was simple. Outside the house stood a small incubator, and the chicks breaking out from their shells passed by a tiny lamp to cast a reflection that could be seen from the sky!

After Dunkirk, few people were unaware of the scanty equipment in the country, and many there were who expected an early invasion. Yester itself was situated in a highly strategic area near the Firth of Forth, and it was thought that among the first German objectives would be the naval base at Rosyth and the shipping at Glasgow. In spite of the menace over our heads, I never noticed any sign of anxiety on the part of the villagers. Was their composure due to stolidity and want of imagination or to native toughness? Perhaps something of both, for in Great Britain, unlike France, the habit of invasion has been forgotten, and few people understood what it would really mean. Certainly

Americans were far more apprehensive of a German invasion of Britain than were the English, for no trace of transatlantic anxiety could be discovered among the latter. In the early autumn of 1940 I expected a landing almost any day. My only preparation for this was to discover a suitable place in the shrubbery in which to bury my wife's jewellery. The difficulty was not the place but how to inform the proper person in order later to recover this in case we should both be killed.

Many now sent their children to America, and my grandchild, who was 13, left Yester in the company of another little girl, a governess, and her retriever so that she should keep some tie with her home. Winston Churchill soon vetoed this children's exodus in the case of members of his own family who were planning the same, and he was angry with one Cabinet minister who had sent his son. There was an implication of defeatism in this, and it might also have provoked a certain class feeling. Evacuation schemes tended to divert attention from winning the war at a moment when a feverish haste was necessary to make up for the arrears in preparation.

All over Great Britain a Home Guard was then being organised. At Yester the men were mostly farmhands and labourers but also included Sir George Clerk, who had lately retired as British Ambassador in Paris. He who had been the best dressed of diplomats, who looked like an eighteenth-century worthy and spoke like a Victorian Cabinet minister, now became private clerk and responded to the military orders given by the family butler, who had been a former sergeant major in the Life Guards. At first all were drilled with sticks, until a very few American rifles arrived. The men wore armlets but later were given boiler suits. They were taught to throw "Molotov cocktails," which were bottles containing some explosive fuel that was supposed to destroy German tanks, and on the hill roads tank traps were erected.

At first our sergeant major was very sceptical about his men. He called them yokels and declared that it was impossible to get any intelligent idea into their thick heads. But among them there was a sprinkling of gamekeepers and foresters who were good shots and would have made useful guerillas. Later this unit was supplied with armoured cars and Lewis guns, and in time it became a good little organization whose efficiency grew as fast as the need for it disappeared.

The importance of the Battle of Britain was hardly realized by us until much later. The casualties inflicted on the Nazi bombers were impressively comforting but we had no inkling on how slender a margin depended the fate of the invasion. We knew in fact very little beyond the bare official statements. Yet it was splendid to observe the high spirits of the young airmen who came frequently to Yester to enjoy a brief relaxation, which their officers encouraged so as to get their minds away from the air.

In the midst of the crisis, I was much impressed by the tactful handling on the part of his superiors of a young flight lieutenant who stayed at the house for some time. He had behaved very gallantly at Dunkirk, where he had shot down several German planes, but then unknown to himself his nerves had been affected, and he was on the verge of a breakdown. He would have been heartbroken had he been told this. He had just then been slightly poisoned after eating a lobster patty. The doctor deliberately exaggerated the effects of this and sent him to an oculist who, tipped off as to what he should say, reported adversely. The boy was then sent to his home for a long rest, and when he returned he was at first given flying duties of a noncombatant kind and never had any inkling of what his real condition had been.

In addition to my work with pigs and potatoes, I gave a couple of talks at Edinburgh on American affairs and joined the committee of the Scottish-American Centre, which was one of the mushroom organisations that grew up during the war. One day Tom Johnson, the Secretary of State for Scotland, announced his visit to this centre. We began to think that we were really important, but our bubble was soon pricked, for his only purpose had been to borrow a copy of Damon Runyon!

When I returned to London, I found the Embassy so overstaffed that there was even less opportunity than before of doing anything. A friend of mine, Ned Coke, had just started a factory which was running on a part-time basis for those who were only able to put in a few hours of work during the day. For some months I went there, helping to turn out some small parts which required little mechanical skill but were supposed to be useful for aeroplanes and submarines.

I doubt if our factory output helped the progress of the war very much, but it gave a number of people the feeling that they were doing something. Air raids, which for a time had become less frequent, started again. I recall watching a few from the roof of the Ritz and felt rather like Nero without a fiddle at the grim spectacle of burning buildings. London is so vast that it was hard to realize the lottery of bombing, for nearly always the explosions were far away. The sensation of noise and blast when a stick of bombs fell close was the reverse of pleasant. In spite of V-1s and V-2s, most people by that time had become fatalistic. No one I met admitted to any ambition of being thought a hero, but in compensation for this no one was any longer called a slacker because he was not in uniform, as often happened during the First World War. Life carried on in the way that life will always carry on, principally because there is no better alternative. The effect of war on nerves of civilians was more one of fatalism and of necessity than any trial of courage. Similar dangers, some greater, some less, existed then in many parts of Europe, but at least in England there was no Gestapo to fear.

With American troops coming over in increasing numbers, the feeling towards these varied. Such resentment as there was remained hidden and seemed to be caused less by their conduct, which on the whole was remarkably good, or their higher rates of pay, but rather by a subconscious feeling on the part of some that the presence of these troops indicated how greatly England needed another nation's help. A well-known woman who was a friend remarked to me that it was not pleasant to see so many Americans in Grosvenor Square. I answered that it would be still less pleasant if there were none. Alongside the feelings of a few that were usually kept in the background were the innumerable acts of kindness, particularly on the part of small people, toward American boys who often felt lonely and homesick. The canteens and soldiers' clubs did good work, but many an unrecorded touch of human sympathy was also extended less conspicuously but more effectively in villages where American soldiers found a homelike welcome.

The effect of a world war on the home front is not easy to describe. Much of it wears off after the crisis is over, but something remains that changes people's lives. What this is may be hard to answer except by some sweeping and useless generalisations. Gallup polls and tables of statistics have in them an intermittent and provisional nature for which usually an insufficient allowance is made. The feelings of today are never quite those of tomorrow. The war certainly finished in victory, but some will ask whose. We cannot even assert with any confidence that we are right in giving proper values to events whose importance will only be demonstrated in the future. To most Americans, it came as an immense surprise that the United States was left to share the top of the world with Russia.

International politics are eminently functional by their nature, although such elements as an inherited prestige, the memory of a great tradition, or the exceptional stature of some country's representatives may for a time give that nation a somewhat higher rating than it would otherwise possess. But sooner or later the rougher tests of power will be used to determine its position in the world. America has risen to her present eminence less because of any deliberate plan or ambition than owing to the fact that as a nation the United States has suddenly been pushed into a fresh vacuum. When I entered the Diplomatic Service in 1903, America was regarded on the Continent as a somewhat uncouth trespasser, very inferior to the great European powers. During my own years of service, in a very small way, I had skirted along the outer fringe of several important questions that helped to raise our stature as a nation. I had unexpectedly witnessed the decline of Europe. What has become of the great powers? One by one in the space of a few decades, whether defeated or victorious, they have fallen from their height. Far from contributing to this fall, the United States tried, with wise and unselfish measures, to help Europe recover her strength, knowing well that these measures, if successful, might later be used against her. No nation has in fact been less ambitious for power or for territory than the United States after the Second World War or more generously unselfish in her attitude and policy. No accusation could be farther from the truth than that of American capitalistic imperialism. The hopes of a liberal world now rest with the United States. May we show ourselves worthy of the great task that lies before us.

# *Biographical Directory*

*Abdul Aziz* (1830–76). Son of Mahmoud II; came to the throne on the death of his brother, Abdul Medjid, in 1861. The first Sultan to travel abroad, he visited the Paris Exposition in 1867, then London and Vienna. There was a rapid spread of Western influence during his reign. After the death of liberal statesmen Ali Pasha and Fuad Pasha, Abdul appointed the unpopular Mahmoud Nedim as Grand Vizier. Abdul was deposed in May 1876 and replaced by Abdul Medjid's older son, Murad V. Six days later, he is presumed to have killed himself with a pair of scissors.

*Abdul Hamid II* (1842–1918). Second son of Abdul Medjid, nephew of Abdul Aziz; proclaimed Sultan, August 1876. Abdul Hamid's first Parliament convened in March 1877 but he soon dissolved it and gradually re-established absolute power. A bomb thrown at his carriage by Armenians at Selamlik in July 1905 increased his fear of assassination. He was compelled by the Committee of Union and Progress to restore the Constitution in July 1908. After the counter-revolution of April 1909 he was deposed and lived in Salonica until the First Balkan War, when he was brought back to Istanbul. The most recent biography of Abdul Hamid is Joan Haslip's *The Sultan,* (London, Cassel, 1958).

*Abdul Medjid* (1823–61). Became Sultan in 1839, following the death of his father, Mahmoud II. He inaugurated Tanzimat, or a period of reform, with a decree promulgated in 1839 and strengthened by Hatti Humayun in 1856. Lord Stratford de Redcliffe, the great *Elchi,* was British Ambassador, 1842–58, during his reign. Abdul's extravagances made him unpopular. He died of tuberculosis and was succeeded by his younger brother, Abdul Aziz.

*Abernon, Lord d',* title of Edgar Vincent (1857–1941). English financier and diplomat; President of the Council of the Ottoman Public Debt, 1883; Financial Adviser to Egypt, 1883–89; Governor of the Imperial Ottoman Bank in Constantinople, 1889–97; Conservative member of Parliament, 1899–1906; Ambassador to Germany, 1920–26.

*Adee, A. A.* (1842–1924). American diplomat and State Department officer; appointed Secretary of the Legation in Madrid, 1870, Chargé d'Affaires until 1877; Chief of the Diplomatic Bureau, Department of State, 1878; Third Assistant Secretary of State, 1882; Second Assistant Secretary of State, 1886. In his State Department posts, he supervised the drafting of diplomatic correspondence.

*Ahmed Riza* (1859–1930). Leader of the Young Turks abroad, he joined the revolutionary group in Paris in 1889 and was elected president of the Committee of Union and Progress. From 1895, he edited the party organ, *Meshveret,* published in Paris and smuggled into Turkey. After the Revolution of 1908, he returned to Istanbul to become the first President of the Chamber of Deputies.

# *Biographical Directory*

*Alfonso XIII,* King of Spain (1886–1941). The posthumous son of Alfonso XII, he was proclaimed King at birth, with the regency being entrusted to his mother, Maria Cristina. In the face of Republican victories in the elections of 1931, and the reluctance of the army to continue to support the monarchy, he went into exile that year.

*Almodóvar del Rio, Duc de* (1859–1906). Spanish politician and diplomat; three times Minister of Foreign Affairs; presiding officer at the Algeciras Conference.

*Aynard, Joseph Raymond* (b. 1866). French diplomat; member of the French Delegation to the Algeciras Conference, 1906; Commercial Counsellor, 1909; Deputy Director of Chancelleries, 1911; Minister to Uruguay, 1912; Chairman of the Delegation to the Commission for the Pyrenees, 1913.

*Bancroft, Edward* (1744–1821). Prominent physician in the American colonies who served as Secretary of the American diplomatic mission in Paris during the Revolutionary War. He has been regarded by historians as a double spy—one who worked for, and was paid by, both the British and the Americans. Einstein dealt with Bancroft at some length in his book *Divided Loyalties* (1933).

*Barclay, Sir George* (1862–1921). English Minister to Teheran, 1908; Minister at Bucharest, 1912–19.

*Bedri Bey.* Turkish lawyer, politician; intimate friend of Talaat Pasha; ranked high in Committee of Union and Progress circles; a patriot, strongly opposed to the Capitulations.

*Beelaerts van Blokland, Franz-Jonkeer* (b. 1872). Netherlands Minister in China, 1909–19; delegate to the Washington Conference on the Limitation of Armaments, 1921–22; Director of Netherlands Foreign Diplomatic Affairs, 1917–27.

*Beneš, Edward* (1884–1948). Czech politician and statesman; Foreign Minister, 1918–35; headed the Czech delegation to the Paris Peace Conference, 1919–20; elected President of the Czechoslovak Republic, 1935.

*Bennett, James Gordon* (1841–1918). Succeeded his father as editor of the *New York Herald;* gained worldwide publicity by sponsoring Stanley's expedition to Africa to find Livingstone in 1869–70.

*Berchtold, Count Leopold von* (1863–1942). Austro-Hungarian statesman; Foreign Minister, 1912–15. He was responsible for sending the famous ultimatum to Serbia during the July 1914 crisis.

*Beresford, Lord Charles William* (1846–1919). Author, traveler; appointed Admiral in 1906; Commander in Chief of the British Mediterranean Fleet, 1907–09.

*Billy, Robert de* (b. 1869). French diplomat; Secretary of the Embassy in London, 1896; Algeciras Conference, 1906; Legation in Sofia, 1907, Tangier, 1909, Rome, 1909; Minister to Greece, 1917–24; Minister to Roumania, 1924–26; Ambassador to Japan, 1926.

*Bliss, Howard S.* (1860–1920). Prominent American missionary and educator; ordained Congregational minister; succeeded his father as president of the Syrian Protestant Church in Beirut, Syria, 1902.

*Bordonaro, Antonio Cheramonte* (1877–1932). Italian diplomat; appointed Secretary in Berne, 1907; Consul at St. Petersburg, 1913, Berlin, 1914; Minister to Prague, 1920; Secretary-General for Foreign Affairs, 1926.

*Boris of Bulgaria* (1894–1946). King of Bulgaria, 1918–43. During the Balkan Wars and the First World War, he served as a staff officer. In the 1930s he created a personal dictatorship in Bulgaria and ultimately brought his country under the influence of the Rome-Berlin Axis.

*Bruning, Heinrich* (b. 1885). German statesman; leader of the Center Party during the 1920s; Chancellor, 1930–31.

*Bryan, William Jennings* (1860–1925). American politician; powerful and popular public speaker; Democratic Party nominee for President, 1896, 1900, 1908; Secretary of State in the Wilson Administration, 1913–15.

*Bülow, Prince Bernard von* (1849–1929). German Foreign Minister, 1897–1909; Imperial Chancellor, 1900–09. In June 1905 he was created a prince after he had, in effect, secured the retirement of the French Foreign Minister, Delcassé, whose policy, especially with regard to Morocco, was hostile toward Germany. Von Bülow's diplomacy was influential in bringing about the Conference at Algeciras.

*Burhan-Eddin, Prince Effendi.* Abdul Hamid's eldest son. Talented but weak, he tried to play a role in the pan-Islamic movement, probably at his father's instigation. There is evidence of his participation in the ill-fated counter-revolutionary grand coup of April 13, 1908, which sought to restore the Sultan's authority. He later took pains to deny his involvement. See Francis McCullogh, *The Fall of Abdul-Hamid* (London, Methuen, 1910), pp. 45-51, 189, 207–08.

*Buxton, Charles Rodin* (1875–1942), *and Edward Noel* (1869–1948). Co-authors of several books on the Near East and the Balkans.

*Calhoun, William C.* (1848–1916). American lawyer and diplomat; served on a special presidential Mission to Cuba, 1897; Minister to China, 1909–13.

*Cambon, Jules* (1845–1935). French administrator and diplomat; Ambassador to Germany before 1914; became Secretary General of the Ministry of Foreign Affairs, October 1915.

*Cartier de Marchienne, Baron Emile* (1871–1946). Belgian diplomat; appointed Minister to China, 1910; appointed Minister to the United States, 1917; appointed Ambassador to the United States, 1919.

*Cassini, Count Arthur Pavlovitch.* Russian diplomat; Chargé and Minister Resident for the Free Hanseatic Cities, 1884–91; Minister to China, 1894–98; Ambassador to the U.S., 1898–1905; Minister to Spain, 1905; First Russian delegate to the Algeciras Conference, 1906.

*Chamberlain, Neville* (1869–1940). English politician and statesman; Lord Mayor of Birmingham, 1915–16; Chancellor of the Exchequer, 1923–24, 1931–37; Minister for Health, 1924–29; Prime Minister, 1937–40.

*Charles-Roux, François-Jules* (1879–1961). French diplomat; appointed Secretary in Cairo, 1906; Secretary in London, 1912; Consul in Rome, 1916; Minister to Prague, 1926.

*Choate, Joseph H.* (1832–1917). Lawyer and diplomat; U.S. Ambassador to England, 1899–1905.

*Chukry (Shukru) Bey.* Turkish Minister of Education, 1913–18; active in furthering the education of women; implicated in the assassination attempt against Ataturk and hanged after the Izmir trials.

*Ch'un, Prince* (personal name, Tsai Feng) (b. 1882). Father of the last Manchu Emperor and Regent for his son, 1908–11; deposed by the Revolution, 1911.

*Clerk, Sir George R.* (1874–1951). English diplomat; appointed Chargé d'Affaires in Abyssinia, 1906; Secretary at Constantinople, 1910; appointed Minister to Prague, 1919; Ambassador to Turkey, 1926; Ambassador to Belgium, 1933; Ambassador to France, 1934.

*Cloman, Colonel Sidney A.* (b. 1867). U.S. Military Academy graduate, 1889; Military Attaché in London, Constantinople; member of the U.S. Commission to Liberia and Sierra Leone; Chief of Staff of the 29th Division during the military operations north of Verdun, October 1918.

*Colloredo Mansfeld, Rudolf von* (1585–1657). Austrian General during the Thirty Years' War; as Commander of the Imperial Army, he successfully defended Prague against a Swedish attack in 1648.

*Constans, Jean Antoine Ernest* (1833–1913). French lawyer, politician, and diplomat; elected Deputy, 1876, Senator, 1889; Governor General of Indo-China for a short term during the 1880s; Ambassador to Turkey, 1898–1909.

*Coolidge, Calvin* (1872–1933). Massachusetts Republican leader noted for his laconic and frugal characteristics; Governor of Massachusetts, 1919–21; elected U.S. Vice President, 1921; succeeded Warren G. Harding as President on the latter's death, 1923; elected President for a full term, 1924.

*Couget, Joseph-Robert* (b. 1856). French diplomat; appointed Secretary of Embassy in London, 1897, Vienna, 1901, Peking, 1905, Tokyo, 1906; Minister to Mexico, 1916–20; appointed Minister to Prague, 1920.

*Crane, Charles R.* (1858–1939). American businessman and diplomat; operated a company that manufactured plumbing accessories; member of a special mission to Russia, 1917; American member of the Mandates Commission concerned with Syria (popularly known as the King-Crane Commission), 1919; Minister to China, 1920–21.

*Crane, Richard* (1882–1938). American businessman and diplomat; son of Charles R. Crane; private secretary to Secretary of State Lansing during the First World War; appointed first U.S. Minister to Czechoslovakia, 1919–21.

*Delcassé, Théophile* (1852–1923). French political leader and diplomat. He was principally responsible for bringing the Anglo-French clash over Fashoda to a peaceful conclusion. His intransigence during the Moroccan Crisis, however, caused him to lose support within the French Cabinet, and he resigned in 1905. Delcassé's hostility toward Germany's aspiration was in large part responsible for the conclusion of the Entente Cordiale in 1904.

*Derussi* [Deroussy], *Georges* (d. 1931). Roumanian diplomat; served in Belgrade, Sofia, Constantinople; appointed Minister to Bulgaria, 1913; appointed Minister to Switzerland, 1919.

*Dickinson, Charles M.* (1842–1924). American newspaperman and diplomat; took a prominent part in the formation of the Associated Press; appointed Consul General in Turkey, 1897; appointed diplomatic agent in Bulgaria, 1901; Consul General-at-large with jurisdiction over U.S. consulates throughout the Middle East, 1906–08.

*Dickinson, Jacob McGavock* (1851–1928). Distinguished member of the Bar in Chicago, specializing in railroad law; Counsel in the Alaskan Boundary Dispute with Great Britain, 1903; a founder of the American Society of International Law, 1906–07; president of the American Bar Association, 1907–08; Secretary of War in President Taft's Cabinet, 1909–11.

*Dimitrieff, General Radko* (1859–1919). Prominent Bulgarian Russophile; eventually executed by the Bolsheviks because of his alleged Czarist sympathies.

*Eboul Houda.* An Arab sheik, said to have been Abdul Hamid's "gray eminence" during the early years of his reign. His contacts among Arab religious leaders made him valuable in furthering the pan-Islamic ideal. Later he was supplanted as unofficial adviser to the Sultan by another Arab, Izzet Pasha.

*Eden, Anthony* (Lord Avon) (b. 1897). British statesman; Under Secretary for the Foreign Office, 1931–33; Lord Privy Seal and Privy Councillor, 1934–35; Minister to the League of Nations, 1935; Secretary of State for Foreign Affairs, 1935–38; Prime Minister, 1955–57.

*Edwards, General Clarence Ransom* (1860–1931). American Army Officer; Adjutant General of the Fourth Army Corps during the Spanish-American War; Chief of the Customs and Insular Divisions of the War Department, 1900–12; accompanied Secretary of War Taft on tours in the Far East, 1905 and 1907, and Secretary of War Dickinson, 1910; commanded the 26th Division in France during the First World War.

*Eleanor, Princess of Reuss* (d. 1917). Second wife of King Ferdinand of Bulgaria, whom she married in 1908.

*Enver Bey* (Enver Pasha) (1881–1922). He joined the Committee of Union and Progress in Salonica as a young military officer and became one of its heroes in 1908. He rose rapidly to the rank of general and became Minister of War in 1913. In 1914 he married an Ottoman princess. He was among those responsible for Turkey's entry into the war on the side of the Central Powers, and in 1918 fled to Odessa in a German submarine. Four years later he was killed by the Soviets while trying to organize the revolt in Bokhara.

*Ferdinand of Bulgaria* (1861–1948). Became King, 1887. In 1908 he proclaimed the independence of Bulgaria and assumed the title of Czar. He took the initiative in forming the Balkan League of Bulgaria, Serbia, Greece, and Montenegro as a coalition against Turkey in 1911–12. In 1915 he formed an alliance with Germany.

*Fitzmaurice, Lord Edmond-George Pelty* (1846–1935). English lawyer and diplomat; became a Liberal member of the House of Commons.

*Fletcher, Henry P.* (1873–1959). American diplomat. Second Secretary of the U.S. Legation in Peking, 1903–05; First Secretary at Lisbon, 1905–07; First Secretary at Peking, 1907–09; Ambassador to Italy during the 1920s.

*Franchet d'Esperey, Louis Félix Marie* (1856–1942). French general who led the Allied expedition against Salonika toward the end of the First World War.

*Freer, Charles* (1856–1919). American art collector; donor of the Freer Gallery of Asiatic Art in Washington, D.C. Freer made his fortune by consolidating some thirteen automobile manufacturing companies into the American Car and Foundry Co. He was a friend and admirer of the painter James Whistler and purchased many of Whistler's paintings. His art collection, however, clearly emphasized Oriental objects.

*Fuad of Egypt* (1868–1936). First king of modern Egypt, 1922–36.

*Furstenberg, Prince Karl Emile de* (b. 1867). Austrian diplomat; appointed Consul at St. Petersburg, 1905; Minister to Russia, 1905; Minister to Roumania, 1911; Minister to Spain, 1914.

*Garroni, Marquis C.* Italian diplomat; appointed Ambassador to Turkey, 1913; participated with ambassadors of six powers represented in Constantinople in establishing the new frontier of Turkey in Europe at the Enos-Midia Line.

*Giolitti, Giovanni* (1842–1928). Italian financier and diplomat; Secretary of the Treasury, 1889–90; Prime Minister, 1892–93, 1903–05, 1906–09, 1911–14, 1920–21; opposed to Italian intervention in the First World War and later a violent anti-Fascist.

*Goerdeler, Karl Frederich* (1884–1944). German administrator; Mayor of Leipzig, 1931–36, and Commissioner of Price Stabilization. He became a principal organizer of the resistance in Germany to overthrow the leadership of Adolf Hitler. In 1944 he was arrested and executed by the Nazis.

*Grey, Sir Edward* (First Viscount Grey of Fallodon) (1862–1933). British politician and statesman; Under Secretary for Foreign Affairs, 1892–95; Secretary for Foreign Affairs, 1905–16; a staunch champion of Anglo-French solidarity against Germany during the decade before the First World War.

*Guechoff, Ivan-Stephanov* (1854–1932). Bulgarian diplomat; served in Paris, Constantinople, Vienna, Berlin. He was much concerned about Bulgaria's support of Austria, which stemmed from Russia's preference for Serbia's interests. He was an ardent supporter of the Balkan Entente.

*Gummere, Samuel R.* (1849–1920). Prominent lawyer and diplomat; Secretary to the U.S. Minister at the Hague, 1881–84; appointed Consul General in Morocco, 1898; appointed first U.S. Minister to Morocco, 1905.

*Hamdi Bey* (1842–1910). Distinguished archaeologist and painter; son of Grand Vizier Ethem Pasha. He studied at the Beaux Arts in Paris, and was appointed Director of Istanbul's Archaeological Museum in 1881, remaining in that position until his death, when he was succeeded by his brother, Halil Ethem. On the twenty-fifth anniversary of his appointment the number of telegrams of congratulation sent him from abroad caused great anger in Abdul Hamid's entourage.

*Harris, Walter B.* (1866–1933). Long-time correspondent of *The Times* of London; well-known traveler, explorer, author; stationed in Morocco during the Algeciras Conference. According to Oron J. Hale (*Germany and the Diplomatic Revolution,* Philadelphia, University of Pennsylvania Press, 1931, p. 23), Harris, while in Tangier during 1904–06, "worked hand in glove with the English colony, which was hostile to French ambitions in Morocco. So far as the policy of his paper permitted, he supported the German position against the French."

*Harrison, Leland* (1893–1951). American diplomat; Third Secretary of the Embassy in Tokyo, 1908; Second Secretary of the Legation in Peking, 1909; Diplomatic Secretary of the American Commission to Negotiate Peace at the Paris Peace Conference, 1918–19.

*Hay, John* (1838–1905). American lawyer and diplomat; served in American legations in Paris, Madrid, Vienna; Ambassador to England, 1897–98; Secretary of State, 1898–1905.

*Hilmi Pasha* (1855–1921). Minister of the Interior in Kiamil Pasha's Cabinet; Grand Vizier in 1909; resigned during the counter-revolution, but returned to power when it was suppressed; he became Minister of Justice, 1912, then Ambassador to Vienna, where he died.

*Hodgson, James F.* (Jim) (b. 1890). American Commercial Attaché; District Supervisor of the American Relief Administration at Odessa, 1921–23; Assistant Trade Commissioner in Warsaw, 1924; Commercial Atttaché in Prague, 1925.

*Holmes, Oliver Wendell* (1841–1935). Prominent American jurist; Associate Justice of the U.S. Supreme Court, 1902–32. Lewis Einstein's correspondence with Holmes has been published: *The Holmes-Einstein Letters: Correspondence of Mr. Justice Holmes and Lewis Einstein, 1903–1935,* ed. James Bishop Peabody (New York, St. Martin's Press, 1964).

*Holstein, Friedrich von* (1837–1909). German statesman and close associate of Bismarck during the Iron Chancellor's early years. Holstein later exercised a profound influence on Germany's foreign policy in his capacity as Counsellor in the Foreign Office. He is often assigned responsibility for the German strategy leading to the Moroccan crisis in 1905 and the Algeciras Conference.

*Hontoria y Fernandez Ladrera, Manuel Gozalez* (b. 1878). Spanish diplomat; Secretary of the Embassy in Paris, 1905–06; member of the Secretariat at the Algeciras Conference, 1906; Under Secretary of State for Foreign Affairs, 1911–13; Spanish representative at meetings of the neutral powers at the Paris Peace Conference, 1919.

*Hoover, Herbert C.* (1874–1965). American mining engineer and government official; Chairman of the American Relief Commission, Chairman of the Relief Program for Belgium, U.S. Food Administrator during the First World War; Secretary of Commerce in the Harding and Coolidge Cabinets, 1921–28; President of the United States, 1929–33.

*Hughes, Charles Evans* (1862–1948). American lawyer, jurist, politician; Associate Justice of the U.S. Supreme Court, 1910–16; unsuccessful Republican nominee for the presidency, 1916; Secretary of State, 1921–25; Chief Justice of the Supreme Court, 1930–41.

*Huguenin, Edouard* (sometimes referred to as Huguenin Pasha) (1856–1926). Swiss head of the Anatolian Railroad, from which the Bagdad rail line extended.

*Hull, Cordell* (1871–1945). American lawyer, politician, statesman; U.S. Representative from Tennessee, 1907–21, 1923–31; U.S. Senator, 1931–33; Secretary of State, 1933–44.

*Humann, Captain.* Son of the archaeologist Karl Humann; Naval Attaché at the German Embassy in Constantinople; lived practically his entire life in Turkey.

*Hurst, Leonard Henry* (b. 1889). British consular official; entered the Consular Service, 1908; appointed Vice Consul at Sofia, 1914, Bengasi, 1924, Port Said, 1926, Basra, 1932; retired, 1949.

*Ijuin, M. H.* (1864–1924). Japanese diplomat; Consul in England and Italy; Ambassador in China and in Italy; member of the Japanese Delegation to the Paris Peace Conference, 1918–19.

*Imperiali di Francavilla, Marquis Guglielmo* (b. 1858). Italian diplomat; First Secretary at Berlin, 1885; Second Secretary in Paris, 1885–89; First Secretary at Washington, 1889–1903; held posts subsequently as Ambasador at Berlin, Minister Plenipotentiary in Belgrade, Ambassador in Constantinople, 1909–10.

*Izzet Pasha* (1870–1924). Turkish political figure. He was always referred to in Turkey as "Arab Izzet" and was extremely unpopular because of his unscrupulous devices. He is alleged to have amassed a large fortune by accepting bribes from concession hunters, and fled the country in 1908.

*Jay, Peter A.* (1877–1933). American diplomat; Secretary to legations and embassies in Paris, 1902–03, Constantinople, 1903–07, Tokyo, 1907–09; Diplomatic Agent in Cairo, 1909–13; Secretary and Counselor, U.S. Embassy, Rome, 1913–19; Minister to Salvador, 1920; Minister to Roumania, 1921–25; Ambassador to Argentina, 1925–27.

*Jiménez Oreamuno, Ricardo* (1859–1945). Costa Rican statesman; President of his country, 1910–14, 1924–28, and 1932–36.

*Johnson, Hiram* (1866–1945). American lawyer and politician; a founder of the Progressive Party, 1912, and its nominee for Vice President that year; elected Governor of California, 1910, re-elected 1914; U.S. Senator from California, 1916–45.

*Jonēscu, Take* (1858–1922). Roumanian statesman; founded the Conservative-Democratic Party, 1908; represented Roumania at the Conference of Bucharest, 1913, and played a leading role in bringing about a peace settlement between Greece and Turkey in 1914. From the outset of the First World War, Jonēscu favored intervention on the side of the Allies, and in 1918 he was instrumental in reintegrating Roumania into the Allied camp. He favored a postwar Danubian federation, which did not materialize.

*Jusserand, Jean Adrien Antoine Jules* (1855–1932). French author and diplomat; Ambassador to the United States, 1902–25.

*Kemal, Mustafa* (better known as Kemal Ataturk) (1881–1938). Famed Gallipoli commander, he was a national hero and commander-in-chief of the Turkish War of Independence. He was founder and first President of the Turkish Republic,

1923, and initiator of a comprehensive program of reforms which accelerated the modernization of Turkey. For a recent biography, see Lord Kinross, *Ataturk: The Rebirth of a Nation* (London, Weidenfeld and Nicolson, 1964).

*Keyes, Admiral Roger J. B.* (1872–1945). Chief of Staff, British Eastern Mediterranean Squadron, 1915.

*Khilkoff, Prince Mikhail Ivanovich* (d. 1909). Russian engineer; studied railroad construction in the United States during the early 1870s; became Chief Engineer for a Venezuelan railway before returning to Russia, where he served as Minister of Communication, 1895–1905; while at this post supervised the planning and completion of the Trans-Siberian Railway.

*Kiamil Pasha* (1832–1912). Pro-British Turkish statesman; twice followed Mehmed Said Pasha as Grand Vizier, in 1884 and after the Revolution of 1908 (both expressed dislike of each other in their memoirs); author of a three-volume political history of the Ottoman Empire.

*Kiderlen-Wächter, Alfred von* (1852–1912). German diplomat; involved in the Agadir Crisis in 1911 and in the Congo dispute with France in the same year.

*Kien Lung,* Emperor of China. During his reign, A.D. 1735–95, Ili and eastern Turkestan were added to the Chinese Empire. He composed much prose and poetry. His reign was notable for improved commercial relations between China and Europe.

*Klehmet, Reinhold.* German Consular Chief in the Ministry of Foreign Affairs, 1896–1906.

*Knox, Philander C.* (1853–1921). Prominent corporation lawyer; U.S. Attorney General, 1901–04; U.S. Senator from Pennsylvania, 1904–09; Secretary of State in the Taft Administration, 1909–13; after returning to the U.S. Senate in 1917, became a principal opponent of American ratification of the Treaty of Versailles and membership in the League of Nations.

*Kolmar von der Goltz, Baron* (1843–1916). Prussian General and Turkish Pasha who reorganized and modernized the Turkish Army, 1883–95.

*Kolowrat, Count* (b. 1881). Member of the Austrian Parliament; active in Czech conservation programs during the 1920s and 1930s.

*Koziebrodski-Bolesta, Count Leopold* (b. 1855). Austro-Hungarian diplomat; Secretary at legations at Bucharest, 1888–90, Belgrade, 1890–92, Rio de Janeiro, 1892–96; Consul at Brussels and Madrid, 1896; Minister to Argentina, Uruguay, and Paraguay, 1900–04; Second Austrian Plenipotentiary to the Algeciras Conference, 1906; Minister to the Sultan of Morocco, 1907; Minister to Portugal, 1909; member of the Ministry of Foreign Affairs in Vienna, 1910–13.

*Labouchère, Henry du Pré* (1831–1912). English Liberal politician and journalist; in the British Diplomatic Service, 1854–64; in Parliament, 1865–68, and 1880–1905; became a Privy Councilor, 1905.

*Leishman, John G. A.* (1857–1924). American businessman and diplomat; executive of the Carnegie Steel Co. during the 1890s; Ambassador to Turkey, 1900–06; Ambassador to Italy, 1909–11; Ambassador to Germany, 1911–13.

*Li Hung Chang* (1823–1901). Perhaps the most important Chinese statesman of the nineteenth century.

*Lichnowski, Prince Charles-Max* (1860–1928). German Ambassador to England, 1912–14; German representative at the peace conference following the First Balkan War.

*Liman von Sanders* (1855–1929). German general who directed his country's military mission in Turkey during the First World War; led the defense of the Dardanelles against the British invasion, 1915.

*Litvinoff, Maxim* (1876–1951). Soviet politician and statesman; People's Vice Commissar for Foreign Affairs, 1918–30; Commissar for Foreign Affairs, 1930–39; Soviet Ambassador to the United States, 1941–42. In eloquent speeches at the League of Nations, he advocated a policy of collective security in opposition to Italian and German aggression.

*Lobkovicz, Prince Max* (b. 1888). Lawyer, diplomat, and landowner; Magistrate, 1913–14; administrator at Prague, 1918–19; Secretary to the Czech Ministry in London, 1922.

*Lodge, Henry Cabot* (1850–1924). Historian, lawyer, politician; for many years U.S. Senator from Massachusetts; adviser to Theodore Roosevelt, particularly on foreign policy.

*Louis Alexander, Prince of Battenberg* (1854–1921). Became British subject, 1868; Admiral of the British Navy; appointed Second Sea Lord, December 1911. Members of the family living in England renounced the name Battenberg during World War I and adopted the name Mountbatten.

*Lowther, Sir Gerard* (1858–1916). British diplomat; Minister to Chile, 1901–04; Minister at Tangier, 1904–08; Ambassador to Turkey, 1908–13.

*Lung Yü,* Dowager Empress of China. Widow of Emperor Kwang-Su.

*McCabe, Colonel Edward R. W.* (b. 1876). Appointed American Military Attaché in Rome, 1924.

*Margerie, Pierre Jacquin de* (1861–1942). French diplomat; Counsellor of the Embassy at Madrid, 1906.

*Marling, Sir Charles Murray* (1862–1933). British diplomat; Attaché at Athens, 1888–1904; Chargé in Madrid, 1904–05; Chargé in Athens, 1905–06; Consul at Teheran, 1906–09; Consul at Constantinople, 1909–15; Minister to Persia, 1915–16; Consul General in Paris, 1916–19; British delegate on the International Commission for Schleswig, 1919; Minister to the Netherlands, 1921–26.

*Marschall von Bieberstein, Baron Adolf Hermann von* (1842–1912). German diplomat. He served as Ambassador from Baden to Berlin and in the 1890s, as Foreign Secretary, drafted the famous telegram of congratulations sent by the Kaiser to Paul Krueger following the Jameson Raid. He became Ambassador to Turkey in 1897 and was the prime mover behind the Berlin-to-Bagdad Railway scheme. In 1912 he was appointed Ambassador to England, where he remained until his death.

*Martin, Fredrik Robert* (1868–1933). Swedish art critic; wrote *History of Oriental Carpets Before 1800* (1908), *The Miniature Painting and Painters of Persia, India and Turkey from the Eighth to the Eighteenth Century* (1912), and other works.

*Masaryk, Jan* (1886–1948). Czechoslovak diplomat; entered the Czech Ministry of Foreign Affairs, 1918; served in various capacities until his tragic death by murder or suicide after the Communist coup in Czechoslovakia.

*Masaryk, Tomáš* (1850–1937). Leader of the Czech independence movement during the First World War; first President of the Czechoslovak Republic, 1918–35.

*Matsuoka, Yosuke* (1880–1946). Japanese politician and diplomat; graduated from the University of Oregon in the U.S.; entered the Japanese diplomatic service; elected to the Diet, 1920, and was also an officer of the South Manchurian Railway; delegate to the League of Nations at the time of the Manchurian Crisis, 1931–32; later Foreign Minister when the nonaggression pact with the Soviet Union was signed; died before he could be brought to trial as a war criminal after World War II.

*Mehmed V* (Mehmed Reshad) (1844–1918). Became Sultan at the age of 65. He was an ineffectual ruler completely under the influence of the Young Turk leaders. He was succeeded by a still younger brother of Abdul Hamid, Mehmed Vahdettin.

*Melvill de Carnbee, J. P. R. A.* Netherlands Minister to Bulgaria during the First World War; appointed Minister to Switzerland, 1921.

*Mensdorff-Pouilly-Dietrichstein, Count Albert* (1861–1945). Austrian diplomat; Ambassador to London, 1904–14. His real name was Pouilly, but he married into royalty and acquired the title Count de Mensdorff.

*Mittag-Leffler, Goa* (1846–1927). Distinguished Swedish mathematician; also served in Sweden's diplomatic service.

*Mizza Mahmoud Khan.* Persian Ambassador to Turkey, 1894–1901; reappointed 1912.

*Morgenthau, Henry* (1856–1946). American lawyer, banker, diplomat, philanthropist; Ambassador to Turkey, 1913–16; Vice-Chairman of Near Eastern Relief, 1919–21; father of Henry Morgenthau, Jr., Secretary of the Treasury in Franklin D. Roosevelt's Administration.

*Moukhtar Pasha, Mahmoud* (1867–1935). Distinguished Turkish military officer, diplomat, statesman; chiefly remembered for his courage in the face of the counter-revolutionary troops at Bayezid Square; Minister of Marine, 1910–12; appointed Ambassador to Berlin, 1912, resigned 1914.

*Nazim, Dr.* Prominent member of the Committee of Union and Progress; fled with Enver in 1918 but later returned to Turkey; was hanged after the Ankara treason trials in 1926.

*Neurath, Baron Constantin von* (1873–1956). German diplomat; Consul at Constantinople, 1911–16; Minister to Denmark, 1919; Minister for Foreign Affairs, 1932–39; convicted at the Nuremberg trials of committing crimes against humanity and against peace, and sentenced to fifteen years' imprisonment.

*Newton, Sir Basil-Cochrane* (b. 1889). English diplomat; served at the Foreign Office, 1912–25; delegate to the Conference on Tariffs in Peking, 1925–26; Minister to Prague, 1937–39.

*Niazi Bey* (1873–1912). A hero of the Young Turk Revolution. Unlike Enver Bey, he had no political ambitions. He was pensioned off and retired to his native town in Macedonia, where he was assassinated by a personal enemy.

*Nicolson, Sir Arthur* (Lord Carnock) (1849–1928). British diplomat; helped revive British interest in Persia; Consul General in Turkey, Bulgaria, Morocco; Minister in Tangier, 1895–1904; Ambassador in Madrid, 1905; appointed Permanent Under Secretary of State of the British Foreign Office, 1910.

*O'Conor, Sir Nicholas* (1843–1908). British diplomat; Ambassador in Constantinople after 1898; favored administrative reforms in the Turkish governmental machinery.

*Oliveira, Regis de.* Brazilian diplomat; Minister to Italy and England before the First World War; Under Secretary of State for Foreign Affairs, 1913–14; Ambassador to Portugal, 1914–25; Ambassador to England, 1925.

*Oxford, Lady* (1865–1945). Second wife of the Earl of Oxford, Herbert Henry Asquith, British Liberal Party leader who served as Prime Minister, 1908–16.

*Page, Walter Hines* (1885–1918). American journalist, editor, diplomat; appointed by Wilson Ambassador to England, 1913; regarded as an extreme Anglophile by most present historians.

*Paget, Lady Muriel Evelyn Vernon* (1876–1938). Philanthropist; wife of Sir Richard A. S. Paget; organized the Anglo-Russian Hospital in Russia, 1915–17; founded and administered a hospital and child welfare programs in Czechoslovakia and elsewhere in Eastern Europe, 1919–22; organized relief for British subjects in Russia, 1924–38.

*Palacky, František* (1798–1876). Czech politician and historian, whose major contribution to historical scholarship was *The History of the Bohemian People* (5 vols., 1836–67).

*Pallavicini, Jean, Comte de* (1848–1928). Austrian diplomat; Ambassador at Constantinople, 1906–18; Acting Minister for Foreign Affairs, 1911. During the First World War, he tried to persuade the Turkish government of the wisdom of opposing the Entente, though he warned his government of the grave difficulties involved in accomplishing this mission.

*Palmerston, Henry John Temple* (1784–1865). English statesman; Foreign Secretary in the Grey Ministry of the 1830s and in Lord John Russell's Cabinet in 1846. He generally pursued a policy of active intervention in European and Asian affairs.

*Peet, William W.* In his *Forty Years in Constantinople* (London, Herbert Jenkins, 1916, p. 299), Sir Edwin Pears describes Peet as follows: "An American who acts as business manager, banker, and general factotum for all the American missions in Asia Minor, a man of untiring energy and of good business capacity."

*Peter, King* (1844–1921). Became King of Serbia, 1903; chosen first monarch of the new triune Yugoslav nation, 1918–21.

*Pilsudski, Josef* (1867–1935). Polish statesman; active in revolutionary movement before and during First World War; became head of new Polish state, 1918; retired 1922, but re-entered public life and served as premier, 1926–28, 1930–35, increasingly as a military dictator.

*P'u-i* (Hsuan Y'ung) (b. 1906). Boy Emperor, named to the throne by Hsiao Ch'in; ruled through the Regency, 1909–12; restored to the throne for 12 days in 1917 by a military coup, and then, overthrown by republican forces; allowed to live in the Imperial Palace at Peking, 1912–24, and then moved to the Japanese Concession in Tientsin until the Manchurian Incident, 1931; brought out of retirement by the Japanese to become nominal monarch of Japanese-sponsored Manchukuo; captured by the Russian Army, 1945.

*Púlun* (P'u-lun), *Prince*. Eldest son of Tsai-chih. In 1875 and again in 1908, Prince Púlun was suggested as heir to the throne but was rejected by Dowager Empress Hsiao-Ch'in.

*Raczinsky, Count Edward* (b. 1891). Polish diplomat; appointed diplomatic representative to Copenhagen, 1919; later served in a similar capacity in London, where he showed particular interest in the minorities and disarmament questions; appointed Ambassador to England, 1934; Minister of Foreign Affairs with the Polish Government-in-exile in London, 1941–43.

*Radolin, Prince Hugo Leszczc* (1841–1917). Prussian and German diplomat; entered the Prussian Diplomatic Service during the Russo-Turkish War as Chargé at Constantinople; became Ambassador to Turkey, 1892, Ambassador to Russia, 1895, Ambassador to Paris, 1900; German representative at the Algeciras Conference, 1905–06.

*Radoslavoff, M. Vasil* (1854–1929). Bulgarian Minister of Justice, 1884–87; Prime Minister, Minister of Foreign Affairs, President of the Council during the First World War.

*Radowitz, Joseph Marie* (1839–1912). Entered the German diplomatic service, 1860; became Ambassador at Constantinople, 1882, and Ambassador at Madrid, 1892.

*Rahmi Bey*. A wealthy and cultured Salonican; one of the first members of the Committee of Union and Progress; deported to Malta after the Armistice, though he had protected British subjects during the war.

*Raouf Bey* (Raouf Orbay) (1881–1964). Famous for his exploits as commander of the cruiser *Hamidiyeh* during the Balkan Wars; last Minister of Marine of the Ottoman Empire; first Prime Minister of Turkey; Ambassador to London, 1942–44.

*Regnault, M. Eugene Georges* (b. 1857). French diplomat; Governor General at Tunis, 1886; Consul at Salonica, 1892; Chairman of the French Mission to the Orient, 1895; Consul General at Geneva, 1898; Second Plenipotentiary at the Algeciras Conference, 1906; Minister to Morocco, 1906; Ambassador to Japan, 1913.

*Reid, Whitelaw* (1837–1912). Journalist and newspaper editor; U.S. Commissioner at the Paris Peace Conference after the Spanish-American War, 1898–99; U.S. Ambassador to England, 1905–12.

*Révoil, Amedée Joseph Paul* (1856–1914). French politician and administrator; French representative at Berne, 1905–07; Ambassador in Madrid, 1907–10.

*Ribbentrop, Joachim von* (1893–1946). German wine merchant; became a prominent diplomat after the Nazis' rise to power; Ambassador to London, 1936–38; Minister of Foreign Affairs, 1938–45; executed after conviction by the Nuremberg Tribunal.

*Robilant, Mario Nicolis de* (b. 1855). Italian general; commanded the international garrison force in Macedonia and then in the Ottoman Empire; Commander of the Twelfth and then the Sixth Army Corps during the First World War.

*Rockhill, William W.* (1854–1914). American orientalist and diplomat. He conducted research expeditions to Mongolia and Tibet. He was interested in compiling bibliographies and in collecting Oriental literature. Secretary of State John Hay considered Rockhill among the two ablest American diplomats of their time, the other being Henry White. In 1899 Rockhill collaborated with the Englishman Alfred Hippsley to prepare early versions of what later became the "Open Door Notes." In 1905 Rockhill returned to China as U.S. Minister.

*Root, Elihu* (1845–1937). Prominent New York lawyer; Secretary of War, 1899–1903; Secretary of State, 1905–09; U.S. Senator from New York, 1909–15; a very influential Republican adviser and spokesman on foreign affairs during the first three decades of the twentieth century.

*Rouvier, Maurice* (1847–1911). French diplomat; Premier and Minister of Foreign Affairs, 1905–06. Rouvier was a political antagonist of Delcassé. He advocated an entente with Germany in order to avoid a war, which, in his opinion, Delcassé was coming close to provoking by his uncompromising attitude on Morocco. When Delcassé was compelled to resign in 1905, Rouvier became Foreign Minister.

*Russell, John H.* Officer in U.S. Marine Corps; served in Haiti, 1917–18; appointed Commandant of Marine Brigade in Haiti, 1919; U.S. High Commissioner in Haiti, 1922–30.

*Said Halim, Prince* (1863–1921). Grandson of Mehmed Ali of Kavala; Minister of Foreign Affairs, 1911; became Grand Vizier on the assassination of Nazim Pasha. He resigned in protest when Turkey entered the war, but was asked to remain in office until 1916, when Talaat Pasha replaced him. He was assassinated in Rome by an Armenian.

*Said Pasha the Kurd.* Not to be confused with the better-known Nehmed Said Pasha (1838–1914), who was nine times Grand Vizier under Abdul Hamid, then again when the Young Turks were in power.

*Schiff, Jacob Henry* (1847–1920). Financier, philanthropist, important leader in the American Jewish community; in 1885, as head of Kuhn, Loeb, and Co., placed large blocks of American securities on the European market; was heavily involved in the financing of railroad construction and operations in Mexico, Japan, and China.

*Schober, Johann* (1874–1932). Austrian political official; Chief of the Austrian Police, 1918; Bundeschancellor, 1921–22, and 1929–30; Vice Chancellor and Foreign Minister, 1930–32; attempted unsuccessfully to bring about the Customs Union of Austria with Germany, 1931–32.

*Selim the Grim* (1478–1520). Ninth of the Ottoman Sultans; consolidated and enlarged the Empire, conquering Aleppo, Damascus, the Holy Places in Arabia, and Egypt.

*Sforza, Count Carlo* (1873–1952). Italian statesman and writer; entered the diplomatic service in 1896; Secretary of the Italian Delegation to the Algeciras Conference; later, during the Fascist era, a principal leader of the Free Italian Movement.

*Shevket, General Mahmoud* (1856–1913). Minister of War in Hakki Pasha's Cabinet; became Grand Vizier, 1912; assassinated, 1913, by a member of a political group opposed to the Young Turks.

*Sonnino, Baron Giorgio-Sidney* (1847–1924). Italian diplomat; elected deputy, 1880, and occupied a seat in the Italian Parliament until 1919; became Minister of Foreign Affairs, 1914.

*Speck von Sternburg, Herman* (1852–1908). German diplomat; Ambassador to the United States, 1903–08.

*Stambulitzky* (Stambolisky), *Alexsandr* (1879–1923). Bulgarian political leader of peasants' causes; responsible for introducing numerous agrarian reforms; Prime Minister, 1919–23.

*Stone, Ellen* (1846–1927). American missionary teacher who went to Bulgaria in 1878. She and another woman were kidnapped on a mountain road in Macedonia in 1901. Brigands demanded $110,000 in ransom, of which more than 50 percent was raised by public subscription in the United States. After six months of captivity, the two ladies were released.

*Straight, Willard D.* (1880–1918). Graduate of Cornell's School of Architecture; served in the Chinese Imperial Maritime Customs Service, 1902–04; covered the Russo-Japanese War as a newspaper correspondent; Consul General at Mukden, 1906–08; Acting Chief, Far Eastern Division, Department of State, 1908. Straight represented the American Banking Group in China in connection with the Taft-Knox dollar diplomacy policy, of which he is often called the father. In 1913 he became a partner in J. P. Morgan and Co. He was later a financial "angel" in the launching of the *New Republic.*

*Stratford de Redcliffe, Lord* (Sir Stratford Canning). British Ambassador to Turkey, 1842–58.

*Švehla, Antonín* (1873–1933). Czech political leader of the Agrarian Party, active in the opposition to Austria-Hungary; Vice President of the National Council at Prague during World War I; later a member of the National Assembly; first Minister of the Interior in the Czechoslovak Republic; Prime Minister in several coalition governments, 1922–29.

*Taft, William Howard* (1857–1930). Secretary of War in Theodore Roosevelt's Cabinet, 1904–09; succeeded Roosevelt as President, 1909–13; appointed Chief Justice of the U.S. Supreme Court, 1921, retiring shortly before his death.

*Talaat Pasha* (1872–1921). Turkish politician; leader of the Young Turks after the Revolution of 1908; Minister of the Interior at the time of the most infamous Armenian massacres.

*Tarnowski de Tarnow, Count Adam.* Appointed Austro-Hungarian Minister to Bulgaria, 1911. He tried to persuade Bulgaria to become an ally of Austria, but the Bulgars were reluctant to break their ties with Russia and Roumania. In the end, his efforts proved successful.

*Tattenbach, Count Christian* (1846–1908). German diplomat; appointed Minister in Tangier, 1892.

*Tcharykoff, Nicholas* (1855–1930). Russian diplomat; Minister at Belgrade, 1901–04; delegate to the Second Peace Conference at the Hague, 1907; Adjutant to the Minister of Foreign Affairs, 1908–09; Ambassador to Constantinople, 1909–12.

*Tewfik Pasha* (1845–1936). Ottoman statesman for nearly sixty years; delegate to the Suez Conference in Paris; Ambassador to Berlin; Foreign Minister, 1895–1909; Grand Vizier after the counter-revolution of April 1909, again in 1918, and again in 1920 until the dissolution of the Empire; headed the Turkish Delegation to the London Conference of February 1921.

*Torres, Sid Mohammed El.* Moroccan diplomat; represented the Sultan of Morocco at Tangier, 1904–08; Moroccan delegate to the Algeciras Conference, 1906.

*Tree, Sir Herbert Beerbohm* (1853–1917). English actor and theatrical producer especially known for his productions of poetic dramas.

*Tsai Tao* (Tsai T'ao) (b. 1886). Brother of Tsai Feng (Prince Ch'un); Superintendant of the Chinese Navy, 1908; appointed Chief of the Chinese General Staff Council, 1909; sent to study military affairs in the U.S., Japan, and several European countries, 1910; threw in his lot with Yuan Shih Kai during the Revolution and was given the title General Kung-wei.

*Tuan Feng* (1861–1911). Chinese administrator; Financial Commissioner of Honan at the time of the Boxer Uprising, 1900; Governor of Hopei, 1901–04; Acting Governor General of Hu Kuang, 1902–04, and of Liang and Kiangsu and Honan Provinces. Tuan Feng supported policies of moderate reform as inaugurated by Chang Chih-tung. In 1911 he was appointed director of the proposed Canton-Hankow-Chengtu Railway. Strong opposition developed, and he was assasssinated.

*Tzu Hsi* (1835–1908). Chinese Dowager Empress; a powerful ruler who encouraged the Boxer Uprising. She was a political reactionary, hostile to foreign influence.

*Verduynen Michiels, Edgar Van* (1885–1952). Dutch diplomat; served in the Ministry of Foreign Affairs, 1920–23; Minister to Prague, 1927–29; appointed Chief of Diplomatic Affairs, 1939.

*Vergara, Carlos.* Chilean Minister to Panama and Central America, 1909–15; appointed Minister to Bolivia, 1915.

*Visconti Venosta, Marquis Emilio* (1829–1914). Italian politician and diplomat; considered a Francophile in Italian circles, particularly on the Moroccan question.

*Walker, William* (1824–60). American promoter and adventurer. He received an M.D. degree in 1843, moved quickly to the law, and then into journalism. He became interested in colonizing the Mexican states and, on his own authority, proclaimed in 1853 that lower California (part of Mexico) would be an independent state. He further declared that he would be president of the new political entity. In 1855 Walker helped the Nicaraguans in their revolution, ultimately assuming the presidency the next year. Later driven out, he invaded Honduras but was captured, condemned to death by court martial, and executed.

*Wallace, Lewis* (1827–1905). American lawyer, diplomat, author, known popularly as "Lew" Wallace; elected to the Indiana State Senate, 1856; Brigadier and Major General in the Union Army during the Civil War; Minister to Turkey, 1881–85. *Ben Hur: A Tale of the Christ* (1880) is his best-known book. He had a keen interest in art, music, and literature.

*Wangenheim, Baron de.* German Ambassador at Constantinople, 1912–15. During the formation of the Entente of Balkan States (Bulgaria, Greece, Montenegro, Serbia) and the war between these states and Turkey, 1912–13, he had a difficult diplomatic assignment, for the sympathies of the Triple Alliance (Austria, Germany, Italy) were with Turkey while the Entente (Britain, France) was sympathetic to the Balkan Entente, operating under the auspices of Russia.

*Washburn, George* (1833–1915). Ordained Congregational minister; missionary in Constantinople, 1858–62; Acting President and then President of Robert College, an American-sponsored college in Constantinople, 1870–1903; author of several books on modern Turkey.

*Welserheim* (Welsersheimb), *Count Rudolphe.* Austro-Hungarian diplomat; Chief of Section in the Foreign Ministry, 1895–1900; delegate to the Hague Peace Conference, 1899; Ambassador to Spain, 1904–11; First Austrian Delegate to the Algeciras Conference, 1906.

*White, Henry* (1850–1927). United States diplomat; Senior U.S. Commissioner at the Algeciras Conference; later Commissioner Plenipotentiary on the U.S. Delegation to the Paris Peace Conference, 1918–19.

*White, John Campbell* (Jack) (b. 1884). American diplomat; son of Henry White; private secretary to U.S. ambassadors in Rome and Paris, 1906–07; appointed Secretary of Legation at Santo Domingo, 1914, Petrograd, 1915, Athens, 1916, Tokyo, 1917; appointed Chargé d'Affaires at Bangkok, 1918; assigned to Warsaw, 1919; Assistant Chief of the Division of Near Eastern Affairs, Department of State, 1920; appointed to Prague, 1923, to Riga, 1924.

*Williamson, Howell S., Jr.* (b. 1890). American lawyer and diplomat; appointed to the Diplomatic Service, 1916, and assigned as Secretary to the Legation at San José, Costa Rica; clerk at the Embassy in London, 1917–18; Secretary at London, 1918–19, Prague, 1920–22, Panama, 1924–25; First Secretary at Warsaw, 1925.

*Winant, John G.* (1889–1947). American politician; Governor of New Hampshire, 1925–26, 1931–34; Chairman of the Social Security Board in the 1930s; Ambassador to Great Britain, 1941–46.

*Winslow, Alan F.* (b. 1895). After joining the U.S. Diplomatic Service, he was assigned to Prague, 1919–22, Department of State, 1922–23, Berne, 1923.

*Yulang* (Yü-lang), *Prince and Princess.* Prince Yulang, son of P'u-hsü, inherited a princedom of the third degree in 1907 and was subsequently made Grand Councillor in 1910–11.

# *A Bibliography of Lewis Einstein's Published Writings*

## Books

*The Italian Renaissance in England,* New York, Columbia University Press, 1902.
*Luigi Pulci and the Morgante Maggiore,* Berlin, Felber, 1902.
*Napoleon III and American Diplomacy at the Outbreak of the Civil War,* London, private printing, 1905.
*Thoughts on Art and Life by Leonardo da Vinci,* trans. Maurice Baring, ed. Lewis Einstein, Boston, Merrymount Press, 1906.
*American Foreign Policy by a Diplomatist,* Boston and New York, Houghton Mifflin, 1909.
*Inside Constantinople: A Diplomatist's Diary During the Dardanelles Expedition, April–September, 1915,* London, Murray, 1917.
*A Prophecy of the War 1913–1914,* foreword by Theodore Roosevelt, New York, Columbia University Press, 1918.
*Tudor Ideals,* New York, Harcourt, Brace, 1921.
*Italian Gardens in Prague,* London, Eyre and Spottiswoode, 1925.
"Lewis Cass," in *American Secretaries of State and Their Diplomacy, 6,* ed. Samuel Flagg Bemis, New York, Knopf, 1928–29, pp. 297–384.
*Roosevelt: His Mind in Action,* Boston and New York, Houghton Mifflin, 1930.
*Divided Loyalties: Americans in England During the War of Independence,* Boston and New York, Houghton Mifflin, 1933.
*Verses,* London, De La Mare Press, 1938.
*The Winged Victory and Other Verses,* London, De La Mare Press, 1941.
*Historical Change,* Cambridge, The University Press, 1946.
*Scattered Verses,* Florence, Ripografia Giuntina S. A., 1949.
*Looking at French Eighteenth Century Pictures of the National Gallery, Washington,* Paris, Gazette des Beaux-Arts, 1958.
*Looking at Italian Pictures in the National Gallery of Art,* Washington, National Gallery of Art, 1958.

## Letters, Articles, Reviews

1902

"The Relation of Literature to History," *Journal of Comparative Literature, 1* (April–June 1903), 105–19, privately reprinted by the author, New York, 1903.

1905

"Exhibition of Mezzotints at the British Museum," *The Nation, 81* (August 3, 1905), 94–95.

1908

"The New Era in Turkey," Letter to the Editor, *The Times* (London), August 9, 1908, signed "A Diplomatist at Constantinople."

1912

"British Shipping and the Canal," Letter to the Editor, *The Times* (London), July 17, 1912.

1913

"The United States and Anglo-German Rivalry," *National Review, 60* (January 1913), 736–50.

1914

"The War and American Policy," *National Review, 64* (November 1914), 357–76.

"Germany and the United States: Relative Importance of American Newspapers," Letter to the Editor, *Morning Post* (London), December 21, 1914.

"The Contraband Difficulty: An American Difficulty," Letter to the Editor, *The Times* (London), December 31, 1914.

1915

"American Peace Dreams," *National Review, 64* (January 1915), 837–50.

"Japan at Tsingtao and American Policy," *Journal of the American Asiatic Association, 14* (January 1915), 359–62.

"A Great Danger," Letter to the Editor, *The Spectator, 114* (January 30, 1915), 153–54.

"The Contraband Dispute: An American's Admonitions," Letter to the Editor, *Morning Post* (London), February 5, 1915.

1917

"How the United States Could Establish Friendly Relations with Japan," *New York Sun,* March 1, 1917.

"Au Tourant de la Route," *Revue Des Nations Latines, 2* (March 1, 1917), 93–98.

"The Armenian Massacres," *Contemporary Review, 111* (April 1917), 486–94.

"The Origin of the War," Letter to the Editor, *The Times* (London), August 4, 1917.

"The Late Queen of Bulgaria," Letter to the Editor, *The Times* (London), September 14, 1917.

1918

"An American Opportunity," *Ararat, 4* (April 1918), 373–75.

"Our Siberian Policy," Letter to the Editor, *New York Sun,* October 2, 1918.

"The Turkish Problem," *Westminster Gazette,* November 1, 1918, signed "A Diplomatic Correspondent."

"La Lega delle Nazione e gli Stati disorganizzati," *La Vita Britannica, 1* (November–December, 1918), 305–11.

1919

"L'America e l'Europa," *Nuevo Giornele* (Florence), February 21, 1919.

"A Way Out of Mandates," *The New York Times,* November 2, 1919.

"Loss in the Exchange Situation," Letter to the Editor, *The New York Times,* December 2, 1919.

"The Mandate for Constantinople," *The Nation, 109* (December 6, 1919), 727–29.

"One Reservation Only: A General Statement to Cover Debatable Treaty Points," Letter to the Editor, *The New York Times,* December 27, 1919.

1920

"The Mandate for Armenia," *Republican Campaign Textbook for 1920,* issued by the Republican National Committee, pp. 115–17.

"Reorganization of the State Department," *Republican Campaign Textbook for 1920,* issued by the Republican National Committee, pp. 231–32.

"The Italian Situation," Letter to the Editor, *The Nation, 110* (May 1, 1920), 592, signed, "A Traveler."

"The Armenian Mandate," *The Nation, 110* (June 5, 1920), 762–63.

"Our Policy in the Consortium," Letter to the Editor, *The New York Times* August 18, 1920.

"Harding Nuggets—A Complaint That They Misrepresent Candidates' Views," Letter to the Editor, *The New York Times,* September 20, 1920.

"Essay," in Symposium on the League of Nations, *Chicago Daily News* and *New York Globe,* October 20, 1920.

"A Correction," Letter to the Editor, *The New York Times,* November 2, 1920.

1922

"The Germans in Czechoslovakia," Letter to the Editor, *The Nation and the Athenaeum, 31* (May 27, 1922), 307, signed "A Traveller."

1923

*The Character of Henry VIII,* pamphlet, London, V. Praze, 1923.

1925

"Italian Gardens in Prague," Part I in *Architectural Review, 57* (June 1925), 253–55; Part II in *Architectural Review, 58* (August 1925), 68–72.

1926

Introductory Note to "Recollections of the War of 1812" by George Hay, in *American Historical Review, 32* (October 1926), 69–78.

1927

"The Tuscan Garden," *Architectural Review, 61* (February 1927), 46–49.

1931

"Our Still Dubious Foreign Policy," abridgment in *International Digest, 2* (November 1931), 14–16.

1932

"Germany and Armaments: French Security," Letter to the Editor, *The Times* (London), September 10, 1932.

1933

"The Conference," Letter to the Editor, *The Times* (London), July 3, 1933.

"Uneasy Europe: Peace Revision of Treaties," Letter to the Editor, *The Times* (London), November 18, 1933.

"The Cult of Force," *North American Review, 236* (December 1933), 501–07.

1934

"Herr Hitler's Middle Europe Plans," *The Spectator, 152* (January 1934), 39–40.

Untitled Letter to the Editor, *The Times* (London), March 7, 1934.

"Germany—Former U.S. Minister's Apt Question," Letter to the Editor, *Morning Post* (London), December 1, 1934.
"Middle Europe," Letter to the Editor, *The Times* (London), December 7, 1934.

1935

"Germany and Britain's Defences; Problem of Hitler's Objectives," Letter to the Editor, *Morning Post* (London), March 14, 1935, signed "Herbert Languet."
"Chinoiserie," *The Spectator, 155* (December 13, 1935), 981–82.

1936

"Danger Zones—Value of League Supervision—The Lucarno Treaty," Letter to the Editor, *The Times* (London), March 26, 1936.
Untitled Letter to the Editor, *The Times* (London), May 16, 1936.
"Spanish Descent of the Irish," Letter to the Editor, *The Times* (London), June 11, 1936.
"Spaniards in Ireland," Letter to the Editor, *The Times* (London), June 22, 1936.
"German Question in Czechoslovakia," *The Spectator, 157* (July 24, 1936), 135–36.
"The Balkans Today: Non Interference by the Great Powers," Letter to the Editor, *The Times* (London), November 16, 1936.

1937

"Czech and German," Letter to the Editor, *The Times* (London), February 2, 1937.
"Germany's Designs on Czechoslovakia: The Obstacle in the Way of a Gigantic Nazi Empire," Letter to the Editor, *Manchester Guardian*, February 9, 1937.
"Czechoslovakia's Confidence," Letter to the Editor, *The Spectator, 158* (February 12, 1937), 270.
"Storing for Emergency," Letter to the Editor, *The Times* (London), April 8, 1937, signed "Georgina Hay."

1938

"Sudeten Germans," Letter to the Editor, *The Times* (London), April 21, 1938.

1939

"The Munich Agreement: A Retrospect," *History, 23* (March 1939), 331–40.
Review, *Foreign Office Archives, Select Documents on Britain and the Independence of Latin America 1812–1830,* ed. C. K. Webster, in *History, 24* (September 1939), 169–70.
Review, *The Great Powers and the Balkans 1875–1878,* by M. D. Stojanovic, in *History, 24* (September 1939), 167.
Review, *Munich and the Dictators,* by Robert Seton-Watson, in *History, 24* (September 1939), 186–88.
Untitled Letter to the Editor, *The Times* (London), November 18, 1939.

1940

"The Sumner Welles Mission: A Fight for Freedom—America's Traditional Appeal," Letter to the Editor, *The Times* (London), February 14, 1940.
Review, *A Diary of the French Revolution,* by Gouverneur Morris, in *History, 24* (March 1940), 356–57.
"The War in a Scottish Village," *The Outpost,* Letter No. 4, September 15, 1940.
"A Farmer's Red Cross Sale in Scotland," *The Outpost,* Letter No. 10, December 15, 1940.
Review, *British Foreign Policy Since Versailles,* by W. N. Medlicott in *History, 25* (December 1940), 272–73.

Review, *Pro-Fascist Italy: The Rise and Fall of the Parliamentary Regime,* by Margot Hentze, in *History, 25* (December 1940), 274–75.
Review, *The Paths That Led to War in Europe 1919–1930,* by John Mackintosh, in *History, 25* (December 1940), 281–82.

1941
"The Elgin Marbles," Letter to the Editor, *The Scotsman,* January 8, 1941.
"Mr. Eden as Foreign Secretary and the War of Ideas," *The Outpost,* Letter No. 12, January 15, 1941.
"What To Tell Italy," *The Spectator, 166* (February 7, 1941), 145.
Review, *A Spanish Tudor: The Life of Bloody Mary,* by H. F. M. Prescott, in *Journal of Modern History, 13* (March 1941), 84–86.
Review, *The Habsburg Monarchy,* by A. J. P. Taylor, in *History,* 26 (June 1941), 83–85.

1942
Review, *History as the Saga of Liberty,* by Benedetto Croce, trans. Sylvia Sprigge, in *Law Quarterly Review, 58* (January 1942), 140–42.
"Address on Modern American Poetry," *Poetry Review, 33* (July-August 1942), 267–68.

1943
"Isolationist Prospect," *The Spectator, 170* (February 12, 1943), 144–45.

1944
"Shelley and Stendhal," Letter to the Editor, *The Times Literary Supplement* (London), July 22, 1944.

1945
"Potsdam, Russia and Central Europe," *The Fortnightly, 164* (September 1945), 154–60.

1946
Review, *Federal Government,* by K. C. Wheare, in *The Fortnightly, 166* (September 1946), 218–19.
"The Next Allied Talks," *The Fortnightly, 165* (January 1946), 13–20.
"Anglo-American Relations and Security," *The Fortnightly, 166* (July 1946), 42–48.

1947
"Declining Values in Civilization," *The Fortnightly, 167* (February 1947), 101–04.
"Communists in Tuscany," *New English Review, 14* (June 1947), 551–54.

1954
"What is Great Art?"*Gazette des Beaux-Arts, 43* (May 1954), 275–98.

1955
"Orphan Island," Letter to the Editor, *The Economist, 176* (July 2, 1955), 28.

1956
"End of an Alliance," Letter to the Editor, *New York Herald Tribune* (Paris), March 14, 1956.

1958
"Arsenal of Ideas," Letter to the Editor, *Washington Post,* October 1, 1958.

1961
"Conversations at Villa Riposa; With French Summary," *Gazette des Beaux-Arts, 58* (July 1961), 6–20.

1964
"British Diplomacy During the Spanish-American War," *Massachusetts Historical Society Proceedings, 26* (1964), 30–54.

1965
"The Unseen in Art," *Gazette des Beaux-Arts, 65* (May 1965), 359–66.

# Index


Abdul Aziz II, 40, 233
Abdul Hamid II, xxxiv, 27, 29–30, 36–37, 39–52, 56, 60, 64–71, 74–76, 78–79, 132, 233
Abdul Medjid, 47, 233
Abernon, Lord d', 119, 233
Adana, Turkey: massacres, 68; governor, 69
Adee, A. A., 83, 233
Adrianople, Turkey, 72, 146
Aegean Sea, 224
Agrarian Centre, Bulgaria, 153
Agrarian Party, Czechoslovak, 177
Aidin Valley, 42, 59
Albania, 148, 157, 158–59
Aleppo, Syria, 43, 122
Alexander II, Czar, 148
Alexandretta, Gulf of, 141
Alexandria, Egypt, 75
Alfonso XIII, King, 20, 234
Algesiras, Duke of, 20
Algesiras, Spain, 4, 92
Algesiras Conference (*1906*), xii, xvii, 3 ff., 188
Algiers, Algeria, 51
Allied Powers (World War I), 144, 146, 147, 159–60, 192; interests in Turkey, 143; medical mission in Serbia, 156; at the Paris Peace Conference (*1919*), 199
Allies (World War II), 222–23
Almodóvar del Rio, Duc de, 20, 234
America, American. *See* United States
American College for Women at Constantinople, 157
American Red Cross, 148, 151; in Serbia, 157
Anatolian Railroad, 76
Anglo-French Entente (*1904*), xvi–xvii
Anglo-German Convention (*1913*), 12
Annam, Emperor of, 61
Antwerp, Belgium, 101
Archbishop of Prague, Catholic, 184
Armaments, viii
Armenia, Armenians, xxiv, xxviii, 32, 45, 59, 132; massacres, xxxiv, 50, 60, 68, 133 ff., 146, 147; Patriarchate, 39; plot assassination of the Sultan, 43–44; cemeteries, 66
Arno Valley, xxvi
Arnold, Benedict, 212
Arslan, Emin, 72
Art: Oriental, 96–99; dealers in Peking, 97
Arthauer, R. N., xv
Arvers, Felix, 19–20
Asia Minor, 70
Asilo, Baron, 161
Asquith, Herbert Henry, 219
Asquith, "Margot," 219
Athens, 35, 111–12
Atlas Mountains, 6 n.
Augustus, Emperor, 104
Austerlitz, Column of, 179
Austria, 80, 173, 192, 216
Austria-Hungary, x n., 192–93, 196, 199; annexation of Bosnia-Herzegovina (*1908–09*), 36; policy towards Turkish sovereignty over Eastern Roumelia, 69
Austro-Russian rivalry, 35–36
Avon, Lord, 225
Axis Alliance, 91 n.
Axis Powers, xxix
Aynard, Joseph Raymond, 15, 234
Azarian, 39

Bagdad Railway, 42, 60
Baker, Ray Stannard, xxv
Baku, U.S.S.R., 222

# *Index*


Balance of power, viii, x, xxii, 212
Balkan, Balkans, 119, 145, 151, 160, 166; Wars (*1912–14*), 36, 51, 80, 119, 145, 148, 169–70; negotiations among, 146; Alliance, 149; racial hatreds, 156; winter, 165
Baltic Sea, 70, 224
Bancroft, Dr. Edward, 214–15, 234
Barclay, Sir George, 150, 234
Bassorah, 59
Battle of Britain, 228–29
Batum, U.S.S.R., 222
Bavaria, 185
Bebek, Turkey, 57
Bedri Bey, 131–32, 138, 234
Beelaerts van Blokland, Franz-Jonkeer, 88, 234
Beethoven, Ludwig von, 174
Beirut, Lebanon, 32, 38
Belgian sporting guns, 21
Belgium, ix, 216; rape of, 125
Belgrade, Serbia, 35
Beneš, Eduard, 175, 184, 191–92, 198–204, 224–25; prestige in Switzerland, 201, 234
Beneš, Madame Eduard, 183, 199–200
Bennett, James Gordon, 102, 234
Berchtold, Count Leopold von, 192, 234
Beresford, Lord Charles, 12, 234
Berlin, Congress of (*1878*), 23; Treaty of (*1878*), 69 n.
Berne, Switzerland, 158
Bible House at Stamboul, Turkey, 129
Billy, Robert de, 15, 234
Bismarck, Prince Otto von, 23,91
Black Sea, 81
"Blacks," the, 175–76, 187
Bliss, Howard S., 32, 234
Blücher, Gebhard Leberecht von, ix
Boddy, Dr., 156
Boer War, 73
Bohemia, Bohemians, 174, 177, 181, 184–85, 190, 197; forestry, 178; captains of industry, 182–83; Crown, 198
Bolsheviks, Bolshevism, xxviii, 176, 203
Bordonaro, Antonio Cheramonte, 187–88, 235
Boris, Prince, 166–67, 235
Bosnia-Herzegovina, 69
Bosporus, 25, 56, 58, 79, 81, 118, 121
Boulanger, George, 61
Boulanger bubble, 61
Boxer Indemnity, 88
Brambilia, Dora, 92–93
Brandis, Castle of (Prague), 180
*Breslau,* the, 125
Britain. *See* Great Britain
Bruning, Heinrich, 216, 235
Bryan, William Jennings, x, xxiii, 26–29, 89, 118, 235
Bubonic Plague, Manchuria, 90–91
Buchanan, James, policy towards Mexico, 85
Bucharest, Roumania, 35, 60, 147, 150, 164
Buckingham Palace, 40
Bucknam, 51
Buenos Aires, Argentina, 29
Bulgaria, Bulgars, x, xxiv–xxv, xxxiv, 69, 118, 143, 145, 156–59, 162, 164–65, 167; terrorist organizations, 35; Mohammedans, 68; politicians, 144, 166; negotiations with Turkey, 146; Ministry at Bucharest, 147, 150; Foreign Office, 147, 158–59, 169; Alliance with Turkey, 148; Army, 148; territorial claims, 148; Ministry of War, 149, 167–69; intervention in World War I, 149; Cabinet, 151, 153, 160; officialdom, 152; Parliament, 152–53; police, 152; Post Office, 152; Government, 159–62, 172; Minister at Washington, 160; Prime Minister, 161, 166; Agency at Bucharest, 163–64; Consul at Salonika, 164; winter, 166
Bulgarian Red Cross, 157
Bülow, Prince Bernard von, 13, 235; Memoirs, 16–17
Burhan-Eddin, Prince Effendi, 46, 235
Buxton, Charles R., 35, 235
Buxton, Edward N., 35, 235
Büyük Menderes River, 42 n.

Cahun, Leon, 70
Cairo, Egypt, 122, 183

Calais, France, 119
Calhoun, William C., 84, 88–90, 235
California vote, decisive in Presidential Election of *1916*, 209
Caliphate, the, 49
Cambon, Jules, 22, 235
Campo Segrado, Marquis of, 62–63
Canton, China 106
Cape Spartel, Morocco, 8
Capitulations, 37–38
*Carbonari*, Italian, 13
Carnegie, Andrew, xxi
Carnock, Lord. *See* Nicolson, Sir Arthur
Carpathians, the, 145
Cartier de Marchienne, Baron Emile, 88, 218, 235
Casablanca, Morocco, 22
Casanova, 174
Cassini, Count Arthur Pavlovitch, 10–11, 235
Castiglione, 96
Castro, Cipriano, 7 n.
Catholic Church, 60
Caucasus, the, 78, 123, 142; Southern, 134
Cavour, Count Camillo, 13
Central America, xxxiv, 112; solidarity, 108
Central American Court of Justice, xxi
Central Asia, 70
Central Europe, x n., xi, 180, 186, 188, 191–93, 195, 198, 203, 216, 224–25; Soviet opposition to union, 204, 224; Einstein's lectures on, 217
Central Powers (World War I), 144, 146, 155–56, 159; isolation, 119
Cercle d' Orient, 31
Chamberlain, Neville, 216, 220–22, 235
Chamonix, France, 223
Chang the Eunuch, 103
Charles, Archduke, 180
Charles, Emperor, 181
Charles IX, King of France, 133 n.
Charles V, Emperor, 19
Charles-Roux, François-Jules, 188, 235
*Chasseurs Alpins*, 223
Chicago, Illinois, 84; newspapers, 89
Ch'ien-lung, Emperor, 105 n.
Chienmen Gate, 88
Chile, 84
China, Chinese, xii, xix, xx, 70, 83 ff.; resources, 85; Revolution (*1911*), xxxiv, 89, 97, 105; anti-opium crusades in, 89; servants, 93–95; Supreme Court, 96; banquets, 100–01; Board of Finance, 103; nationalism, 106
Ch'ing, Princess of, 103
Chios, massacre of, 53
Choate, Joseph H., 7, 236
Christian missionaries, xviii; in Turkey, 32–33; in Bulgaria, 152
Christian Ottomans, 69
Christian population in Turkey, 142
Christians in Ottoman service, 43
Chukry Bey, 131–32, 236
Ch'un, Prince Regent, 101–04, 236
Churchill, Winston, 220, 228
Civil List, Turkish, 45
Clerk, Sir George, 187, 228, 236
Cloman, Colonel Sidney A., 72–73, 236
Coke, Ned, 229
Colloredo Mansfeld, Rudolf von, 174, 236
Columbia College, xv
Columbia University Press, 213
*Comitadjis*, Bulgar, 34, 65–66
Commercial Academy at Prague, 199
Committee of Union and Progress, 68, 123, 133–34
Communism, 176, 212, 223
Congo, the, 16 n.
Constance, Council of, 183
Constantinople, Turkey, xix, xxiv, xviii, 25–27, 31–34, 39, 43, 49–51, 54–55, 57, 61, 64–65, 67, 73, 76–77, 79, 81, 105, 118 ff., 145–47, 158–59, 171, 188; Einstein's diary of, vii; gossip of, 41; charm of, 56; neutral zone in, 129
Constans, John A. E., 60–61, 236
Coolidge, President Calvin, 29, 236
Costa Rica, Costa Ricans, viii, xx–xxi, 108 ff.; inhabitants, 108; army, 112; Minister of Foreign Affairs, 112; hospitality, 114 ff.; notables, 116
Couget, Joseph-Robert, 184, 236

Crane, Charles R., 83, 236
Crane, Richard, 174, 236
"Crane Incident," 83–84
Crete, 42
Crimean War, 49
Crown Council (*1914*), 128
Curzon, George N., 201
Cyprus, 141
Czechoslovakia, Czechs, xxviii, 173 ff., 193–94, 197–98, 202, 216; aristocrats support the Republic, 174; officials, 175; currency depreciation, 176; Land Reform Act, 176–77, 179; land tenure, 176; language, 177; nationalism, 177, 185–86; Ministry of Agriculture, 179–81; National Arboretum, 179; Parliament, 181, 192; politicians, 181; democrats, 182; newspapers, 184; pride in Prague, 190; political parties, 192; university appointments, 195; students in Prague, 199; relations with Britain and France, 201; views of Germany, 201; Communists, 203; lacking in social graces, 199, 205; proposed union with Poland, Yugoslavia, Greece, 204, 224–25

Damascus, Syria, 53
Danube: River, 147, 150, 192, 198; Valley, 185, 224–25; states, 225
Dardanelles, xxiv n., xxxiv, 122, 125, 128, 133–34, 145; British blockade, 126; naval attack (*1915*), 132; fighting, 140
Dawes Plan (*1924*), 201
Dedéagatch, Bulgaria, 139
Delcassé Théophile, 16, 236
Democratic Party (U.S.), xxvii–xxviii, 209
Denmark, Minister at Madrid, 161
Depression (*1930s*), 211
Derussi, Georges, 150, 237
Dickinson, Jacob M., 84, 101–02, 237
Dickinson, Mrs. Jacob M., 102
Dimitrieff, General Radko, 149, 237
Diplomats, 162; as nomads, 55; as viewed by Czar Ferdinand, 153–54; their participation in hunting, 179 ff.
Disraeli, Benjamin, 23
Dobrovitch, Czar Ferdinand's secretary, 166
"Dollar diplomacy," xix–xx, 85, 89
Doiran front, 164–65
Dolma Bagtché, Palace of, 79
Drem, Scotland, 227
Dreyfus Affair, 3
Dropmore, England, 95
Dual Monarchy, 196
Dunkirk, France, 227, 229
Dux, Castle of, 174–75

Earl Li, 97
Eastern Europe, x n., xi, xxiv
"Eastern Question," 41, 58
Eastern Roumelia, 69, 169
Eboul Houda, 48, 66, 237
Ecclesiastical Court, Constantinople, 39
Eden, Sir Anthony (Lord Avon), 225, 237
Edinburgh, Scotland, 225–27, 229
Edward VII, 98
Edwards, Mrs. Clarence R., 102
Egan, Maurice, vii
Eger, District of, 198
Egypt, Egyptians, 3 n.; anti-British group in Constantinople, 122; Legation at Prague, 183
Einstein, Caroline, xvi n.
Einstein, Helen (Mrs. Lewis), xxi, xxv, 110–11, 117, 138–39, 171, 212
Einstein, Lewis: literary achievements, vii; prescience of, x; U.S. government's relations with, xi; Junior Secretary in Paris and London, 24; at Constantinople, 25; confidential reports, 171–72; in U.S. on holiday, 182; in Prague, 189 ff.; plan for Central Europe, 203–04; departure from Prague, 207; retirement from the Diplomatic Service, 207 ff.; lectures on Central European problems, 217; writings on the international situation during the *1930s*, 217; plan for an American-British-Russian committee (*1941–42*), 225; grandchild, 228

Einstein, Lewis (*cont.*)
*A Prophecy of the War,* viii
*Divided Loyalties,* vii, 213
*Historical Change,* vii
*Italian Gardens in Prague,* vii
*Italian Renaissance in England,* vii
"Lewis Cass," vii, 85 n.
Sofia Diary, xxiv n.
Einstein family, xv
Eleanor, Princess of Reuss, 154, 237; Queen of Bulgaria, 154–55, 167, 171
England. *See* Great Britain
*Entente Cordiale,* 3, 11, 15, 17, 144, 145, 147, 149
Enver Bey, 67, 122–23, 126–27, 131, 138–39, 237
Eski Chehir, Turkey, 129
Eunuchs, 44, 103–05
Europe, xxix, 230; American attitudes towards, viii, 8; balance of power, xvii–xviii; attitude toward U.S., 231
Executive Agents, xxviii

"Face," in China, 94
Fairchild, Lucius, 8 n.
Falloden, England, 118
Far East, viii, 86; American policy in, xxvi
Fashoda, crisis of (*1898*), 16
Ferdinand, Czar of Bulgaria, 144–45, 152–55, 166, 237
Fez, 70
Finland, 222–23
Firdausi, language of, 64
Fitcheff, General, 149
Fitzmaurice, dragoman at the British Embassy, Constantinople, 74
Fletcher, Henry, xix, 84, 238
Florence, Italy, xxv, 111–12, 200
France, French, ix, xvi–xviii, 3, 37, 49, 144, 149, 158–59, 180, 193, 223, 227; at Algesiras Conference (*1906*), 6 ff., 15–17, 20–21; dependence on British sea power, 12; Congo, 22; claims over Syria, 42; Embassy in Constantinople, 49; loan to the Sultan, 49; interests in Turkey, 60; Revolution, 66, 177; financial interests in China, 86; Legation at Peking, 87; cuisine

France, French (*cont.*)
in Peking, 93; nuns in Constantinople, 131; envoys at Sofia, 144; Army in Serbia, 153; prisoners of war in Bulgaria, 164, 166, 171; interests in Bulgaria, 165; recognition of Czechoslovak Republic, 197; generals during the *1930s,* 216; Embassy in London, 221; General Staff, 221
Franchet d'Esperey, General Louis, 157, 238
Francis Ferdinand, Archduke, murder at Serajevo (*1914*), 36, 181–82, 192–93
Francis Joseph, Emperor, 19, 173
Franco-American Alliance (*1778*), 214
Franklin, Benjamin, 214
Frederick, Archduke, estate of, 179–80
Freer, Charles L., 53–54, 98, 238
Freer Museum, Washington, D.C., 53–54, 98
Freud, Sigmund, xiii
Fuad, King, 182–83, 238
Fuad, Reshad, 55
Furstenberg, Prince Karl Emile de, 194, 238

Galata Bridge, 25, 79–80
Gallipoli, Battle of, 125, 129, 140–41, 145
Gallup polls, 230
Galtier, Joseph, 19
Gardening, Oriental theory of, 95
Gargiulo, Mr., 33
Garroni, Marquis C., 128–30, 138, 238
Gates, Caleb Frank, 32
Geneva, 191, 200–02; political refugees living in, 65
George III, 214
George V, 111, 181
Georgia, U.S.S.R., 78
Germany, Germans, xvi, xviii, xxii, xxvi, 3, 37, 144, 146, 167, 193, 211, 216, 220, 222–23; rivalry with Britain, ix; relations with U.S., xxii; at Algesiras Conference (*1906*), 3 ff.; policy towards Venezuela (*1901–02*), 7; fear of encirclement, 15; policy towards Morocco, 15, 17, 22; policy towards Britain and France, 18;

Germany, Germans (*cont.*)
interest in Bagdad Railway, 42; and Pan-Islamism, 49; influence at Constantinople, 60, 81; relations with Turkey in World War I, 67, 121, 124; policy towards Turkey, 81, 126; financial interests in China, 86; Legation at Peking, 91; prisoners of war in England, 119; military mission at Constantinople (*1914*), 124; Embassy at Constantinople, 127; White Book on Belgian atrocities, 134–35; attitudes towards Armenian massacres, 137; submarines, 139; Army, 148; influence in Bulgaria, 152; minority in Czechoslovakia, 184, 198; influence in Czechoslovakia, 185 ff.; influence in the Danube Valley, 185; nationalism, 195; universities, 195; education, 200; in World War II, 222 ff.
Gibraltar, Bay of, 4; Rock of, 12
Giolitti, G., 129, 238
Gladstone, William E., 167
Glasgow, Scotland, 227
Gobineau, Joseph A. de, 70
*Goeben*, the, 121, 125
Goerdeler, Dr. Karl, 216, 238
Golden Horn, 58–59, 142
Goltz, General von der, 60
Great Britain, viii, xi, xvi, xviii, xxii, 49, 144, 147, 149, 167, 193, 203, 212, 216, 219–21, 222–23, 226–28, 230; rivalry with Germany, ix; Navy, xxiv, 12, 132–33, 141; interests in Bulgaria, xxxiv; prisoners of war in Bulgaria, xxv, 164 ff.; opposition to France in Morocco, 11, interests in Africa, 12; Embassy in Constantinople, 35, 58, 67, 74; Foreign Office, 35–36, 118, 203; interest in Aidin Valley, 42; policy in India, 50; interests in Turkey, 59; policy towards China, 85, 86; Legation at Peking, 98–99; merchant class in China, 107; defeat at Gallipoli, 141, 145; subjects in Bulgaria, 151; language, 152, 205; Legation at Sofia, 164–66; interests
Great Britain (*cont.*)
in the Balkans, 167; diplomats at Prague, 180–82; cuisine, 222; in World War II, 223 ff.
Great Wall of China, 102
Greece, Greeks, 42 n., 159; archbishops, 66; in Constantinople, 132; Minister to Bulgaria, 158; proposed union with Czechoslovakia, Poland, Yugoslavia, 204, 224–25
Grenville, Lord George, 95
Grey, Sir Edward, xxiv n., 12, 118–19, 126, 219, 238
Guechoff, Ivan-Stephanov, 149, 157, 238
Gummere, Samuel, xvii, 7, 238

Habsburg Empire, 36, 175, 177, 185, 192–93
Habsburgs, 94, 176, 183, 196, 202; dynastic characteristics, 41; estates, 180–82
Haddington, Scotland, 226–27
Haidar Pasha, Turkey, 128
Haiti, 91
Halil Bey, 53
Hamdi Bey, 53–54, 238
Harbin, Manchuria, 90
Harem, Abdul Hamid's, 79
Harding, Warren G., xxviii
Harris, Walter, 6, 239
Harrison, Leland, 91, 239
Hatamen Gate, 88
Hay, Helen, 155, 171
Hay, John, vii, xvi, 38, 239
Hayes, Rutherford B., xvii
Hedjaz Railroad, 49
Hereké, imperial factory of, 79
Hilmy Pasha, 68–69, 239
Hitler, Adolf, x n., xxix, 175, 211, 216–17, 219–20, 222–23
Hodgson, Jim, 188, 239
Hohenzollerns, 19
Holland. *See* Netherlands
Holmes, Oliver Wendell, Jr., vii, xiii, xxxi, 108, 207–08, 217, 239
Holmes, Mrs. Oliver Wendell, Jr., 108
Holstein, Friedrich von, 18, 239

Holy See, 183
Honda, Japanese Counsellor at Peking, 91
Hontoria y Fernandez Ladrera, Manuel, 20, 239
Hoover, Herbert C., x–xi, 195, 207, 239
Hospitals at Sofia, 167
House, Edward M., xxvi
Hradcany (Hradschin), castle of the, 173, 182, 194
Hughes, Charles Evans, xii, 196, 201, 208–10, 217, 239
Huguenin, E., 76, 240
Hull, Cordell, xi, xxix n., 215–16, 240
Humann, Captain, 126–27, 240
Hungarian Plain, 145
Hungary, 142, 148, 198; food supplies, 120; irredentism, 198
Hurst, Leonard Henry, 159–64, 240
Huss, John, 183–84, 196

Ijuin, M. H., 91, 240
Imperiali, Marquis, 66, 240
Imperialism, American capitalistic, 231
India, 50, 165
Indian Moslems, 49
Indochina, 61
Inquiry, the, xxvi
International Banking Consortium, xviii
International congresses, American opinion towards, 8
Ireland, 165, 168, 198
Islam, 72, 74
Italy, xviii, 121; defection from Germany, xvii; policy towards North Africa, 13; interest in Libya, 42; Legation at Peking, 88; Embassy at Constantinople, 120, 127; intervention in World War I, 136; colonial ambitions, 138; diplomats at Prague, 182
Izzet Pasha, 48, 66, 240

Japan, xix–xx, 3, 81; military activities in Siberia, xxvi; occupation of Shantung, xxviii; press, 83; policy towards China, 85; obstruction of U.S. rail-
Japan (*cont.*)
way schemes in Manchuria, 89; Legation at Peking, 91; concept of Emperor, 101–02
Jay, Peter, 25–26, 28, 240
Jefferson, Thomas, 211
Jews: in Morocco, 10; in Constantinople, 132
Jiménez Oreamuno, Ricardo, xxi, 109, 114, 240
Johns Hopkins University, 217
Johnson, Hiram, 209–10, 240
Johnson, Tom, 229
Jonēscu, Take, 147, 240
Joseph, Archduke, 181
Jusserand, Jean A. A. Jules, 9, 108, 240

Kellogg, Frank B., 202; attitude towards Czechoslovakia, 202
Kellogg-Briand Pact (*1928*), 202
Kemal, Mustafa (Atatürk), 142, 240
Keyes, Admiral Roger J. B., 132, 241
Khan, Mahmoud, 122
Khedive, the, 57
Khilkoff, Prince Mikhail I., 86–87, 241
Kiamil Pasha, 66, 241
Kiderlen-Wächter, Alfred von, 22, 60, 241
Keil, Germany, 51
Kien Lung, Emperor, 96, 241
King, Mr., 96
Kinsky, Count, 174
Kipling, Rudyard, 170
Kitchener, Horatio H., 16 n.; new army, 165
Knights of Malta, 168, 173
Knox, Philander C., xx, xxvii, 83–86, 105, 117, 241
Kodok, 16 n.
Kolowrat, Count, 178, 241
Konopisht, estate near Prague, 181–82
Korea, 86
Kovatcheff, General, 170
Kosseff, Bulgarian Undersecretary for Foreign Affairs, 150–51, 159–61, 165
Koziebrodski-Bolesta, Count Leopold, 19–20, 241

*Index*


Kremlin, 203
Kut, 125

Labouchère, Henry, 113, 241
Lafayette Squadron, 188
Lansing, Robert F., xxiv–xxv, 162
Lany, castle at, 194, 196
Latin America, viii
Lawyers as diplomats, 7
League of Nations, xxvii
Ledebur, Count Eugene, 175
Leipzig, Colonel von, 145
Leishman, John G. A., 29–30, 34, 38, 50–52, 57, 61, 72, 241
Leishman, Mrs. John G. A., 46
Levant, the, 58
Li Hung Chang, 97, 242
Li Lung Mien, 98
Libya, 42
Libyan War (*1912*), 139
Ligne, Prince Eugene de, 218
Liman von Sanders, General, 133, 242
Lincoln, Abraham, 211, 223
Little Entente, Treaty of the, 202
Litvinoff, Maxim, 216, 242
Lloyd George, David, 198
Lobkovicz, Prince Max, 174, 242
Lobkowicz, Prince Zdenko, 175
Lodge, Henry Cabot, xxvii, 9, 209, 242
London, England, 64, 188, 144, 159, 166, 171–72, 201–05, 212–16, 224–25, 229–30; Lord Mayor of, 183
London Economic Conference (*1933*), 215
Loti, Pierre, 56
Louis Alexander, Prince of Battenberg, 12, 142
Lowell, James R., vii
Lowther, Sir Gerard, 67, 75, 242
Loyalists during the American Revolution, 213
Luli Chang, 96
Lung Yü, Dowager Empress, 103–04, 242
Lusatian Serbs, 198
*Lusitania,* the, 127, 208

McCabe, Warner, 188
Macedonia, 35, 37, 64–65, 71, 80, 149;
Macedonia (*cont.*)
brigands in, 33–34; reforms, 36
Madrid, Spain, 5; Conference, xvii, 8; British Embassy at, 11
Magyars, 198
Mahdists, 16 n.
Mala Strana, 173
Manchu Emperors, 92; Princes, 99
Manchuria, xix–xx, 85–86, 89; railways in, 85
Manchus, xxxiv
Margerie, Pierre Jacquin de, 15
Margerie, Madame Pierre de, 92, 242
Maria Theresa, Queen, 180
Maritza River, 146
Marling, Sir Charles Murray, 76, 242
Marmora, Sea of, 133
Marne, Battle of the, 125–26
Marschall von Bieberstein, Baron Adolf, 37, 59–60, 67, 75, 81, 125, 243
Martin, Fredrik, 86, 243
Masaryk, Jan, 204, 243; apprehensiveness about Soviet policies, 205–06
Masaryk, Tomáš, 177, 181, 183–84, 188, 191–92, 194–98, 201, 243
Masaryk Station, Prague, 173
Masonic lodges, 65
Matsuoka, Yosuke, 91–92, 243
Mayfair, 168, 223
Mecca, Arabia, 49
Medici, Catherine de, 133 n., 134
Mehmed V, 79, 122, 139, 243
Melvill de Carnbee, J.P.R.A., 165, 167, 169–70, 243
Mensdorff-Pouilly-Dietrichstein, Count Albert, 168, 243
Mesen, Brenes, 113
Mesopotamian Desert, 135
Messina, Strait of, 125
Metternich, Prince Klemens Wenzel von, 13, 187
Mevlevi sect of dervishes, 55
Mexico, xxiii, xxviii; Army of, 116
Michaeloff, Dr. Kara, 167
Michiels, Edgar, 188
Middle East, xxviii
Miletus, Turkey, 42 n.
Ming Dynasty, 92
Missionaries, 68; in Turkey, 137

Mittag, Baron, 153
Mohammed II, 44 n., 57
Mohammedans, 49, 68, 69
Mombelli, Colonel, 138
Monastir, Serbia, 148, 157–58
Mongols, 70
Monte Carlo, casino at, 79
Montenegro, 148
Moore, Lionel, 40
Moravia, 179, 194
Morganatic marriages, 182
Morgenthau, Henry, 128, 130, 243
Moroccan Conference (*1880*), xvii, 8; (*1906*), *see* Algesiras Conference
Moroccan dispute (*1911*), 60
Morocco, xvi–xviii, 3, 6, 15–17
Morton, Captain, 132
Moscow, 86
Motley, John L., vii
Moukhtar, Mahmoud, 70, 72–73, 242
Munich Crisis (*1938*), 202–03, 221
Mussolini, Benito, 195, 211
Mytilene, 52–53

Nabbatean: antiquities, 53; forgeries, 98
Naidenoff, General, 165, 168–69
Napoleon Bonaparte, ix, 12, 83, 106, 123, 179
Napoleon III, vii
*National Review* (London), 212–13
Nazi bombers, 212
Nazim, Dr., 123, 243
Nazim Pasha, 80
Neapolitan Revolution (*1820*), 13 n.
Near East, 66, 70–71, 118; balance of power in the, xviii
Near Eastern Question, xviii
Nelson, Admiral Horatio, 138
Nero, Emperor, 39, 229–30
Netherlands, 37, 147; Minister in Bulgaria, xxiv; Inspector in Morocco proposed, 21; Legation at Peking, 88; Legation at Constantinople, 121; Minister at Prague, 180
Neurath, Baron Constantin von, 145, 243
New York, New York, 173, 209
Newspapers, Czechoslovak, 184; in Sofia, 163
Newton, Sir Basil-Cochrane, 171–72, 244
Niazi Bey, 67, 244
Nicaraguans, 112
Nicholas II, Czar, 10, 42, 78, 145
Nicolson, Sir Arthur, 11, 12 n., 18, 244
Nisch, Serbia, 147–48, 156–57, 164
North, Lord Frederick, 214
Norway, 128
Nostitz Palace, Prague, 186

O'Conor, Sir Nicholas, 38, 58–59, 244
"Old Buddha," 104
Oliveira, Regis de, 218, 244
"Open Door," xx, 15, 17, 20, 22
Opium, 89
Orient: fatalism, 77; art, 96–99; cuisine, 100–01; festivals, 107
Orient Club, Constantinople, 73, 76–77
Orthodox Church, 34–35
Othman, House of, 41, 46, 123
Ottoman Bank, Constantinople, 73
Ottoman Empire, xviii, 36, 42, 51, 59, 69, 74, 79, 130. *See also* Turkey
Oxford, Lady, 219, 244

Page, Walter Hines, xxiv n., 172, 244
Paget, Lady Muriel, 156–57, 244
Palacky, František, 202, 244
Pallavicini, Count Jean de, 138, 244
Palmerston, Viscount Henry J. T., 59, 244
Pan-German ideas, 176–77
Pan-Islamism, 49–50, 69
Pan-Turanianism, 69–70
Papal Nuncio in Prague, 183–84
Paris, France, 144, 199, 201, 214; bankers' investments in Bagdad Railway, 60; political refugees in, 65
Paris Peace Conference (*1919*), xxvii–xxviii, 193, 198
Parthian sarcophagi, 53
Pasadena, California, 209
Peacock Throne, 63
Peddlers in Peking, 95–96
Peet, William W., 32, 244

Pei-ta-Ho, 107
Peking, China, xxxiv, 49–50, 87, 90–91, 218; U.S. Legation in, xix; Imperial Palace, 105
Pera, Turkey, 58, 131, 143
Persia, 57; Ambassador in Constantinople, 63
Persian Gulf, 42
Peter, King, 170, 245
Philadelphia, Pennsylvania, 215
Philippopolis, Bulgaria, 169–70
Phillips, William, xix
Pilsudski, Josef, 34 n., 245
Pittsburgh, Pennsylvania, 30, 190
Plotz, Dr., 168–69
Poincaré, Raymond, 201
Poland, Poles, 192, 193, 221–24
Porto Rico, 117
Potsdam, Crown Council, 128
Prague, Czechoslovakia, xxxiii, 210, 212; Italian gardens, vii; Einstein as Minister at, x; Einstein's arrival in, 173; ancient buildings, 174; aristocrats in, 175; woods near, 179; U.S. Legation garden, 190; municipality, 192; pre-World War 1, 192
Princeton University, 217
Prison camps, 165, 170–71
Prisoners of war: Einstein and, x, 164–68; treatment of, 167–71
Procopius, 41
Progressive Party (U.S., *1912*), 209
Protestant powers, 184
Prussian Guard, 70
Public opinion, 6–7, 193; Bulgarian, 160
Puerto Limon, Costa Rica, 109
P'u-i (Hsuan Y'ung), Emperor, 103, 245
Púlun, Prince and Princess, 99, 245
Putney, England, 202

Racial hatreds, Balkan, 156
Racism, German, 184–85
Raczinsky, Count Edward, 218, 245
Radolin, Prince Hugo Leszczc, 3, 245
Radomir, Bulgaria, 168–69
Radoslavoff, M. Vasil, 150–51, 153, 160, 162, 164–67, 171, 245
Radowitz, Joseph Marie von, 17–18, 22, 245
Rahmi Bey, 126, 245
Ralli, Helen. *See* Einstein, Helen
Raouf Bey, 51, 74, 245
Regnault, M. Eugene Georges, 15, 245
Reid, Whitelaw, 10, 245
Republican Party (U.S.), xv, xxvii, 209, 212; Campaign Text Book (*1920*), xxviii
Reshad Fuad, 56, 121–22
Révoil, Amedée, 14, 20, 246
Ribbentrop, Joachim von, 219, 246
Riza, Ahmed, 67
Robert College, xviii, 32, 40, 152
Robilant, Mario Nicholis de, 36, 246
Rockhill, W. W., 84, 246
Roman Catholic Church, 183
Roosevelt, Franklin D., 62, 224; Einstein's interview with, xi, 216
Roosevelt, Theodore, vii–viii, xv, xvii, xxiii, xvii, 4, 7, 17, 196, 213, 217; attitude towards the Moroccan Crisis (*1905–06*), 9; concern for Jews in Morocco, 10–11; and the Open Door policy, 15; influence on French policy, 16; development of a career diplomatic service, 25–26; relations with U.S. diplomats, 38; Einstein's biography of, 212
Root, Elihu, xv, xvi n., 9, 21, 84, 109, 184, 209, 246
Rosyth, Scotland, 227
Roumania, Roumanians, xxiv, 121, 142, 157, 193; frontier, 119–20; intervention in World War I, 130, 150; Ententophiles, 147; Minister to Bulgaria, 171
Roustchouk, Bulgaria, 147, 151
Rouvier, Maurice, 17, 246
Runyon, Damon, 229
Russell, John, 91, 246
Russia, Russians, x n., xi, 3, 42, 49, 80–81, 87, 126, 142, 149, 193, 203, 211, 222, 223, 225, 231; war with Japan, 7, 154; war with Turkey, 42 n.; Turkish fear of, 60; Revolution, 66; policy towards China, 85; obstruction of U.S. railway schemes

Russia, Russians (*cont.*)
in Manchuria, 85; subjects in Constantinople, 132; Army, 145, 149; prisoners of war in Bulgaria, 149; Grand Mistress of the Court in Sofia, 154; steppes, 192; strategic railroads, 193; relations with Czechoslovakia, 202–06; censorship, 203; war with Finland, 222

Said Halim, Prince, 122, 246
Said the Kurd, 52–53, 246
Salerno, Francesco da, 14
Salonika, Turkey, 35, 65, 74, 76–77, 80, 147, 159, 165
San Francisco, California, 84
San José, Costa Rica, xxi, 109 ff.
San Stefano, Turkey, 76
Saxony, 185, 188, 198
Schiff, Jacob, 10–11, 246
Schober, Johann, 200, 246
Schönborn Palace, 174
Schwarzenburg, Prince, 175–76
*Scorpion,* the American Guardship, 129, 132
Scotland, Scots, xi, 147, 225 ff.
Selim the Grim, 49, 247
Selim Pasha, 64, 66
Serajevo, Austria-Hungary, 181, 192
Serbia, Serbs, 145, 147, 153, 156, 164, 193; front in World War I, 142; Army of, 148, 157, 170; Legation at Sofia, 148; money, 156
Sforza, Count Carlo, 4, 14, 23, 247
Shanghai, China, 107
Shantung, xxviii
Shevket, General Mahmoud, 76, 80
Siberia, xxvi, 87, 197; Siberian Express, 86–87
Sinaia, Roumania, 150
Slavs: sympathy for Serbia, 148; in Austro-Hungarian Empire, 192–93
Slovakia, 181, 194, 197–98
Smyrna, Turkey, 38; harbor at, 126
Sofia, Bulgaria, 34–35, 143 ff.; Cathedral, 153; topography, 155
Sonnino, Baron Sidney, 138, 247
Southend, England, German prisoners at, 119
Soviet-Japanese Non-Aggression Pact (*April 13, 1941*), 91 n.
Spain, xviii; Delegation to the Moroccan Conference (*1906*), 5; claims in Morocco, 15
Speck von Sternburg, Baron Herman, 9, 22, 247
Spender, J. A., 220
Spring Rice, Sir Cecil, xxiv n.
St. Bartholomew's Day Massacre (*1572*), 133
St. Germain, Treaty of, 193
St. Petersburg, Russia, 35; Japanese Embassy in, 61
St. Sophia, Cathedral of (Constantinople), 28
Stalin, Joseph, 203
Stamboul, Turkey, 25, 55, 72, 80, 120, 129
"Stamboulin," 44
Stambulitzky, Alexsandr, 153, 247
Stone, Ellen, 33–34, 247
Stormont, Lord, 214
Straight, Willard, xix–xx, 86, 89, 247
Stratford de Redcliffe, Lord, 49, 247
Streater, Mrs. Jasper, xxxii
Sublime Porte. *See* Ottoman Empire
Sudan, 16 n.
Suez Canal, 142
Suleymanieh Mosque, Stamboul, 55–56
Sung Dynasty, 97–98
Suvla, Turkey, fighting at, 141
Švehla, Antonin, 186, 247
Sweden, 37, 223
Switzerland, 158–59, 199; Inspector in Morocco proposed, 21; frontier, 164
Szechuan, China, 101

Taft, William Howard, xix, 9, 83–84, 117, 247; Administration of, xix, 83
Talaat Pasha, 67–69, 122–24, 133, 138, 247
Talfilelt, Morocco, 6
T'ang Dynasty, 98
Tangier, Morocco, 10–11, 16, 18, 21
*Tanin,* the, 72 n.
Tarnowski de Tarnow, Count Adam, 153, 247
Tarouca, Count Silva, 179

Tatar Bazardjik, Bulgaria, 167–68, 170–71
Tattenbach, Count Christian, 8, 18, 248
Taxim barracks, 77–78
Tcharykoff, Nicholas, 80, 248
Teheran, Persia (Iran), 31, 63
Tennessee Valley Authority, 225
Teschen, Czechoslovakia, castle at, 175
Tewfik Pasha, 51–52, 75, 248
Therapia, Turkey, 26, 64, 66, 81, 120
Thirty Years' War (*1618–48*), 174, 177
Thun, Prince, 175
Thun Palace, 174
Tientsin, China, 90
Tirard, Pierre, 61 n.
Topolcanky, forest of, 181
Torres, Sid Mohammed El, 10, 248
Tree, Sir Herbert Beerbohm, 170, 248
Trianon, Treaty of, 193
Tsai Tao, Prince, 101–02, 248
Tuan Fang, Viceroy, 96–97, 248
Turanian nationalism, 50, 70
Turkestan, 89
Turkey, Turks, x, xii, xix, xx, xxiv, xxxiv, 26, 37, 50, 119, 142, 145, 152, 159; Grand Vizier, 6, 44–47, 51, 53, 55, 66, 68, 74–75, 122, 138, 151; anticipated break-up, 35; Revolution (*1908*), 36, 43, 48, 67, 78; paternal administration, 42 ff.; Sheik-ul-Islam, 44, 78, 122; reception of foreign diplomats, 45; decay, 46; army, 50, 65–66, 70, 77–78, 123, 124; fear of Russia, 60; nationalists, 70; National Assembly, 78; Constitution, 71; Counter-Revolution (*1909*), 71, 74–75, 77; language, 76; intervention in World War I, 124, 126; police, 131; Ministry of Education, 131; Ministry of the Interior, 131; racism, 134; Consul at Dedéagatch, 139; Minister of War, 139; wartime reign of terror, 142; cession of territory to Bulgaria in World War I, 145–46; alliance with Bulgaria, 148; baths, 150
Typhus epidemic, 156
Tzu Hsi, Dowager Empress, 103, 248
"Union and Progress," Committee of, 68
United Kingdom. *See* Great Britain
United States, 193, 212, 213; economic interests, ix; military power, ix; neutrality (*1914–17*), ix; foreign policy, x, xi; Foreign Service, xii; Department of State, xv, xxiii, xxviii, 26, 32–33, 89, 118, 160, 162, 172, 211; Diplomatic Service, xv, xx–xxi, xxiii, 26, 231; at the Algesiras Conference (*1906*), xvi, 7, 9–10; Congress, Congressmen, xxvii, 191, 210–11, 215; Embassy in Constantinople, xviii, 38, 72, 118, 129; proposed mandate over Armenia, xxviii; "Dollar Diplomacy," xix, 20, 85, 89; "Open Door" Policy, xx, 15, 22; Senate, 8, 83; Diplomatic Bureau, 26; interests in the Balkans, 36 ff.; Fleet in the Mediterranean, 38; Consular Court in Constantinople, 39; Department of the Navy, 50–51; policy towards China, 83; Legation at Peking, 83, 87, 89–91, 102–03, 105; policy towards Europe, 84; policy towards Far East, 85; capital investments in China, 85; Legation at San José, Costa Rica, 110; Department of War, 116; asked to protect German and Austrian interests in Turkey, 128–29; interests in Turkey, 136 ff.; missions in Turkey, 137; policy in Bulgaria, 147; Legation at Sofia, 149, 159–62, 171; attitude towards First Balkan War, 152; medical personnel in Bulgaria, Serbia, 156–57; Legation at Prague, 175, 187, 189, 191–92, 194; importation of cars into Czechoslovakia, 192; recognition of Czechoslovak Republic, 197; Embassy in London, 203, 211, 223, 225, 229; Presidential campaign, *1916*, 208–10, *1920*, xxviii; Supreme Court, 209; Embassy in Paris, 211; Revolution, 214; Presidency, 217; capitalistic imperialism, 231; troops in Britain, 230
Uskub, Serbia, 156

Valideh Mosque, 25
Vallombrosa, Italy, xxv
Van, Turkey, 134
Van Dyck, Sir Anthony, 175
Varna, Bulgaria, 118
Vassar College, 217
Vatican, the, 183–84
Venetian craftsmen of the Renaissance, 57
Venezuelan Debt Dispute (*1902*), 7
Venizelos, Eleutherios, 120
Verdun, France, 15
Vergara, Carlos, 114, 248
Versailles, 214; Court of, 55; Treaty of, 86
Vidal, Mrs. Bancroft, 214–15
Vienna, Austria, 35, 119, 173, 185, 200, 216
Visconti Venosta, Marquis Emilio, 13, 19–20
Vopicka, Charles, xxiv–xxv
Vultava River, 173

Wai Wu Pu, 102–03
Waldstein, Count, 174
Wallace, General Lewis, 75, 249
Walsingham, Sir Francis, 11
Wangenheim, Baron de, 121, 125, 127–28, 249
Washburn, George, 32, 249
Washington, D.C., 159, 212, 215–16
Weitz, Paul, 125
Wellington, Arthur Wellesley, Duke of, ix
Welserheim, Count Rudolphe, 19, 249
Western Europe, 192, 221
White, Henry, xvii, 7, 9–12, 22, 190–91, 249
White, Jack, 188, 190–91, 249
White House, 194
William II, Emperor, xvii, 3 n., 7–9, 15–17, 19, 22, 49, 58–60, 128, 181; correspondence with President Theodore Roosevelt, 12
Williamson, Howell, 188, 249
Wilson, Huntington, xix
Wilson, Woodrow, xxiii, xxv, xxviii, 86, 89, 137, 193, 209
Winant, John G., xi, 223–24, 249
Windischgrätz, Princess, 119
Windsor, England, 95; castle at, 58
Winslow, Alan, 188, 249
World War I, xxii, xxxiv, 3, 36, 50, 67, 119, 128, 145, 181, 201, 212, 230; social consequences, 176
World War II, xi, xxxiv, 203, 211, 221, 230–31
Wylie, Doughty, 68–69

Yalchin, Hussein Djahid, 72 n.
Yangtse Valley, xx
Yellow Sea, 70
Yester, Scotland, 147, 225–27, 229
Yildiz, xxxiv, 29–30, 40, 43, 45, 67, 74, 78, 81
Young Plan, 201 n.
Young Turks, xviii, 69, 71–72, 74–76, 78, 81
Yugoslavia, Yugoslavs, 173, 193, 224
Yulang, Princess, 100, 249
Yung Ching, 97

Ziedlochowice, estate of, 179–80
Zimmerman, Marcia, xix n.